Anticipation and Anachrony in Statius' *Thebaid*

Also published by Bloomsbury

Statius, Poet Between Rome and Naples, Carole E. Newlands
Silver Latin Epic, H.M. Currie
Statius: Silvae IV, edited by K.M. Coleman
The Poet Lucan: Studies in Rhetorical Epic, Mark P.O. Morford
Lucan: Bello Civili I, edited by Robert J. Getty

Anticipation and Anachrony in Statius' *Thebaid*

Robert Simms

BLOOMSBURY ACADEMIC
LONDON • NEW YORK • OXFORD • NEW DELHI • SYDNEY

BLOOMSBURY ACADEMIC
Bloomsbury Publishing Plc
50 Bedford Square, London, WC1B 3DP, UK
1385 Broadway, New York, NY 10018, USA
29 Earlsfort Terrace, Dublin 2, Ireland

BLOOMSBURY, BLOOMSBURY ACADEMIC and the Diana logo are
trademarks of Bloomsbury Publishing Plc

First published in Great Britain 2020
Paperback edition first published 2021

Copyright © Robert Simms, 2020

Robert Simms has asserted his right under the Copyright, Designs and
Patents Act, 1988, to be identified as Author of this work.

For legal purposes the Acknowledgements on p. vii constitute
an extension of this copyright page.

Cover design: Terry Woodley
Cover image © Cover image: Etruscan urn depicting the struggle between
Eteocles and Polynices for the throne of Thebes (4th–3rd centuries bc),
Archaeology Museum of Barcelona, Spain. Prisma/UIG/Getty Images

All rights reserved. No part of this publication may be reproduced or
transmitted in any form or by any means, electronic or mechanical,
including photocopying, recording, or any information storage or retrieval
system, without prior permission in writing from the publishers.

Bloomsbury Publishing Plc does not have any control over, or responsibility for,
any third-party websites referred to or in this book. All internet addresses given
in this book were correct at the time of going to press. The author and publisher
regret any inconvenience caused if addresses have changed or sites
have ceased to exist, but can accept no responsibility for any such changes.

A catalogue record for this book is available from the British Library.

Library of Congress Cataloging-in-Publication Data
Names: Simms, Robert, author.
Title: Anticipation and Anachrony in Statius' Thebaid / Robert Simms.
Description: London : Bloomsbury Academic, 2019. |
Includes bibliographical references and index.
Identifiers: LCCN 2019010447 | ISBN 9781350082571 (hb) |
ISBN 9781350082595 (epub)
Subjects: LCSH: Statius, P. Papinius (Publius Papinius). Thebais. | Statius,
P. Papinius (Publius Papinius)–Criticism and interpretation.
Classification: LCC PA6698 .S56 2019 | DDC 871/.01–dc23
LC record available at https://lccn.loc.gov/2019010447

ISBN: HB: 978-1-3500-8257-1
PB: 978-1-3501-9139-6
ePDF: 978-1-3500-8258-8
eBook: 978-1-3500-8259-5

Typeset by RefineCatch Limited, Bungay, Suffolk

To find out more about our authors and books visit
www.bloomsbury.com and sign up for our newsletters.

Contents

Preface		vii
	Introduction: notum iter ad Thebas	1
	Prisca Nomina	2
	An Audience for Thebes	5
	Suspense, Anticipation, and Surprise	8
	Epic and Drama	12
1	Beginning with the End	15
	They Call Me Jocasta	16
	The *Thebaid*'s Prologue	24
2	Portentous Beginnings	31
	Argos and the Seeds of War	31
	Interlude: Eteocles' Dream (2.1–83)	35
	The Wedding Portents	37
	The Necklace of Harmonia	39
	Argia's Unease	41
	Amphiaraus and the Flight of Birds	42
	The Bacchant and the Necromancy	45
3	Hypsipyle and the Army at Nemea	49
	Hypsipyle's Lemnian Narrative	51
	The Death and Funeral of Opheltes	58
	Funeral Consolations	62
4	Jocasta	67
	Tisiphone's Fears	68
	Jocasta and Polynices	69
	Jocasta and Eteocles	73
	Chronology and Suspense	74
	Strategies of Elision	76
	Jocasta's Hope and Death	79

5	iam pater est	83
	The Curse	83
	Anticipation	89
	Outcome	93
6	Portentous Ends	99
	Amphiaraus	100
	Tydeus	102
	Hippomedon	105
	Parthenopaeus	107
	Capaneus	110
	Adrastus	114
	Menoeceus	121
7	hic imperat, ille minatur	125
	The Anonymous Critic	126
	The End of Polynices	128
	The End of Eteocles	134
8	Theseus and Concluding the *Thebaid*	143
	The Idalian Doves	144
	The Edict of Creon	146
	The Choices of Ornytus	147
	ubi incluta fama Antigone?	148
	The Twin Flames	151
	Choosing Theseus	152
	fidissime Phegeus	154
Notes		161
Bibliography		193
Index		207

Preface

Statius' *Thebaid* has been a long and rewarding preoccupation and I am grateful to have worked with many encouraging and helpful friends and colleagues along the way. Bill Dominik read and guided the dissertation that sprouted a scrappy little seed which, in the fullness of time, would become the present book. A kinder and more patient Doktorvater could not have been hoped for. John Garthwaite, Neil Bernstein, and Antony Augoustakis were also enthusiastic and helpful supporters. I have carried this book from Dunedin, New Zealand, to the hinterlands of Oman, to Tokyo, Japan and most recently, Oslo, Norway, where I am especially grateful to the Institutt for filosofi, ide- og kunsthistorie og klassiske språk at UiO for providing a welcome postdoc and *koselig* environs in which to complete this study. Here, in particular, I am indebted to Silvio Bär, Mathilde Skoie, Eirik Welo, and visiting from Uppsala, Ingela Nilsson. I was as much professionally as personally privileged to receive gracious funding that allowed five weeks at the Norwegian Institute in Rome. Just to be there, ah! Lastly, I thank my children (Mira Jo, Camilla, and Noah) who made it all worthwhile and matter most. As I close this project I am struck, and a little saddened, by how long it took, and by how much longer I wish it could have taken.

R.C.S.
Reno, Nevada
February 2019

Introduction: notum iter ad Thebas

In the first book of Statius' *Thebaid* Oedipus begs Tisiphone to fulfill the vengeful imprecations he makes against his sons, Eteocles and Polynices. The Fury leaves the banks of Cocytus and travels to Thebes: "arripit extemplo Maleae de ualle resurgens | notum iter ad Thebas," "Straightaway she rises from Malea's valley and hurries along the familiar road to Thebes" (1.100–1).[1] Statius describes the road to Thebes as "notum," which probably makes an oblique reference to the continual mischance and suffering that plague that city.[2] It is also possible, however, that Statius' description of the road as "known" may stress the familiarity of the myth, since this was a very well-trod road indeed, as well as Statius' own fidelity to that myth's tradition—what the audience may expect in his *Thebaid* is not likely to differ much from the other retellings.[3] When Statius commenced his epic poem on the quarrelsome sons of Oedipus he was well aware that this was a popular tale, one that if not done properly would be tiresome to his audience. When Statius' Tisiphone travels this "notum iter ad Thebas" and infests the home with its usual pestilence ("adsuetaque infecit nube penates," 1.124), there is the suggestion that in terms of literary reproduction this story has been done many times before.

Despite the continued eagerness among Roman audiences for Greek myth, its continual reproduction did not please everyone. Martial, Statius' contemporary under Domitian, twice disparages the value of mythic stories. In the first instance he berates Mamurra for delighting in such shallow trash and he indicts a catalog of works for being unable to address or improve readers (10.4.1–12).[4] Additionally, in a mock aporia to his fourteenth book of epigrams Martial comments on the ineffectual quality of mythic literature by declaring: "uis scribam Thebas Troiamve malasve Mycenas? | Lude, iniquis, nucibus: perdere nolo nuces," "You would have me write about Thebes? Or Troy? Or wicked Mycenae? You say, play with nuts. But I don't want to waste my nuts" (14.1.11–12). Martial's knowledge of trading in trifles aside, he makes a clear indication that the familiarity of myths and their routine iterations veers toward tedium. By the time of Statius' writing, the Theban legend remained popular enough to be found in circulation, but familiar enough to be scoffed at as trifles. Martial is critical of stories that are so well-known that they have become tiresome, no longer able to hold philosophical or aesthetic interest. Thus, the inherent predictability of recycled narratives was clearly a hazard for Roman poets. Notably, the desire for novelty and the difficulty of attaining it within a highly recidivist literary system was by no means unique to the Romans; their Greek forbears were similarly aware of this issue. In a fragment recorded in Aristotle's *Rhet.* 1451a, the poet Choerilus suggests: ἆ μάκαρ, ὅστις ἔην κεῖνον χρόνον ἴδρις ἀοιδῆς, | Μουσάων θεράπων, ὅτ' ἀκήρατος ἦν ἔτι λειμών, "he's blessed, that one, who in those days was servant to the Muses and sang skilled songs, while the meadow still lay unmown" (fr. 317.1–2). It must have taken some maneuvering to reconstitute familiar stories in such a way as to make them compelling. Thus, it is not unreasonable to suppose that when Statius brought out his *Thebaid*, which treats a well-known myth and was certain to be measured against familiar antecedent versions, the epic could well have flopped, but it did not, and it is worth considering why not.

Prisca Nomina

Statius knew that his *Thebaid* was competing for a place within an established literary tradition. In the invocation to his unfinished *Achilleid* he reflects on the reception of his Theban epic: "scit Dircaeus ager meque inter prisca parentum | nomina cumque suo numerant Amphione Thebae," "The fields of Dirce know my song, and Thebes numbers me among the ancient names of her parents and with her own Amphione" (1.12–13). In no place is Statius specific about which of the "prisca nomina" his *Thebaid* should be, or even could be, counted among. His hope to rival the greatest of the ancient epic poets, however, can be observed at *Silvae* 5.3.61–3 and in the coda to the *Thebaid* (12.816–7) where he expresses the wish that his work be second only to Virgil's.[5] Since treatments of the "Oedipodionidae fratres" were undertaken in epic, dramatic, and lyric poetry his comments in the *Achilleid* suggest he had chosen to contend with a varied poetic corpus. Statius' confident standing among other poets and genres that produced treatments of the conflict between Eteocles and Polynices raises several questions, foremost of which are these: what is it about Statius' epic that warrants a place among these "prisca nomina" and which of the several treatments might he have had in mind? These questions cannot be fully answered, certainly, but a brief survey of possible candidates and what is known of their work demonstrates a rich and suggestive repository of potential influence. We cannot be unconditionally certain about Statius' knowledge of any of these works, but a few undoubtedly influenced his conceptualization, as well as Roman awareness of, the myth.

The conflict at Thebes may possibly have had historic origins;[6] however, the literary record of the Theban narrative begins with the Cyclic *Thebais* attributed to Homer. An *Amphiaraou Exelasis*, also attributed to Homer, might have been part of the same work. Antimachus' name stands out prominently among Attic treatments.[7] Once bursting with song (Catullus notes his tumescence, 95.10), only a scant sixty-six fragments survive from his hefty twenty-four volume work on the *Septem* mythos.[8] Since Antimachus rivaled Homer in popularity it is unlikely that Statius was unfamiliar with his *Thebais*.[9] Pollmann suggests that it is improbable, given the range of Statius' knowledge and learning, that he was unfamiliar with Antimachus, or the lost works of Hellenists about whom even less is known: Antagoras of Rhodos, Antiphanes of Colophon, or Menelaus of Aegae.[10] We can also add to this list Ponticus' highly regarded Roman epic about which we know only that it was sad ("tristia").[11] There is also Novius' antithetically parodic play, which would be a delight to have.

One influential collection of fragments to set alongside Statius' *Thebaid* is the Lille-papyrus attributed to Stesichorus. The papyrus fragments, used as packing material for a mummy case, were discovered in 1976 and preserve over one-hundred continuous verses treating the conflict. In *Silvae* 5.3 Statius cites several ancient authors that formed part of his literary education and his father's curriculum, but of the authors known to have produced works on the Theban saga only Stesichorus is cited (5.3.154).[12] There is no comment on which of Stesichorus' works was used for instruction, and some scholars doubt that the Lille-papyrus should be attributed to him.[13] While the fatherly advice to Statius concerns epic, it is unlikely that a genre like tragic drama was wholly absent from the curricula. More likely, these texts were taught by another magister.[14] The Lille fragments present a scene in which Tiresias delivers unfavorable omens about Oedipus' sons and a female speaker—most certainly Jocasta—attempts to curtail the outcome. Essentially, the poem reveals the maternal intercession that establishes the alternate reigns and the division of wealth that unwittingly leads to the conflict. Arguably, it is Jocasta's misuse of masculine power here as elsewhere that hastens the conflict between the brothers.[15]

Seneca's *Phoenissae* is incomplete, which makes discussion of the final outcome speculative. As it survives, his *Phoenissae* appears to be in two halves with the first half reminiscent of Sophocles' *Oedipus at Colonus* and the second recollecting later scenes of Euripides' *Phoenissae*, which treats Jocasta's intervention.[16] The play breaks off with a *pro et contra* on the nature of power that resembles their rhetorical back and forth in Euripides' *Phoenissae*. Arguments for the play's incompleteness are more convincing: the end lacks resolution, by the end Oedipus still remains in the woods waiting for news of the conflict between his sons, choral passages are absent. The two large sections that comprise the play are poorly integrated and thus lend themselves to speculation that what we have as the *Phoenissae* is actually two fragments of two seperate plays. Most importantly, the enmity between the brothers never reaches a point of conflict. Indeed, if Seneca elected to have the brothers not slay one another, then this is a spectacular departure from traditional telling, though a likely disappointment for audiences familiar with the story and anticipating the climactic duel that ends the brothers' lives. Nevertheless, even if Seneca is not among the "prisca nomina," Statius shares much with the substratum of Senecan tragedy generally.[17]

Several dramatic treatments focus on specific characters that Statius could have had in mind as he conceived his *Thebaid*. Carcinus the younger and Cleophon of Athens both wrote an *Amphiareos*. Achaeus of Eretriam, who likely competed against Sophocles and Euripides, brought out an *Adrastus*. Timesitheus produced a *Kapaneus*. Theodectes of Phaselis, privileged to study under Plato, Aristotle, and Isocrates, retired from rhetoric to write tragedies; among his titles we find a *Tydeus*. Spintharus wrote a *Parthenopaeus*, as did Astydamas whose production was so well received that a bronze statue was erected in the dramatist's honor. It is difficult to imagine such a work becoming completely obscure and neglected. Sophocles wrote a *Lemniai*. Aeschylus and Cleaenetus produced lost versions of *Hypsipyle*, though those need not necessarily have included her encounter with the Argives; Euripides' version survives in sufficient fragments to discuss the overall trajectory of his play, though with some mindfulness of its gaps. We will have considerable recourse to what survives of this work in Chapter 3. On the Roman side, we have two lines on the "Dircaeum fontem" from Accius' *Thebais*. He also wrote a *Phoenissae* and an *Antigona*. There is also an anonymous *Amphiaraus* and an *Adrastus* by C. Julius Strabo. The inclusion or exclusion of these names, conjectural though it may be, remains critical to how Statius can be regarded as a "doctus poeta." It goes without question, and certainly beyond dispute, that far more iterations of the myth were available to him than us.

Of all these potential "prisca nomina," however, one incontestable candidate is the *Phoenissae* of Euripides, since considerable evidence suggests that Statius was familiar with the work.[18] It is hard to imagine that Euripides is not among those "prisca nomina." Statius also treated episodes found in Euripides' *Suppliants* and *Hypsipyle*, though their influence is not as apparent. Euripides' *Phoenissae* offers a rich array of episodes and responds to Aeschylus' *Sephem* at several turns.[19] In all likelihood Statius and his contemporaries encountered Euripides' *Phoenissae* as part of their education. The extractable passages and gnomoi made the play a popular school text. As Cribiore notes, the *Phoenissae* was not simply a one-time visitation, but returned to at successive stages throughout a student's education.[20] The evidence is papyrological, with sententiae surviving in fragments and quotes, as well as sundry Latin authors.[21] Given the extensive familiarity and use of Euripides' *Phoenissae* at Rome, it is possible that Statius' claim that his *Thebaid* had become a school text (12.815) sets his epic in rivalry not only with Virgil, but Euripides as well. And if not the *Phoenissae*, then other works treating the same myth.[22] More importantly, the story that Statius produces is not likely to be an unfamiliar one to, at the very least, educated audiences and readers. Outside of education, however, we can only speculate on the conditions of dissemination and its attraction as an entertainment. Nevertheless, for many, Euripides' *Phoenissae* was a convenient touchstone and basis for comparison.

Still, who, if any, can be counted among the "prisca nomina" will remain an insuperable matter of speculation. For Statius' audience, there were still other ways to become familiar with the story. Within schools, and possibly outside, the basic outlines of the myth were condensed for introduction through mythographical handbooks like those of Hyginus, and Pseudo-Apollodorus. In addition to studying Euripides' *Phoenissae*—or similar works on the fratricidal conflict—there were even other ways to become acquainted with the story. Lucian lists several scenes, all of which are treated in Statius' *Thebaid* except the death of Antigone, that are necessary to the actor's tragic repertoire (*De Saltatione* 43.6–44.2). Mime and pantomime performances, as well as revival plays, allowed circulation among both the educated and the less-educated, familiarizing them with significant characters and episodes. It is not surprising that references to the myth are legion among Greek and Latin authors, and not in ways so elusive and recherché that the point of the allusion is missed.

An Audience for Thebes

For as much as these works may or may not have contributed to Statius' own *Thebaid*, we must bear in mind, as much as possible, that these works also contributed to the audience's familiarity with the myth, and ultimately the reception of Statius' work. Granted, how well the Theban story was known would vary considerably, and it would be necessary for authors to compensate for the degrees of familiarity with referential devices, expositions, and so forth to accommodate recall. For my purposes, however, the presumed hypothetical audience would fall somewhere within the middle to upper range of familiarity with the Theban mythos; a reader familiar with the bare outlines and significant plot points of the story, either through education, performances, or oral transmission. Perhaps a reader not unlike Cicero who recalls Caesar routinely reciting passages from Euripides' *Phoenissae*, and who can stammer out a few lines translated into Latin to make a rhetorical point (*De Officiis* 3.83). Or Caesar himself, for that matter. Or a reader like Ovid who regrets that his licentious muse did not lead him to write on the mutual wounds of the brothers instead of the erotic verses that caused his exile so far from his beloved Rome (*Tristia* 2.313-20). Or perhaps someone like Aemilius Scaurus, who was compelled to commit suicide under Tiberius. While speciously for a tryst with Livilla, the penalty was more likely for including a few lines from Euripides' *Phoenissae* on enduring the stupidity of tyrants in Scaurus' *Atreus* (Dio Cassius 58.26). Or Virgil, who populated his underworld with a few of the characters (*Aen.* 6.479-80). These and other witnesses demonstrate familiarity with actions and themes in the story. The recollection of every particular detail may elude them, but knowledge of the broad outline is present.

When the *Thebaid* first emerged at Rome it was merely another production of a familiar story—albeit by a prominent poet—competing with previous literary productions, whose success or failure would be measured against its antecedents. Yet we know from Statius' own comments that the *Thebaid* was favorably received in its own time. Indeed, Statius describes the reception of his epic at Rome: "iam certe praesens tibi Fama benignum | stravit iter coepitque nouam monstrare futuris," "already Fate undoubtedly presents to you the kindly path she lays out, and begins to reveal your novelty to what will be" (12.812-15). It is certainly possible that "nouam" means "young," "fresh," or "recent" but being composed and performed publicly over more than a decade may disqualify this; early parts, perhaps, but not the whole, and it is the whole *Thebaid* that Statius addresses here. A more accurate sense of "nouam" is probably "novel" or even "original," though admittedly "original" is too heavily freighted to hang on so slender a word.[23] Indeed, such a term appears even more peculiar because the story itself is so revisited. How could Statius possibly declare originality when there appears to be nothing particularly unique about his iteration of the myth when compared to surviving sources? Yet, not only was the epic well received, but it continued to influence poets across Europe well into the early modern period.[24] To what then might we attribute this reception and success? Or to put the question more broadly: how was it possible for Statius to make his narrative compelling when it was drawn from something akin to what Segal describes as a "megatext?"[25]

Statius makes a bold claim and we might be inclined to accuse him of excessive bravura, but the *Thebaid* had an enthusiastic public regard:

> curritur ad uocem iucundam et carmen amicae
> Thebaidos, laetam cum fecit Statius urbem
> promisitque diem: tanta dulcedine captos
> adficit ille animos tantaque libidine uolgi
> auditur.
>
> 7.82–6

Once Statius has promised the day and made the whole city happy they rush to hear his pleasing voice and his song of beloved Thebes. He holds their spirits captive with such sweetness in with such rapture he is heard by the mob.

This brief testimony fires the imagination; it is the closest we will ever come to knowing what it was like to listen to Statius' *Thebaid* from the poet himself. While the passage gives sufficient evidence to consider the epic's successful public reception, what is more pressing of our attention in this study is Juvenal's description of the power and influence exerted over the audience. The verb "adficit" suggests that Statius takes possession of his audience, with especial reference to their "animos." While it is possible to separate the content and the form, the singing (what is possibly just Juvenal's commendation of Statius' dulcet warbling) from the song, the content of that song, the story itself, is equally relevant in his description. He notes specifically the poem as well as the poet. Unfortunately, no term in antiquity approximates our contemporary definition of suspense, though Fuchs catalogs enough instances to demonstrate that there was a disposition toward states of anticipation and suspense.[26] Juvenal's comment here is the closest we come to knowing how audiences experienced the *Thebaid*. Juvenal informs us, perhaps not in the clearest way, that his work was eagerly anticipated: a day for performance was posted and audiences rushed to hear him. While they listened they were captivated either because his voice was so rapturous, or because his meter was so astounding, or because the content of his song was so compelling, or most probably all three. Thus it seems a perfectly reasonable question: How is it possible to make a narrative engaging within an overwhelmingly revisionist enterprise? How does Statius negotiate the complex interplays of certainty and uncertainty over twelve books, and reintroduce canonical characters, themes, episodes, and locations in a way that will be engaging to his audience? Indeed, if we take uncertainty of outcome, suspense or anticipation, as fundamental features of a compelling narrative, as they conventionally are, how is it possible to achieve or manipulate these cognitive states when the outcomes are already known?

Suspense, Anticipation, and Surprise

Suspense, anticipation, and surprise create a compelling narrative; there is no reason to presume that any of these states were not enjoyed by Statius' audience. Understanding how these states could be created within literary traditions in which events and outcomes are so well-known is a challenge. Prior familiarity enables audiences to anticipate what is likely to occur, and of the three anticipation is perhaps the easiest to understand. As I discuss in the next chapter, the prologue creates for the reader an implied contract that key events that feature in the mythos will be presented, and thus readers proceed in anticipation of them. What the audience will know of the mythos before encountering the *Thebaid* can be brought into line with the expectations of the work at hand. Thus anticipation can be understood as a heightened sense of expectation for familiar and likely outcomes; it is a state dependent on a level of familiarity and certainty. In contrast, surprise occurs completely contrary to expectation. Suspense, however, is more problematic.

The point of departure for discussions of suspense (among theorists generally) is the now classic definition put forward by Ortony, Clore, and Collins which situates suspense within the ambit of "prospect emotions," meaning that suspense—along with other similar emotions like hope, dread, or relief—is contingent on a future condition and depends on the confirmation or disconfirmation of an event or outcome regardless of whether or not that outcome will be pleasing. Ortony, Clore, and Collins maintain that suspense involves "a Hope emotion and a Fear emotion coupled with a cognitive state of uncertainty."[27] Notably, the prospective nature of suspense imparts a temporal and sequential nature to its experience. As scholars are quick to point out, however, not all instances of suspense require the state of "cognitive uncertainty" critical to validating this definition, and widely assumed to be a primary element of suspense. The fact that audiences frequently experience suspense despite already knowing the outcomes of stories they have read or films they have seen gives rise to the so-called "suspense paradox." Simply stated, the paradox claims that if uncertainty is required in order to experience suspense, then audiences should not experience suspense in the absence of uncertainty. Yet, they do. A leading attempt to resolve the suspense paradox comes from Richard Gerrig, who argues that the human mind is wired to respond to "moment-to-moment" situations. When audiences participate fully in narrative they are "transported" and so engrossed with the action that their awareness, their access to knowledge of what will happen next, becomes impeded.[28] Statius does create uncertainty, which plays against anticipation, so Ortony's notion of suspense can be maintained, especially where we might consider first-time readers of the *Thebaid*. There are also, however, moments that are so engaging that even where an outcome is certain Gerrig's notion of immediacy can also be applied, especially where a scene is particularly "spectacular." Certainly spectacle affords advantages to drama for which epic will have to compensate through narration rather than immediate visualization, so this does raise questions on how rightfully the *Thebaid* can be set against its surviving antecedents, which are on the whole dramas. In general, suspense has two fundamental aspects: there is the cognitive experience of suspense, the state that emerges within a reader (or spectator) and the prompts, cues, and discourse states that compel the emergence of that experienced state.[29] Certainly, the prompts that *could* create suspense are simpler to isolate than the experience itself. Nevertheless, it would be shortsighted not to remain sensitive to both levels.

Anticipation, for the purpose of this study, is understood as the experience of an audience member or reader who enjoys through previous iterations familiarity with the constituent features of the narrative: the characters, their actions, canonical events, and so forth. The experience of Statius' *Thebaid*, after being acquainted with the myth through any of the above mentioned sources compels, or allows, Statius' audience to anticipate the coming of events, their order, and the breaches in their familiarity with the narrative. Suspense, on the other hand, will be taken to indicate the expectation of events where the outcome is uncertain, where familiarity with say Euripides' *Phoenissae* or any antecedent version is not helpful.[30] And, of course, we have surprise, where the outcome of events occurs contrary to what the audience might (have been led to) suspect. The *Thebaid* does not have any wild divergences from the myth's consistent outline, though it does present several unique features. Statius is faithful to the horrible end in which the principal heroes die in the march against Thebes just as they had in Aeschylus' *Septem* and Euripides' *Phoenissae*. And certainly one of the pleasures of Statius' epic is that the ends are not kept from the reader. Indeed, Statius repeatedly reminds readers of coming misfortunes. He plays on that sense of anticipation, the eagerness to experience the great end of the story, the horrible doom, and the tragic deaths. A reader in Statius' Flavian audience is no doubt aware from experience and familiarity with the myth that the march on Thebes will end in disaster, with the deaths of several heroes. Yet, Statius goes to great lengths to build a sense of anticipation by prefiguring the misfortunes that await the Argive army. For this reason, Ogilvie's criticism, while not meant favorably, is particularly astute: the basic structure of the narrative is a front loaded epic of anticipation and the delivery of a violent end.[31] Portentousness and a sense of unavoidable catastrophe drives the narrative forward. It is not, then, uncertainty but certainty and the anticipation of the fulfillment of events that makes the *Thebaid* compelling. Yet, much of that sense of certainty and anticipation is manipulated by the narrator.

The *Thebaid*'s initial success and its extended shelf-life from late antiquity into the early modern period may have as much to do with its themes and world-view as the thrill of reading it. Unable to arouse its audience the *Thebaid* would have surely fizzled like a damp squib. Readers do not suffer tedium gladly as the long historical list of literary and dramatic failures reveals. Cicero, to take a fitting instance from among those who composed a Theban work, notes in his comments on Antimachus that audiences do not want to be exasperated with the excessively abstruse. Antimachus' failed to keep the attention of anyone in the audience (apart from Plato) while reading his *Thebais* (*Brutus* 191.1–7). The point Cicero makes is that a few readers for such a recondite work are sufficient for a poet like Antimachus, but the orator needs to "move" his audience: "oratio popularis adsensum volgi debet movere" (191.8–9). Cicero well knew that which seemed not to concern Antimachus: audiences don't want to be bored. Such notions can also be inferred in Catullus' assessment of the same poet, whose tumescence creates a contrast to his own poetry: "Parva mei mihi sint cordi monimenta . . ., | at populos tumido gaudet Antimacho," "Let there be for me the small works . . ., but people adore that swelling Antimachus" (95b). Thus, when we consider Statius' comments on the reception of his epic and Juvenal's comments, we might wonder too about Statius' audience, and the testimony we have would indicate a wide and enthusiastic audience and readership.

The myth's narrative tensions accrue between Eteocles and Polynices as they vie for the ruling power over Thebes. Both brothers make their claims and both demonstrate through armed conflict the lengths they will pursue to gain the kingdom. In the end their positions are irreconcilable and they perish at each other's hands. Their deaths, their mutual slaughter—driven by pride, enmity, greed—is the crisis toward which the Theban story aims and was long established by tradition as the canonical scene under which other narrative features like characters, episodes, actions, and the like are subsumed.³² That is to say, the outcome governs the construction and reader's interpretation of the narrative. None of this is particularly new to Statius' scholars who have long been sensitive to his handling of suspense, or at the very least the *Thebaid*'s propulsive momentum. As Moore observes: "[Statius] keeps the great climax before us and seldom turns our thoughts away from the ultimate tragedy."³³ Yet, discussion of suspense, anticipation, and surprise has never been systematically applied to the *Thebaid*. Rather, these aspects of forward momentum have been overshadowed by discussions of the poem's structure.³⁴ Scholars have been occupied with the structure of Statius' *Thebaid*, while ignoring the epic's overall trajectory and the strategies of anticipation developed through scenes of portentousness and doom that carry the reader from beginning to end. Narrative trajectory in the *Thebaid* is certainly a fluid operation that develops to a conclusion, not a static model of correspondences. This does not mean we should be indifferent toward the importance of connections between books, episodes, and themes. Often, however, these structural treatments imply that Statius frames a fragmented and episodic narrative,³⁵ a view further emphasized in discussions of its initial composition for performance.³⁶ Feeney, however, argues against the notion of a loose episodic structure by demonstrating the close command that Statius demonstrates over his material in the frequent signaling within the "eddies and drifts of his narrative."³⁷ Indeed, fostering a sense of "what next?" appears to be a dominant strategy for Statius. The *Thebaid* is not inert, nor does it shift convulsively; it has a plot and a forward trajectory that hinges on anticipation for its major (and minor) ends.³⁸ Discussions of structure can be limited because of the inability to translate schemes of complementary structure into linear experience. Looking at the interconnections between books, resolving the discussion into parts, dissipates awareness of the narrative momentum and detracts from the temporal succession and linearity between episodes that is so critical to the creation of suspense and anticipation in the *Thebaid*. Thus, focus on the end of Statius' *Thebaid* is vital to evaluating its potency as the plot leads inexorably toward the fratricide.

Hitherto antecedent versions of the Theban story have been used, in as much as we can make use of them, to consider the source relationships and influence between the *Thebaid* and its predecessors. A critical aspect of the narrative, however, remains overlooked. How might an audience's familiarity with previous story versions impact the design of a new narrative? Such extensive saturation of characters and episodes would have provided Statius' readers a model on which to place probable actions in the narrative trajectory, which would allow organization and anticipation of familiar material in its temporal order. A particular matter in dealing with suspense, uncertainty, and anticipation, then, is how prior familiarity shapes interpretation of the plot. Previous experience with the Theban tradition undoubtedly impacts expectations and interpretation. Statius' audience would posses an interpretive schema for organizing and anticipating narrative material. The level of familiarity can vary considerably, but even where only knowledge of a final combat between the brothers is known, a short crib from a mythographer like Hyginus has the potential to influence awareness of outcomes and audience anticipation of events. Indeed, in Hyginus' narrative sequences on Polynices, Eteocles and Polynices fight and kill each other in all three versions, which reinforces anticipation of that event (Hyginus 68). The interplay between expectation, gained through familiarity with similar treatments, and experiencing Statius' *Thebaid* can be highly dynamic and fluid as the audience adapts and reorganizes expectations as they move through a narrative. Moreover, the degree of probability that particular events will be realized is subject to a continual process of confirmation or invalidation (until the event state is either arrived at or disconfirmed).[39] This is an avoidable feature Statius must be sensitive to in his reconstruction.

Epic and Drama

Much of the discussion throughout this study relies on drawing comparisons between epic and other genres in which the Theban myth had been presented, especially drama. Thus, a brief word on the relationship between tragic drama and epic seems warranted. Aristotle, in making an analog of the *Margites* to comedy, indicates that the Homeric epics are comparable to dramatic tragedies (*Poet.* 1448b38).[40] For Aristotle, the *Iliad* merits high esteem alongside tragic drama because the epic has similar formal properties.[41] As Hogan points out, there are more references to Homer in Aristotle's *Poetics* than to tragedians, suggesting Aristotle saw a strong link between the two genres in their "structural principles" and in their "effect and function."[42] The most critical point of formal difference between epic and dramatic tragedy is the amount of compression or expansion allowed between the two genres. While this might appear on the surface as a distinction merely between lengths, what is gained and lost in the expansion of an epic narrative is significant; the allotment of space governs the narrative. Aristotle suggests that it is to the advantage of epic to be expansive because it is difficult to represent (or rather stage) multiple events at the same time (*Poet.* 1459a35–b2).⁴³ Epic has nearly unlimited space in which to develop its narrative (*Poet.* 1449b17–20). He also cautions against adapting epic structures to dramatic tragedies since epic is by nature *polymython* (*Poet.* 1456a12).⁴⁴ Despite apparent differences in form, the two genres often share similar narrative objectives, subject matters, and effects. Aristotle points out that epic and tragedy can hardly be distinguished from one another in their effect when read (*Poet.* 1462a11–13). No matter what difficulties are found in a comprehensive view of tragedy, ultimately the aesthetic pleasure of tragedy lies in the effect it has on the participant. Between the two genres there is a shared effect in the ends toward which their narratives drive. Ultimately, as critics we should take some comfort that if we are capable of discerning the good or the bad effect in one genre, we are equally competent in judging the other (*Poetics* 1449b17–20). It is not possible to separate the two genres from one another beyond their formal qualities and their medium of presentation. Rather, the two forms are interdependent, drawing often from the same sources and aiming quite often for similar impacts, especially in the development of scenes intended to influence the spectator or reader.

Narrative is much easier to identify than define. For our purposes, Patrick O'Neill offers a convenient, base-line definition, which he equates with story. As he plainly puts it: "... stories essentially amount to the doings of particular *actors* involved in various *events* at particular *times* and in particular *places*, and a narrative discourse is thus merely a matter of saying who did what, and when, and why they did it."⁴⁵ Thus, O'Neill identifies four constituent features in the presentation of a narrative (or interchangeably story): actor, events, times, and places. Likewise, in Miecke Bal's seminal work on narratology, she identifies the following elements under consideration: Events, Actors, Time, and Location.⁴⁶ Thus, the purpose of this study is to consider the narrative construction of Statius' *Thebaid* in light of these four constituent parts, with particular emphasis on how their reconstitution, when set against previous story-versions, enables the poet to create and manipulate anticipation, suspense, and surprise. Indeed, the *Thebaid* is the best available work for a study of this kind because it offers more surviving versions with which to make comparison than any other extant work from Classical antiquity. It is, in short, the most ideal case study for trying to understand how poets attempt to create novelty and compelling narratives. I will further argue that of these four elements, the most critical to Statius' revision is time, or more precisely, the temporal ordering of events.

1

Beginning with the End

Stories seldom begin at the beginning. When poets begin *in medias res*, as Horace suggests at *Ars Poetica* 146–50, they leave much undisclosed and must set aside, at least initially, the events that inform that opening moment. Nevertheless, a sense of causality persists. As Aristotle defines *mythos*: there needs to be a beginning, middle, and ending, and the beginning is not to be preceded by anything other than itself (*Poet.* 1450b21–b34). The manipulation of how and when events occur are a traditional resource for story-telling and one of its most readily manipulated features.[1] Narrative anachrony, or non-chronological modes of narration, refers to the narrative presentation of action that has taken or will take place outside the present moment. Gerard Genette defines these as "all forms of discordance between the two temporal orders of story and narrative."[2] Anachrony can also posit temporal boundaries, providing a sense of what to expect within the work at hand, and what lays beyond its scope or interest. Narrative anachrony comes in two basic flavors. Analepsis corresponds to events that precede the "present" (commonly known as exposition or back shadowing). Genette defines this device as "any evocation after the fact of an event that took place earlier than the point in the story where we are at a given moment."[3] The logical counterpart to analepsis is to be found in references to the future, or prolepsis, defined as "any narrative maneuver that consists of narrating or evoking in advance an event that will take place later."[4] This device is commonly associated with notions of "foreshadowing."[5] While complementary, analepsis and prolepsis are far from mirror-images of each other.[6] The notional use of analepsis is to provide background information;[7] however, as I address in this chapter, references to the past often cue anticipation for events to come. This is done by exploiting a sense of continuity, where events happen, as Aristotle notes, "because of" one another (*Poet.* 1452a). Indeed, as Peter Brooks notes, perhaps with Aristotle in mind, it is necessary to the beginning to start with the end.[8] The present chapter thus considers how the canonical ending of the conflict between Eteocles and Polynices influences the openings of Euripides' *Phoenissae* and

Statius' *Thebaid*. Both Euripides and Statius are preoccupied with creating anticipation for the fratricide; however, I am most interested in how temporal ordering and the references to the past and/or the future create anticipation for the outcome. The openings of the Theban narratives under consideration here use anachrony to create both connections and gaps that manipulate anticipation for the ending.[9]

They Call Me Jocasta

One advantage that canonical narratives have for poets is that mere reference to key events, places, or characters often relieve some of the burden of exposition for the poet, since the audience already has some understanding of the causal circumstances to likely lead to the narrative's opening. In a surviving fragment of his *Poesis*, the comedian Antiphanes begrudges tragedians the ease with which they can index considerable background information with the use of a single name.[10]

> μακάριόν ἐστιν ἡ τραγῳδία
> ποίημα κατὰ πάντ,' εἴ γε πρῶτον οἱ λόγοι
> ὑπὸ τῶν θεατῶν εἰσιν ἐγνωρισμένοι,
> πρὶν καί τιν' εἰπεῖν· ὥσθ' ὑπομνῆσαι μόνον
> δεῖ τὸν ποιητήν· Οἰδίπουν γὰρ ἂν μόνον
> φῶ, τἄλλα πάντ' ἴσασιν· ὁ πατὴρ Λάιος,
> μήτηρ Ἰοκάστη, θυγατέρες, παῖδες τίνες,
> τί πείσεθ' οὗτος, τί πεποίηκεν.
>
> Fr. 191.1–8

Tragedy is blessed in every way. First, the audience knows the stories even before a character says a word, so all a poet has to do is remind them! Let me mention Oedipus and they know the rest: his father was Laius, his mother was Jocasta — they know who his daughters were, and his sons, and what will happen to him, and the things he has done.

For Antiphanes familiarity with mythic material influences the poet's narrative constructions, especially with regard to what need or need not be supplied. Antiphanes notes of Oedipus that by the mention of his name not only is his genealogy referenced, but the events of his life: what he has done, what he will do (τί πείσεθ' οὗτος, τί πεποίηκεν). These buttresses of past and future imply a present moment, a point in the characters' biography to separate these two, which is the time of the story being told. Thus, once a character has been situated temporally in a narrative retelling the audience will know what events led the character up to his or her present state, and they can also anticipate what events may befall them in the narrative at hand. Pratt persuasively argues that among Greek audiences the narrative material for tragedies was not as well-known as is often supposed, especially when considerable space is given to the establishment of identities.[11] He argues as evidence the emendation of εἴ γε for ἧς γε in the second line of Antiphanes' *Poiesis* fragment, a difference that favors "if" for "since." Pratt translates the passage as: "Tragedy is in every respect fortunate . . . *if*, in the first place, the stories are known by the spectators before anyone speaks, so that the poet has only to remind the audience."[12]

The way in which the revelation of identity impacts readers' or audiences' initial sense of expectation is evident in Jocasta's prologue to Euripides' *Phoenissae*. Euripides, and Statius as I discuss later, use the past to anticipate future events in their narratives. Jocasta's opening lines, while delimiting the location of the play as Thebes, arouse initial curiosity in the audience for the identity of the speaker. Once that curiosity is satisfied with the revelation of her name the audience must speculate on the time of her speaking. Moreover, since the audience cannot know from what point in her biography she is speaking, it is impossible to determine whether she should be alive or dead, which precludes the possibility of surprise largely held to be created by her appearance.[13] The initial inability to bind her identity to the chronology of her life at the outset of Euripides' *Phoenissae* creates anticipation or curiosity for the resolution of that unknown. When Jocasta recounts the events that bring the audience current she frames her backstory to be so suspenseful and compelling that her narrative occludes the intrusion of the variant tradition. In addition, Euripides employs strategies to create anticipation for the fratricidal conflict through the Apollonian prophecy, Oedipus' curse, and her concluding prayer.

Prologues frame a narrative's necessary features. At the start of his *Phoenissae* Euripides presents the lone figure of a lamenting woman,[14] who begins with an 87-line monologue, the longest extant, that recounts Thebes' distant past from Cadmus' founding to the present moment of crisis in which her sons Eteocles and Polynices vie for sole rule of their father's kingdom.

[Ὦ τὴν ἐν ἄστροις οὐρανοῦ τέμνων ὁδὸν
καὶ χρυσοκολλήτοισιν ἐμβεβὼς δίφροις]
Ἥλιε, θοαῖς ἵπποισιν εἱλίσσων φλόγα,
ὡς δυστυχῆ Θήβαισι τῆι τόθ' ἡμέραι

ἀκτῖν' ἐφῆκας, Κάδμος ἡνίκ' ἦλθε γῆν
τήνδ,' ἐκλιπὼν Φοίνισσαν ἐναλίαν χθόνα·
ὃς παῖδα γήμας Κύπριδος Ἁρμονίαν ποτὲ
Πολύδωρον ἐξέφυσε, τοῦ δὲ Λάβδακον
φῦναι λέγουσιν, ἐκ δὲ τοῦδε Λάιον.
ἐγὼ δὲ παῖς μὲν κλῄζομαι Μενοικέως,
[Κρέων τ' ἀδελφὸς μητρὸς ἐκ μιᾶς ἔφυ,]
καλοῦσι δ' Ἰοκάστην με·

Phoen. 1-12

Gliding your path through the heavenly bodies, on a chariot inlaid with gold, Helios, swift horses and whirring flame. Thebes, unfortunate on that long ago day when you directed your gaze as Cadmus came to this land, leaving the Phoenician shores. He wed Aphrodite's daughter Harmonia, and sired Polydorus, and then, so they say, came Labdacus, and then Laios. I am the child of Menoikeos, my brother is Creon, born from the same mother, and they call me Jocasta.

As the first speaker, Jocasta serves two functions. First, she participates within the drama as an integral character, bound to the laws of Euripides' story-world. Second, she establishes the scene; she functions initially as narrator or storyteller.[15] She will establish the space of the drama as Thebes, introduce characters, provide a temporal frame, and create anticipation for coming events.[16] And most of the information she provides depends on her spoken cues because the sparse scene offers little to no identification of the immediate place and time of her oration.[17] Indeed, she reveals the coming conflict only near the end of her speech, which Antigone and the tutor take up in more vivid detail with the flashing armor of the heroes and their armies.

Jocasta prioritizes "where" in the locative Θήβαισι (4) and she presents a vague but painful condition of suffering there through the utterances ὡς δυστυχῇ, which identifies the sorrows that began on the day Cadmus arrived from coastal Phoenicia. The mention of Thebes manifests a space that is remote from and counter to Athens, and liable to bespeak "democracy's mirror opposite, a closed-in, suffocating, xenophobic tyranny whose royalty specialized in making both love and war within their immediate family."[18] Thebes is a place where wicked and unnatural things happen, and its foul and polluted history no doubt rushes to the audience's mind when the place is mentioned. This initial *ponoi* motif reaches far into the remote past, and is reminiscent of the nurse's complaints in Euripides' *Medea* in that both proceed *ab ovo* and augment pathos; establishing plaints long in time.[19] Her lament creates a sense of pervasive woe that magnifies the sorrow of her present moment. She bemoans a state of misfortune that began with Cadmus' founding of Thebes and has not yet, by the time of speaking, resolved. The day of Cadmus' arrival precedes the one on which she speaks, but until she tells the audience we cannot yet know how long ago that was. Additionally, the conventional use of Helios as an overseeing omniscient spectator gazing indifferently on this day and all days before, and to whom Jocasta complains, further emphasizes the sense of endless suffering; the suggestion here is that Thebes and its people have always and will always be unfortunate.[20] Jocasta emphasizes Thebes as a place of persistent woe to the neglect of happier times in its history, which has puzzled some readers.[21] Indeed, the chorus cites some of these μυριάδας δ' ἀγαθῶν in the close of the second stasimon (822–31). But Jocasta's repression of these past glories supports Zeitlin's suggestion that in Thebes "there can be no escape from the tragic in the resolution of conflict."[22] But this selective recollection is not merely histrionic. In the face of misfortune, as Euripides demonstrates, former glories have no value. As Antigone, who by the end of the play becomes *ersatz*-mother to Oedipus, scolds when her father reminisces about his triumph over the Sphinx (*Phoen*. 1733–34).

Antigone at the end, like her mother at the beginning, cannot focus on happy times and perceives such seeming good success as the origin for their reversal. Through the extensive chain of causality all of these events can be traced back to, as Jocasta wails, Cadmus' founding of Thebes.[23] Despite how easily we are pulled into Jocasta's lament, we must be mindful that there are actually two temporal points in play here. One has its origins in the distant mythic past, which she recounts, and the other in the time from which Jocasta speaks. Thus, Euripides approves the later Horatian injunction to begin *in medias res*, to circumvent lengthy exhibition (*Ars P.* 146–50). Such opening plays necessitate the use of non-chronological narration, or anachrony, in order to make the present moment intelligible.[24] Notably, until Jocasta reveals the present moment she would seem to exist outside of time, we are not in the middle of anything as yet, except her suffering.[25] Starting in the middle requires that part of her expository function reconcile the distance between the external analepsis/retroversion and from "when" Jocasta speaks.[26] In hearkening backward, the opening stratagem is to create two conflicting temporal expositions. On the one hand, we have Jocasta, clearly present at an unidentified point in time at the start of the play, and on the other hand, we have Jocasta's story, which begins from a *terminus a quo* of mythic antiquity.

After the patrilineal genealogy that connects the speaker through her marriage to Laios with the Cadmeian line, she identifies herself as Jocasta: καλοῦσι δ' Ἰοκάστην με (12). Jocasta's self-identification in conjunction with the episodes she relates, authenticate her identity. Revelation of her name, however, does not sufficiently indicate at what point in her life she is at the start of the play, so at this point there can be no surprise that she is alive because we do not yet know whether she should be alive or dead. When Jocasta reveals herself to the audience her identity becomes established within the canonical episodes of her life and narrows the temporal range against the sweeping scope of Thebes' history; the audience knows who the speaker is, but does not yet know "when" she is within her own biographical vectors. As a dramatic performance the audience would not know the speaker's identity until 12, though they would have some formulation of her character (i.e. old woman). Later readers, of course, may have peritextual markers like a helpful ΙΟΚΑΣΤΗ preceding the speech, provided that it had been written into the manuscript. The identification of character demarcates a limit whose life generally sets a boundary, so when Euripides gives a "who" there is a great deal of "what" and "when" against which her identity can be aligned. The name is suggestive, it cues what one can expect, but in the end is more anticipatory than revelatory.

Through Jocasta, Euripides uses the past to condition reception and expectation of future events.[27] Embedded within this function is also a creation of anticipation. Her exposition stabilizes the presented versions within mythic tradition. Euripides' opening tactic uses analepsis to provide background and preparations, a feature for which the device is commonly used.[28] The prologue and review are most certainly directed at an audience already familiar with the myth and antecedent story versions. Such an audience, by virtue of exposure, has an operative script regarding the Theban mythos.[29] But as a stabilizing gesture, the prologue serves anyone experiencing the story for the first time by imparting some necessary preparations.[30] As Craik notes: "Euripides seems to rely on familiarity with the myth and with previous dramatic treatments to secure an effective impact for his innovations."[31] An essential function of the analepses provided in Jocasta's speech, however, is to stabilize a tradition in flux.[32] Yet even the notion of competing traditions or varied canonical interests aside, the sheer amount of material available within the Theban saga demands finding and delimiting a notional point at which to reify time, space, and characters from a dizzying panoply of episodes.[33] Creating a stable connection between the mimetic present and the mythic past are critical to Euripides' opening scene in the *Phoenissae*.

After revealing her identity Jocasta recounts her childlessness with Laios and the prophecy of Apollo, then launches a veritable Bildungsroman of Oedipus' conception, exposure, foundling days, adoption, the search for his true identity, and encounter at the crossroads at Pholcis (21–42). As Jocasta recounts these family events she gradually brings us closer to the present point from which she speaks.³⁴ After the death of Laios, Jocasta recounts Oedipus' victory over the Sphinx (45), her status as prize (47), and the fruit of their matrimony. At 59-62 she tells of Oedipus' realization of the incest, μαθὼν δὲ τἀμὰ λέκτρα μητρῴων γάμων (59). Readers should note the sudden detachment and distance in the way Jocasta suddenly refocalizes her narrative to Oedipus' point of view here. Lamari suggests "the narrative position of the heterodigetic narrator grants Jocasta a secure distance from the narrated events."³⁵ While Jocasta's seeming detachment and remove is incontestable in the prologue, the notion of "secure distance" gives some pause; dissociative, to play at clinical diagnosis might be more apt. Psychologically removed, which gives the events more poignancy in her reluctance to insert herself more directly into the narrative until it is to note dramatically the result of her affair with Oedipus. The detachment creates a more dramatic effect, setting up herself as removed from the horror only to suddenly spring the horror of "I" bore him children in the first-person: τίκτω δὲ παῖδας παιδὶ (55). Jocasta then narrates the children, the realization of incest, and the gold brocades with which Oedipus gouges out his eyes.

In the accounts of Homer's *Odyssey* (11.271-9) and Sophocles' *Oedipus Tyrannus* 1223-530 Jocasta ("Epikaste" in the *Nekyia*) commits suicide after the revelation of incest.³⁶ Because of this tradition many readers maintain that Jocasta's presence at the start of the play creates an innovative surprise.³⁷ Identifying a precise point in her opening speech in which surprise can occur, however, is problematized by our inability to position her in time. The problem is not that Jocasta's presentation is unexpected, but that in the presentation of the features of the story, it is difficult to pin down at what point any surprise is likely to have taken place. The narrative structure of Jocasta's prologue, and the chronological revelation of key narrative dimensions that define her present moment, her time "when," do not support this claim. After bringing us to the pitch of "affective intensity"³⁸ Jocasta moves quickly to Oedipus' house arrest by his sons to hide, apparently with little success, the shame related to the incest. In order to experience surprise at Jocasta's presence we must know the story that Euripides tells in order to relate her to a divergence in narrative trajectory. This is not to say that Jocasta's presence is not an innovation, it certainly could be, and perhaps this is what scholars have in mind when they suggest that her presence is a surprise.³⁹ And there is little doubt that Euripides responds to Aeschylus, who does not feature Jocasta in the *Septem*, presumably because she is dead, at several turns.⁴⁰ Her own presence precludes anticipation for her having died shortly after the revelation of their incestuous union, so a condition of surprise in the prologue appears doubtful because it is too quickly set aside to present Eteocles and Polynices hiding him away. Moreover, surprise would deflate the narrative potential of Jocasta's prologue. Granted, curiosity could be aroused, but this too is inconsistent with the trajectory of her discourse. The sequence of engagement conjured here seems to be an anticipation for the speaker's identity, followed by anticipation as she narrates Oedipus and his trajectory, building to the anticipated canonical episode of anagnoresis, the filial disrespect of his sons, declaration of the curse against them, and the present conflict. The problem with surprise at seeing Jocasta as she relates the back-story is that at no point is she presented as though she should not be there; she is so deftly woven into the fabric of her own narrative that it is as though she never could have died.

While readers note the anticipation in Jocasta's opening speech, none have explored the way in which this anticipation is constructed.[41] As mentioned, Jocasta identifies the Apollonian prophecy that attends Laius' siring children which claims: εἰ γὰρ τεκνώσεις παῖδ,' ἀποκτενεῖ σ' ὁ φύς, | καὶ πᾶς σὸς οἶκος βήσεται δι' αἵματος, "if you should bear child, it will kill you and bathe all your house in blood" (19–20). The prophecy has two parts: one specific, the other much less so but equally dire. In the first part any offspring will kill Laios, but in the second there is a vague, albeit graphic, suggestion of continued but unspecified death. Euripides nests prolepsis in the form of prophecy within Jocasta's exposition and casts attention forward. Nevertheless, it is uncertain whether either part of this prophecy has yet been fulfilled. Once Jocasta reveals, παῖς πατέρα καίνει (44), the first part of Apollo's portentous prophecy is resolved and no longer has any anticipatory power; however, the notion that the Labdacid family is to be steeped in blood remains open, and so still as an anticipatory cue.[42] Despite being part of the narrated past, the revelation of the prophecy becomes anticipatory in that it suggests the possibility of completion at some future point. After Jocasta reaches the climax of Oedipus' fateful revelation and his self-blinding she reveals how their sons imprisoned Oedipus.[43] Once imprisoned Jocasta relates that Oedipus is alive, which sets up anticipation for a later encounter.[44] And from his solitary darkness Oedipus curses his sons, that they will divide their inheritance with a sword: θηκτῶι σιδήρωι δῶμα διαλαχεῖν τόδε (68). The precise motivation for this is vague compared to the surviving epic fragments but nevertheless consistent with the theme of filial maltreatment and impiety.[45] Oedipus' curse sets up a second anticipatory moment against his sons and opens another temporal gap while boosting the potency of Apollo's curse recounted earlier. Eteocles and Polynices fearing their father's curse decide on alternate rule, but Eteocles fails to cede the throne after the first year, and

Polynices goes to Argos making a marriage alliance and raising an army against his brother. He has now arrived with his foreign allies to fight against his homeland, which anticipates the fulfillment of Oedipus' curse. Thus, information and action related to past time anticipates future events.[46] Jocasta then closes with a prayer to Zeus that her sons reconcile and suggests that it is unjust for one person to always be unhappy (*Phoen.* 84–7).

Tragically, and with no small irony, the prayer will be fulfilled, just not in the manner hoped. In her prayer, she intends σύμβασιν to mean "agreement," but the word has the root sense of "coming together."[47] This prayer, in fact, complements the prayers of her sons to kill each other.[48] Given that the fratricide of the brothers is so well known, Jocasta directs attention to that outcome by attempting to derail it.[49] Thus, Apollo's prophecy, Oedipus' curse, and Jocasta's prayer, with its ironic germ of completion by coming together, point toward a conclusion, an end.

Anna Lamari raises an important point when she suggests that Jocasta's lengthy analepsis "creates the feeling that the 'clock,' which calculates the time of the story, has not started ticking yet."[50] Once Jocasta begins to relate more recent events the zero-point of the story "clock" would seem nearly begun. As Lamari rightly argues, a sense of the "present" is finally obtained at 66 when Jocasta informs the audience that Oedipus lives in the house (ζῶν δ' ἔστ' ἐν οἴκοις, 66).[51] This line expresses, however, a time and space that is parallel to Jocasta. Oedipus is in the home, Jocasta is outside.[52] Similarly, her later description of Polynices as she references him in the present moment bringing his foreign contingent also reveals their separation in space. Jocasta then reveals how she arranged the truce and was told by a messenger that Polynices will come (81–3). It is at that moment that Jocasta's temporal position is revealed, because we know as the time relates to her, that she is waiting for Polynices. Indeed, this revelation is retrogressive because it allows us to read back against her prologue, it completes the scene. Within narrative or fictive time the start and stop points fit into a global construction of emplotment wherein events are bound by a causal relationship. As Aristotle comments, events should happen "because of" one another (*Poetics* 1452a). The anachrony of Jocasta's narration directs attention away from the "present" moment of her story to a moment that lies outside it. But this activity is also part of what she is doing as she waits. Since analepsis treats past moments, in this capacity it connects the present with the past. Creating temporal connections is critical to the construction of stories. The cognitive ability to reorder information that is temporally disordered, provided the events can be cogently connected, permits extensive flexibility in the order of presentation.[53] Thus, the "clock" that marks that start of the *Phoenissae* began when Jocasta appeared as a dramatic character, but we do not know "when" she is until the end of the prologue when we understand what she is doing. Essentially, the "clock" has been continually running and we are just jumping into things as the misfortune becomes more imminent. Jocasta's lament is thus coextensive with her current activity, waiting. Her present is implied in that she now waits to receive Polynices, and make an effort to forestall or prevent the fratricidal conflict. Here, as we realize that we have been made to wait with Jocasta, we cross the temporal boundary that separates past and present.[54] Notably, now that we know what to anticipate and are properly oriented for events to come, Antigone's *teichoskopia* and the choral *parados* of Phoenician women will delay Polynices' arrival.

The *Thebaid*'s Prologue

Similarly, though in a different way, Statius encourages anticipation for the *Thebaid*'s end. Indeed, the proem is more concerned with ending than beginning.[55] The first lines summon the conflict between Eteocles and Polynices from the recesses of history and myth: "Fraternas acies alternaque regna profanis | Decertata odiis sontisque evolvere Thebas, | Pierius menti calor incidit," "Fraternal lines drawn in battle, the alternate reign decided by wicked hate, and Thebes ever guilty; the heat of Pierian fire burns me tell of these things" (*Theb.* 1.1–3). The prologue delimits its temporal boundaries and imparts knowledge of where the story is to end.[56] In doing so, however, Statius also creates temporal gaps. Statius' prophetic first utterances echo the "cognatas acies" of Lucan (1.4), which may have encouraged a likely misprision of "alternaque" for "cognataque" according to Barthius.[57] As Vessey notes, "euoluere" governs three moments of the story; they are not, however, in an "inverse (chrono)logical order" as he suggests.[58] The "fraternas acies" indicate simply enough the respective battle-lines of Eteocles, with his Theban forces, arrayed against Polynices' Argive contingent. Reference to the "alternate reign fought out with dire hatred" must indicate the actual waging of the war because "decertata" conveys the sense of a completed event. The adoption of the alternate rule to avoid fulfillment of Oedipus' curse reveals at least a momentary accord; the "profane hatred" does not come until later. Indeed, as Dominik notes, Eteocles expresses no concern for the coming sea-change until Laius' eldritch visitation.[59] Nor does Polynices know that his portion is to be denied until Tydeus' embassy. So the initial plan was clearly formulated in a spirit of hope and compromise. Statius then moves to the "sontes Thebas," which proposes the condemnation of these first two events, and inclusively the fratricide.[60] Granted, it would be possible to take Thebes, or the line itself, as guilty but Eteocles and Polynices are notionally innocent outside their filial impiety until they engage one another. The guilt does not, or at least should not, extend back to Oedipus because the gods pardoned him (*Theb.* 1.236-8). So the initial order is progressive toward the end and conclusion of the *Thebaid*, not retrospective. Moreover, the reign fought out in "profanis odiis" and the condemnation of Thebes as "sontes" closes the moral interpretation of these events.[61] In effect, the events are prejudged. As Gary Paul Morson observes, the presentation of events in the past as "backshadowing" imparts to the observer a fundamentally superior position.[62] As a chronotope Thebes is convenient shorthand for pollution, *nefas*, and guilt, so it is understood that what is to be anticipated is quite rotten. Statius is not inviting judgment, at least not yet. While the moral implication and interpretation of these events can be at times ambiguous in the *Thebaid*, the emphatic judgment here conditions an anticipatory response. What will happen here has already happened in the mytho-historic record, and will happen again here in this story-version. The guilt of Thebes is intractable, permanent, or even monumental. A stain that cannot be washed away or forgotten with the passing of time. But while the guilt of Thebes may be boundless and unchangeable, its retellings are not. Statius' first words provide a "metus," a goal in a brief sketch of the *terminus ad quem* toward which his narrative is to be ordered.

The use of "euoluere" expresses the linear process through which the Theban story is to be presented and the sense of a "rolling out" as one would a scroll.[63] The linearity inhibits literary narratives from being presented all at once or in their entirety. Though the entire field of events cannot be taken in at a glance (*totum simul*) this does not mean that the events must be discussed in chronological order. Our cognitive ability to reorder information that is temporally disordered, provided the events can be cogently connected, permits extensive flexibility in the order of presentation.[64] This flexibility offers a convenient resource for the development of anticipation, suspense, and surprise within stories, by presenting elements of the past or future to work with or against the acute sensitivity to sequence and connections between events. Thus integral to the development of suspense and anticipation is the manipulation of expectation through the way in which events are made known, not only in the "present," but in the "narrated" (e.g. a narrator's omniscient whim to discuss what has happened or will have happened, but with the awareness presented tapping into their thoughts, or presenting their speech), but in the reference to what is passed, or will come to pass. So while events and actions revealed in narrative cannot escape their linearity, the flexibility of temporal presentation provide the narrator with a convenient means of controlling the presentation of events and information regarding them. Thus Statius can move freely from the end of his *Thebaid* back to the very origins of Thebes.

In beginning with the end Statius creates the awareness of a temporal gap. We have the end, the future, we know what to look forward to, but what about the beginning, where do we start from? Statius poses this question for us. After establishing in the first lines where, or rather when, he wants his story to end, Statius reels over the sheer scope of where a Theban history can begin. Before launching into a lengthy index of possible points of origin, Statius asks: "unde iubetis | ire, deae?," "From where would you have me begin, goddess?" (*Theb.* 1.3-4). The elliptical summary that follows could be construed as ostentatious bravado, intended to draw attention to the vast store of myth that Statius has at his command. But Statius is not referring to anything with which the majority of his audience was unfamiliar.[65] Indeed, the allusions are only effective where they are already known, since here they are under-developed and presented in only the barest outline, sometimes quite allusively. Most of these instances suffer extraordinary informational gaps, which suggests either Statius assumes audiences are familiar with his oblique references or (far less likely) Statius is being too much the *doctus poeta*. Of course, the possibility exists that some readers were uninitiated, but it is difficult to imagine many within his close circle of educated readers being so. And so we are left to conclude that if Statius is writing for an audience that is not familiar with this material, then much of the exposition here falls short. But if they do grasp immediately how far back Statius threatens to begin then they understand how remote from the fall of Oedipus and the Thebic wars these historical points are. Despite its cursory and elliptical nature, the series progresses forward providing the sense of moving to a point. When he declares the "limes" the reader does not really know how close to that end point, or even the beginning, they may be. Statius maintains a forward looking but elliptical series of prolepses to accelerate through the proem and into the narrative's "present," which will be Oedipus and his curse.[66] Thus, Statius creates anticipation and uncertainty from the start by exploiting the need for and expectation of a present moment. Since Statius here searches for a narrative present with which to begin his narrative thread these backward glances have as yet no present to be associated with; however, they do have a future in the "fraternas acies" which gives them a temporal position, a kind of forward anchoring. Moreover, these mytho-historic mentions reside outside the narrative's reach, which we know because Statius chooses to reject them as possible points of departure. They are also instanced in brief punches, and in the case of Juno, elusive extents, nevertheless, woven into the rich tapestry of the Theban mythos. The designated categories of narration, while extremely helpful in understanding how stories are put together, are also limited. Not all references invoking past or future states, or even present states for that matter, have or will come to pass. External, and yet, not unattached or irrelevant.

The past rushes the audience in the prologue. Without the mediation of the present, the vantage point from which this history can be surveyed properly, Thebes' long history threatens to run amok until the poet can assert control.[67] An audience familiar with the Theban myth would know the tales surrounding Thebes reach far back into the remote past, and a story-version that reaches too far back, and has too much ground to cover before the narrative's expected climax would be trying. Statius unsettles readers when he wonders "gentisne canam primordia dirae | Sidonios raptus et inexorable pactum | legis Agenoreae scrutantemque aequora Cadmum?," "Should I sing first the origins of that hateful line, the Sidonian rape, Agenor's inexorabile pact, Cadmus searching the waters?" (1.4–6). Statius threatens (playfully?) what would surely be a long exposition from the origins of the Theban people.[68] Such ambitious efforts were not unknown. Aristotle criticizes poets who attempt to stuff the whole scope of the Trojan War into the scope of a single tragedy, and names Agathon (the host of Plato's symposium, incidentally) in this particular regard (*Poet.* 1456a13–19).[69] Thus he provides something of an end, but not yet a beginning. In his *Ars Poetica* Horace pleads with poets of epic not to recount stories *ab ovo*. Ovid humorously mocks this injunction by starting his own "perpetuum carmen" from the origin of the world.[70] But Statius catches himself. No, that's all too far back, as he notes of the "longa retro series."[71] Perhaps he could begin with Cadmus' sowing of the seeds, Amphion raising the walls? Bacchus? Athamas? Juno? This has a slight nod to the *Aeneid*. All of these are passed over, but until Statius says "limes mihi carminis esto | Oedipodae confusa domus," "let the confused house of Oedipus set the limits to my song" (1.16–17), the historical reach backward allows any of these to be a possible *terminus a quo*.[72] This opening frustrates the audience's expectations because though the narrative has been initiated, the story has not really begun. The point from which we can move forward has not been found, and we wait in anticipation as Statius fumbles for a thread with which to create the gap, the point that will bind the *Thebaid*'s start to the end which has already been established.

But then, after establishing that the house of Oedipus will mark the boundaries of his epic, Statius redirects attention away from his Theban narrative and toward the epic he will not write on Domitian's military success. In this fulsome *recusatio* he promises to recount later the worthy deeds of the emperor in future song (1.17–33) before returning to the concerns of the *Thebaid* proper. This sudden break away from the development of Theban material proffers an effective strategy for developing anticipation and appears to have an integral function in the prologue's initial strategy.[73] Just at the point where the prologue establishes a temporal boundary for beginning the epic there comes a surprise shift to unrelated material before again focusing on Thebes.

When Statius picks up the trail he again focuses on the end toward which he aims, though with greater specificity. The swift and elliptical presentation of heroes and their dooms reorients the reader toward the end points, as though to counterbalance the distractions presented with Thebes' remote past, and Domitian's recent glories.[74] Like the "fraternas acies," the mention of past events to be retold create a substantial gap and Statius places particular emphasis on the conflict's fallout, presented in a way that extends beyond the height of the conflict to produce the effect that the war was somehow overlooked. The "arma Aonia" (33–34) synecdoche describes the height of the conflict, while the "sceptrum exitiale" favors event over cause where the qualification of "fatal" anticipates the brothers' mutual fratricide. Statius also invokes the familiar trope of competing flames, which anticipates when Argia and Antigone recover the body of Polynices and place it on the one still smoldering pyre they find, which happens to be Eteocles'. Finally, Statius mentions Creon's edict refusing burial to the dead, and a generally lamentable loss of life. Note also the unnaturalness of the war: the blood of heroic corpses changes the color of the Dirce. What proceeds from this point forward hinges on a trust between reader and text (and implicitly author) that a logical sequence of events will close the gap between initial actions up to the fated pyres.

Before Statius closes the proem he invokes the goddess Clio, whose customary purview is history, to give him a hero with which to begin the story.[75]

quem prius heroum, Clio, dabis? inmodicum irae
Tydea? laurigeri subitos an uatis hiatus?
urguet et hostilem propellens caedibus amnem
Hippomedon, plorandaque bella proterui
Arcados atque alio Capaneus horrore canendus

Theb. 1.41–45

> Which of the heroes comes first, Clio? Tydeus unchecked in anger? Or the swallowing of the laureled priest, perhaps? Hippomedon eagerly rushing against the river, his enemy, with corpses? The Arcadian, beautiful and head strong, he must be wept, and Capaneus, to be sung with a shudder.

Statius offers a focused *telos* in the range of ends that the heroes of his epic will meet. In this way, the prologue anticipates horrible events throughout the narrative.[76] The invocation of Clio and allusion to known stories, defined by their outcome, allows Statius to breech the fabula and its history, to reopen what was sealed so that it may contend with the "prisca nomina" that have already sung Thebes.[77] Notably, when the prologue concludes it is with the inference that the story will begin with one of the heroes alluded to, "quem prius, Clio." Contrary to the expectations developed, however, the first hero presented will be Oedipus. Let us now turn our attention to the portentousness Statius uses to develop anticipation for the war.

2

Portentous Beginnings

Statius uses portentousness and the supernatural to create an atmosphere of doom and heighten tension throughout the *Thebaid*.[1] Indeed, prophecy and omens present one of the most convenient expository devices in ancient literature for framing future events.[2] The multi-functional scenes can, as a form of foreshadowing (or prolepsis), reveal the narrative's temporal frame while remaining part of the narrative event. Throughout the *Thebaid*, Statius seeds the narrative with anticipatory cues that signal coming catastrophe, but concentrates portentous events in the first four books. A tension between knowledge and ignorance on the part of the characters underlies all these portents. In creating anticipation for the audience, then, there is a vital interplay between how much the reader knows, and how little the reader knows that characters know. This interplay allows the reader to enjoy a fundamentally superior position. The fates of characters often engenders sympathy and pity, and outcomes are driven as much by what will happen, as by the reaction of characters to the outcome. From that advantageous position we can sympathize, judge, condemn, applaud, or wish things might turn out otherwise.[3] Moreover, these anticipatory moments remind the audience of the impending disaster that will eventually arrive at Thebes. The work of the early books is preparatory, not only in the way they establish logical motives, but also in the way they develop connections between the reader and the characters through portents and omens. The present chapter examines how Statius uses portentousness and a sense of foreboding to create anticipation in readers and anxiety among characters for the conflict.[4]

Argos and the Seeds of War

Preparations for the conflict begin in Argos at the Palace of Adrastus, as Jupiter declares. After Oedipus makes his condemnations against his sons and Tisiphone promptly takes up his cause, Jupiter calls a *concilium deorum* during which he stresses the need to punish humanity. He ratifies Oedipus' prayer and condemns the two houses, Thebes and Argos. At the close of his speech Jupiter resolves to incite a fresh war and to pull out the whole stock at Thebes, which will end the royal line of Laius when power passes to Jocasta's brother, Creon, after the deaths of Eteocles and Polynices. Jupiter identifies the house of Adrastus and the marriage alliance furnished by the king's daughter, Argia, as the flash-point for the conflict.[5] He declares: "belli mihi semina sunto | Adrastus socer et superis ah, iuncta sinistris | canubia," "Let Adrastus' gift of his daughter, to be married in divine disfavor, be seed for battle" (*Theb.* 1.243–5).[6] Indeed, Jupiter's position is intractable, and nothing will turn him from his resolve (1.290-2). This decree anticipates Argos for the origins of the conflict, and provides the stage for ominous scenes that anticipate the war and its tragic outcome for both sides. The union will be made in "superis sinistris," which expresses the divine disapproval under which the wedding is to take place. This disapproval will be revealed in the portents that will haunt Argos after Polynices' arrival and through the wedding festivities until war is decided.

The first violence at Argos is not between enemies, however, but strangers destined to become friends and brothers through marriage. On his return journey Polynices comes to Argos, a peaceful ("tranquille") kingdom where king Adrastus reigns. Adrastus, anxious by disposition and throughout the epic, worries over his lack of a male heir and ponders Apollo's prophecy that fate will lead a boar and a lion as husbands to his daughters, Argia and Deipyl. The full import of this prophecy is beyond the vatic capacities of Adrastus and Amphiaraus because Apollo will not allow full disclosure (1.395–99).[7] When the newcomer, Tydeus, also seeks shelter from the rains and frigid winds he encounters Polynices who had already secured for himself a place on the cold ground. Like his brother Eteocles, Polynices will not share any part of his meager territory. The two combat one another, attacking bare-handed, but the situation escalates to the point where they would have drawn swords had Adrastus not intervened.

The scene offers the *Thebaid*'s theme in miniature. We have two men that are, as upheld by Statius and tradition, brothers; both have the stain of fratricide within their biographies. Tydeus has killed his brother and guilt, his *conscious horror*, drives him into exile. Polynices will eventually kill his own brother. The fight between Eteocles and Polynices takes place for no other reason than hate and covetousness. Neither are moved by notions of glory or praise ("cupidine laudis," 1.425). Their sole motivation is that neither will suffer to share the space ("haud passi sociis defendere noctem | culminibus," 1.409-10). Statius makes them comparable to animals in their territoriality, and presses this association through the description of their clawed hands ("unca manus," 1.427). As feral beasts, a condition improper to men but one brought about by exile, they fight over the scrap of territory with no more motivation than to possess it. As Tydeus later acknowledges, even civilized mythical monsters, Cyclopi and Centauri, share sleeping spaces (1.457-60). On the one hand, this scene reveals Polynices' status as an exile and the mean conditions in which he lives; he fights for the smallest bit of shelter. On the other hand, the fight with Tydeus, destined to be Polynices' brother-in-law, foreshadows the fraternal combat between Polynices and Eteocles. Statius likely models his impoverished Thebes hardly worth the war on traditional claims, which contrast the motivation.[8]

The commotion outside rouses Adrastus who emerges from his palace to quash the fray. Earlier Argos had been honoring Apollo, as he explains in the digression of Coroebus. Adrastus embodies the eidolon of Cato, a man of piety and gravity as described in the first simile of the *Aeneid* (1.148-56), the comparand for Neptune as he settles the storms sent against Aeneas by Aeolus. Adrastus' inquiry "quae causa furoris" 1.438, echoing certainly Lucan 1.8, beseeches them to explain for what reason they fight. Their brawling contrasts with Adrastus' efforts to impose peace and civility.[9] The king has been successful in his own domain and diplomatically flatters them with the suggestion that their anger is noble and makes them appear well-born.[10] This role as peacemaker persists throughout the epic until his ability to do so fails against Tisiphone who supplants him when Polynices seeks his "belated counsel" during the conflict, their best men now lost. The Fury arrives in the guise of Inachian Phereclus and throws Polynices over the horse claiming that Eteocles comes to the gate before Adrastus can offer his sage advice (11.193-204).

As the two strangers reconcile to one another, Adrastus notices the pelts of a boar and a lion that the men use as coverings.[11] Adrastus then understands in the two strangers' fulfillment of the prophecy that neither he nor Amphiaraus could puzzle out (1.398-9). He believes that this is in fulfillment of the prophecy; however, he is unaware that the fulfillment of this prophecy will lead to disaster. There is a tragic tenor to his thinking he understands the gods (1.510). On sighting the cloaks of the two strangers he boldly declares "deprendi, Fortuna, deos!," "Fortune, I have caught the gods!" (1.510). Here, "deprendi" has the sense of "observed" or "seen;" Adrastus supposes that he understands the gods, though his unease will persist throughout the epic. As Horace expresses, even when the gods offer some glimpse of the future they may inhibit full understanding for their own amusement. Offering council to Maecenas, who was worried about political affairs, Horace points out, with the carefully nuanced fatalism of his merry philosophy, that god, to his own amusement, laughs at mortals who pry into knowledge of the future beyond what they are allowed to see.

> prudens futuri temporis exitum
> caliginosa nocte premit deus,
> ridetque si mortalis ultra
> fas trepidat.
>
> Odes 3.29.29-32

The god presses into pitchy night foreknowledge of future's outcomes and laughs if mortals would dare peer beyond what he wills.

The fulfillment of the Lion-Boar prophecy furnishes one seed of the conflict; the fulfillment itself does not create anticipation for the conflict or for the future as much as Adrastus' positive misreading.

At the close of his council after breaking up the bugaboo between Tydeus and Polynices he speculates, "forsan et has uenturas amor praemiserit iras, | ut meminisse iuuet" "perhaps even these things love will forward as delightful something pleasant to remember," (1.472-3).[12] Adrastus' deficiencies in knowledge and authority anticipate an unfortunate outcome; he cannot avoid the danger and ruin of the Theban expedition because of pronounced inability to perceive the signs. This is particularly evident when he tells Polynices, after the young Theban has disclosed his identity, that his lineage is unimportant, that he can be different (1.691.92).[13] Here two things are working against Adrastus: a peaceful disposition that prevents him from realizing that the introduction of his son-in-laws will be anything but consistent with his hitherto good fortune and the inability of the divine powers to be wholly forthcoming on what the fulfillment of the prophecy entails. Adrastus' flaw is to be insufficiently suspicious. He should know that good fortune can be the ruin of kings (*Theb*. 6.691-2) and the sons that Adrastus anticipates in the prophecy of the boar and the lion will bring more suffering and misfortune. Thus, Statius positions Adrastus, as he does Oedipus, in a position of ignorance, but his lack of authority plays out through anticipatory cues keyed to political, rather than supernatural, concerns. Even the stain of Polynices' heredity is something that Adrastus overlooks in his eagerness to see the prophecy fulfilled. Indeed, Adrastus overlooks his own lineage (1.687-690), which Jupiter claims as grounds for punishment because of Tantalus (1.245-7). His hesitant bids toward optimism betray him, which is unfortunate considering how anxious and uncertain Adrastus is throughout the

Thebaid, and his eagerness for an heir factor into the destiny that works against him.¹⁴ Still, the characterizing feature of Adrastus is that he will never be wholly reconciled to the war, nor will he ever be as fully in command as he is when we first find him.¹⁵

Interlude: Eteocles' Dream (2.1-83)

The "interea" that opens *Thebaid* 2 governs the whole sequence of Laius' visitation: his limping travels from the underworld to the palace at Thebes, the presentation of himself as Tiresias in a dream to Eteocles, his grandson, and the revelations of Polynices' plans to move against his brother and countrymen. This shift in place allows the sense of concurrent action; all these events take place within the span of a single night and when we return to Argos dawn will be breaking. The visitation of Laius and his prophetic revelation of Polynices' activities, however, mislead reader expectations by presenting actions that have not yet happened as though they had. In this ellipsis readers might expect these events to be set aside, rather than returned to in the narrative. During the visitation Laius informs Eteocles of the mounting plans against him (*Theb.* 2.108-119). The intensive "iamque" ("even now," 2.1), suggests that the events described to Eteocles are taking place. While "scit Fama" signals the unreliable nature of the information being presented; readers know that all of what is being related is more or less necessary to move the plot forward. None of these things has yet happened, however. Or rather, these things have only begun to take shape when we leave Polynices and Adrastus in the palace of Adrastus. They are canonical matters that the reader can suppose to have taken place, but details that do not require narration. The information that Laius passes to Eteocles also passes to the reader with an elliptical sense in that it covers, quickly and at some remove, the ground that needs to be covered to make the canonical preparations for the conflict, and move the story along. Of course, we know though Eteocles does not, that the full and complete veracity of Laius' information is dubious, especially in his claim to be sent by a sympathetic Jupiter (2.115). This claim undoubtedly leads Eteocles to suppose that he has the might of Jove on his side and in defense of his position. The tone is supportive and Eteocles cannot be faulted for presuming that Jupiter supports his position. And certainly he could not know from this information that the support is implied for the purpose of hastening his own ruin. Laius' claims and the timing in which these claims are presented expresses an underlying tension between the mortal and supernatural spheres. Here the plot gets ahead of itself and expresses an impatience with getting the conflict underway, not unlike the manner in which Tisiphone hurries to Thebes in the first book (1.100–2). She acts even before Jupiter ratifies the prayer of Oedipus. She knows her role and is eager for events to be fulfilled. The supernatural frustration with this tedium ends at Langia where Jupiter, weary with the dallying, bids Mercury command Mars speed along the conflict (7.6–33).

In any event, Laius offers prophetically what the reader can easily read as having happened in the interim, in an unnarrated space between the end of the first book and the start of the second. So it is somewhat surprising that after Laius opens his throat to bathe Eteocles in phantasmagorical blood we are transported back to Argos where what was claimed to have happened is only now beginning to happen. This is not a temporal glitch or short-coming in the sequence. Rather, the surprise is that where events would seem to have been hurried through the dream-prophecy of Laius, the pace is hamstrung by recounting what is already supposed to have taken place: the marriage negotiations and offer of military support to Polynices and Tydeus through the union with Argia and Deipyl. This is very much in line with Statius' ubiquitous strategies of "mora," but one that also creates a surprise as well, in the way prolepsis and ellipsis are used retroactively against itself and the reader. The dream creates an unexpected sequence in that it presents what could just as well have been omitted; it jumps the gun. The return to Adrastus' home and the marriage offer gives a strange pull backward and sense of delay. After the interlude of Eteocles' dream and Laius' visitation the point to which we are returned in the narrative is, minus a few hours of sleep, the point from which we left. Laius' speech offers a cursory short-hand review of things that could just as easily have gone untold or unrepeated. Thus Statius uses narrative ellipse against the reader's expectations.

While Adrastus appears pleased with his initial recognition of the prophecy when he identified the pelts, upon reflection or having had time to mull the significance of what their arrival and his contract with them may mean, concerns and worry resurface by morning (*Theb.* 2.145–8). This unease is consistent with the nervous fretting Adrastus demonstrates throughout the preparations for war, and into the battles.[16] Here, however, we must take him as a worried parent who is anxious to embrace Tydeus and Polynices, despite the prophecy, and join them to his daughters that he deeply loves. We are, perhaps, too harsh if we condemn Adrastus for being overly optimistic. His persistent ill-ease affords him a tragic sensibility, while offering a kind of prolepsis for the reader. Adrastus' doubt at the start of the scene raises the possibility of an alternative to his fated compliance with destiny and mythic tradition. His worry is, of course, pointless; he cannot escape. Yet Statius seeds throughout the epic side-shadows wherein the reader glimpses the possibilities that affairs could have gone otherwise and perhaps without so much lost. Adrastus' worry anticipates and creates tension between the inevitability of what will happen and the possibility that it could turn out some other way. Doubt allows Adrastus to resist his destiny and his resistance further slows, or threatens to slow, the forward progress.

A further drain on the momentum after returning to cover what Laius had already presented is the scene in which Adrastus, Tydeus, and Polynices sit down to talk. Tydeus and Polynices hesitate to speak, being "dubios" (2.151) and Adrastus opens with a proposal of marriage for Argia and Deipyle (2.168–72).[17] Tydeus, speaking first, assents and Polynices seconds, thus securing increased assurance of the outcome, to which Polynices foolishly adds: "iuuat ingressos felicia regni | omina quod superest fati uitaeque laborum | fortuna transire tua," "We delight to enter into promising presages of rule and enjoy our lives and destinies under your grace" (2.195–7).[18] The bond between Polynices and Adrastus is thus secured. The union of Adrastus' daughters Argia and Deipyle with Polynices and Tydeus provide the Theban exile with the resources to undertake armed conflict against his homeland. While Polynices may carry some of Thebes' wealth in exile, evident in his possession of Harmonia's necklace, he does not have the personal resources to raise an army. The union between Argos and Thebes provides Polynices with a means for waging a conflict against Eteocles, should he fail to step down at the end of the year. Adrastus willingly abides the prophecy, yet his reservations and concerns will persist until the end and until it is too late. His worry makes him sympathetic. Though for readers nothing has been propitious nor do the nuptials bode well for Argos or the bridal couples.

The Wedding Portents

Once the happy day ("exspecta dies," 2.214) arrives the expectation of that event, the marriage ceremonies to be conducted, is informed as much by the rumors that have surrounded it as by what will happen as a result of this ceremony. Anticipation for the wedding, as much for the characters of the epic as the reader, is shaped by rumor and speculation that sings of: "hospitia et thalamos et foedera regni | permixtumque genus (quae tanta licentia monstro, | quis furor?) et iam bella canit," "guests and nuptials, loyal vows, and binding family, and now (such license as the monster has, such madness!) of war" (2.211–13). The description of the marriage celebration is joyful, with a strong female presence to the idyllic festivities. The innocence of Argia and Deipyle is in strong contrast with the impending doom and violence to which they are about to be joined. Statius describes the maidens as blushing, modest, taken by a sudden love of their virginity. The bashfulness of first fault anticipates the conjugal relations impending after the ceremonies (2.230–4). This description of the maidens aligns neatly with Roman ideals of virtuous maidenhood.[19] All of which is in stark contrast to the wickedness and doom that is to follow.[20] Statius soon reminds readers of what is to come.

During the wedding procession an unexpected series of portents express an unfavorable future, reflect the ill-will of the gods and cast a dark shadow over the celebration.[21] A sudden fear strikes the wedding party at the behest of fate, "ecce metu subito (Lachesis sic dura iubebat) | impulsae mentes" (2.249–50).[22] The lengthy description of the sisters, which runs 2.213–248, lulls the reader and allows for a more abrupt shift to the ill omens at the wedding.[23] In the midst of the festivities an unexpected series of portents casts a dark shadow over the celebration.

> ...celsam subeuntibus arcem
> in gradibus summi delapsus culmine templi,
> Arcados Euhippi spolium, cadit aereus orbis,
> praemissasque faces, festum nubentibus ignem,
> obruit, eque adytis simul exaudita remotis
> nondum ausos firmare gradum tuba terruit ingens.
> in regem conuersi omnes formidine prima,
> mox audisse negant; cunctos tamen omina rerum
> dira mouent, uariisque metum sermonibus augent.
>
> *Theb.* 2.256–64

As they reached the high citadel, a bronze shield, the spoil of Arcadian Euhippus, fell from the temple's uppermost summit to the steps, knocking over the torches at the lead of the procession, the brides' festal fire; then, while they still dared not go forward, they were frightened by the sound of a great trumpet from within the shrine. At this first terror they all turn to the king, then deny their ears. But the brooding omens of that to come move them all and they increase the fear with various talk.

The shield of Euhippus crashes down from a considerable height and upsets the wedding torches. The procession hesitates and soon after they hear the bellow of a tuba, long connected with "terror," from within the temple.[24] They turn to Adrastus, possibly for guidance.[25] This spooky happening fills the party with fear and foreboding; however, as Statius notes, all are quick to deny they heard anything at all: "mox audisse negant," "but shortly they deny they heard anything at all" (2.263). They hurriedly move on with a collective and voluntary amnesia. And Statius taps into the psychology behind portents and prophecies: what use can they be if the witnesses either cannot discern the truth in the presentation or deny its occurrence. Nevertheless, all remain ill at ease over the ominous events, and they exacerbate their fears and worries with speculative discussions: "cunctos tamen omina rerum | dira mouent, uariisque metum sermonibus augent" (2.263-4).

The Necklace of Harmonia

Statius implicates the necklace of Harmonia in the ill omens that occur at the festivities, and suggests that what has occurred should come as no surprise: "nec mirum: nam tu infaustos donante marito | ornatus, Argia, geris dirumque monile | Harmoniae," "And no wonder. For Argia wears the unhappy adornment that her husband gave, the dire necklace of Harmonia'" (2.265-7). The necklace has a mysterious power that affects the Theban world and it appears to be coterminous with the other supernatural agencies causing the lamentable destruction at Thebes. Indeed, it has the power to sow the seeds of war (4.211-3).[26] Quite possibly the role of the necklace is merely to enhance the image of Argia's innocence against the flood of misery about to engulf her since the ill omens are credited to her having been given the necklace. Despite the "post longior ordo" (2.296), the last named owner was Jocasta, whom Statius shifts out of a narrative retelling of the necklace's genealogy to address directly (2.294-6). The necklace promises the same for its new owner. Notably, Statius indicates the necklace of Harmonia, which Argia wears as a bridal gift from Polynices, as the cause of the portentous signs. It is difficult to determine the role that this necklace might have played in the misfortunes that befell the Theban household in other versions, though it has traditional status. Nor can we be certain if Statius is following a particular source or striking out on his own with compelling invention.[27] To be sure, the necklace threads its way through a series of disasters and upsets.

Statius proceeds from the necklace's origins at Vulcan's forge as he creates the vengeful wedding gift for Harmonia, his unfaithful wife's daughter with Mars.

The bauble was set with secret flame ("arcano igne," 276), ill-omened forms ("infaustas figuras," 277), Gorgon eyes (278), and the ash of a thunderbolt, then entwined with various harms ("varias pestes," 282), a lead snake from Tisiphone's hair (283), and the "pessima vis" of Venus' girdle (283-4). Notably here we find Tisiphone and Venus paired for the purposes of suffering and destruction as they will be again during the Lemnian massacre (5.64-69). The charm is then shaped with personifications of Luctus, Irae, Dolor, and Discordia (287-8). The necklace passes from Harmonia to Semele, then Jocasta, wreaking havoc and doom in the lives of each, before passing to Polynices who takes the movable wealth, like Harmonia's necklace and robe, into exile,[28] and presents it to Argia. Then, it is given to Eriphyle in exchange for persuading her husband, Amphiaraus, to join or encourage the Theban expedition, for whom the cursed finery emanates evil that inflames her covetousness (2.303-5).[29] Notably, Eriphyle does not benefit from the recent omens (2.302). Greed has so clouded her perspective that she cannot see past the groans and slaughter she desires: "quos optat gemitus, quantas cupit impia clades!" (2.303).

At *Thebaid* 4.190-213 the necklace returns again after Amphiaraus' augury and after Eriphyle has traded her husband for gold. Argia claims that it would be unseemly to wear that necklace in a time of war and suggests:

"nunc induat illa
quae petit et bellante potest gaudere marito."
sic Eriphylaeos aurum fatale penates
inrupit <u>scelerumque ingentia semina</u> mouit,
et graue Tisiphone risit gauisa futuris.

Theb. 4.209-13

"For the time being let her who seeks it wear it and be happy with her husband at the in battles." So the fatal gold invaded Eriphyle's home and moved the great origins of crime. Tisiphone smiled darkly, pleased with the future.

Here we have a reflection of Tisiphone in Eriphyle.[30] And an echo of the "sceptrum exitiale" in the "aurum fatale," (210) that invades her home. The "scelurumque ingenta semina" recall Jupiter's decree of "semina belli" to initiate the conflict. Now, however, the seeds have grown in size. The anticipation of all these things gives Tisiphone cause for laughter and Statius closes the section with a proleptic reference to the undeserved suffering that will befall Amphiaraus and their son, Alcmaeon, who will later kill Eriphyle in revenge and who will be pursued, Orestes-like, by Furies. Eriphyle's punishment is an external narratorial prolepsis that will not be satisfied with Statius' epic, though her merit of that punishment is referenced at 2.304, where she is "digna," and when Amphiaraus will humbly request punishment for her from Dis (8.120–22).

Argia's Unease

Shortly after the wedding, Polynices' thoughts again turn toward his restoration at Thebes. Since, as Argia elegiacally expresses, lovers catch everything ("nil transit amantes," 2. 335), she confesses her concern for Polynices, his exile, and his stolen entitlement; however, she also worries about portents that signal doom for a march against Thebes, but will ultimately work to promote the conflict.[31] In this regard she is much like her father Adrastus, who, as Dominik points out "ignores omens that portend disaster."[32] While not explicitly described, unfavorable omens evidently have persisted after the wedding and have become entwined in the general atmosphere at Argos. She expresses to her newly wedded spouse:

> me quoque nunc uates, nunc exta minantia diuos
> aut auium lapsus aut turbida noctis imago
> terret et (a, memini!) numquam mihi falsa per umbras
> Iuno venit. quo tendis iter?
>
> *Theb.* 2.348–51

Now priests frighten me, now entrails threaten of gods or soaring birds or the disturbed appearance of night, Juno too visits me from the shadows, and she has never lied (ah, remember!). Why do you take this road?

Polynices, however, allays her fears and encourages her to dismiss them, promising that not only will everything be for the best but that she shall be queen of not one but two cities, Argos and Thebes (2.356–62). Polynices expresses an optimism that the war will be successful, though his awareness of the role played by the gods is clearly less assured than Argia's in the omens and dreams. He presents his anticipation of victory ("tranquilla dies") in hopeful, albeit abstractedly possible, terms.

Argia's misgivings and anxiousness over the future and Polynices' optimistic reply allow a domestic exchange between husband and wife that inverts the exchange between Hector and Andromache of *Iliad* 6.[33] The scenes from both Statius and Homer anticipate the sorrowful outcome of war. Hector, curiously and more nobly than Polynices, is aware of what will happen to Troy if he fails as its bulwark. Just as he relates to his wife, who urges him not to return to battle, so

Argia conveys her anxiousness over Polynices' machinations to contend against his brother. Hector prophesies the fall of Troy and Andromache led away as a spoil to be a fetch-water along the Messeides. This is why he must fight as the champion of his people. Polynices does not demonstrate similar motivations. He is compelled by his own glory and sense of fair play. This particular instance demonstrates a clear and marked divide between the heroic attitudes of Statius and Homer. Unlike Hector, Polynices' concern for Argia is secondary to his concerns for himself.

Statius never explicitly states that Argia is won over by Polynices. The only evidence provided that she has set aside her concerns and misgivings are to be found at *Thebaid* 3.687–710. By this time Tydeus' embassy to Eteocles has failed, Amphiaraus has beheld the flight of the birds, and the people are stirred for war. Argia goes to her father and begs him to support a war on her husband's behalf. She claims that he groans and sobs. Her support and supplication seem to stem from pity.[34] Argia acts out of seeming compassion for her husband in encouraging the war, pleading with her father: "da bella, pater" (3.696). Whatever her motivations, she has had a change of heart. The reasons could certainly be from her husband's optimism, her own sense of bridal obligation, or even the attractive prospect that she may be the queen of two cities. Argia is far from being as easily enticed by wealth as Eriphyle; however, she does reveal a conspicuous vanity when she agrees to gift Harmonia's necklace to Amphiaraus' wife on the grounds that she will wear even more attractive jewelry when she is Queen of Thebes and Argos: "Fortune will provide more fitting adornments than [Harmonia's necklace] and my trappings will outshine all Argive brides when I am wife to the king," "dabit aptius isto | fors decus, Argolicasque habitu praestabo maritas, | cum regis coniunx" (4.206–7). Argia's motivation to support the conflict is uncertain, but the tragic optimism, which she now shares with her spouse, is evident in her anticipation for a future that she is not destined to have. In the end she laments her decision (12.336).

Amphiaraus and the Flight of Birds

Polynices' increasing ambition for the throne of Thebes and a growing excitement for war among his people leave Adrastus torn and indecisive over an appropriate course of action. As the leader of the Argives, war at this point is the path of least resistance; however, peace among people so enflames by the "nouos stimulus" of conflict would be more difficult to achieve (3.444–6). Unable to resolve the matter independently, he enlists Amphiaraus and Melampus to read the future.[35] Given the mistrust and disdain Statius exhibits for the human practice of sneaking peeks at the future, the king's willingness to consult his augurs in order to reach a decision should be read as an indication of his weakness and indecision, especially where this invites comparison with Lucan's Cato who scorns the oracle of Jupiter Hammon (*BC* 9.511-86).[36]

Initially, the seers attempt a haruspicy but when the entrails present unfavorable omens they consult the open skies of Mount Aphesas instead. Amphiaraus makes a prayer to Dictean Jupiter asking that he reveal his will through the flight of the birds so they may have knowledge of things to come in war (3.471-96). The news is not promising: the expedition will run afoul. Melampus quickly notes the birds do not travel serene courses (3.502) and those representative of Apollo, Jupiter, and Minerva (the raven, eagle, and owl) are absent from the heavens. This might possibly be a prefiguration of the gods' departure from the scenes of battle at *Thebaid* 11.119. Instead, Melampus sees "dirae uolucres" (3.510), hawks and carrion vultures that savagely fight among themselves (3.513-5). Such discordance is consistently demonstrated as a characterizing feature of the army. Amphiaraus notes the great signs of doom, beyond anything he has seen before ("sed similes non ante metus aut astra notaui | prodigiosa magis; quamquam maiora parantur," 3.522-3), and then indicates that "innumeri cygni" (3.525) swarm and prepare for engagement: "nam sese inmoti gyro atque in pace silentes | ceu muris ualloque tenent" (3.529-30), which indicate the walls of Thebes. Against these swans, a line of tawny birds attacks. Melampus Jupiter compels the birds toward death (3.539-45). In seven lines of description Statius compresses the deaths of six heroes. Amphiaraus identifies his own death when he states: "that one who falls, reverend Melampus, I know" ("illum, uenerande Melampu, | qui cadit, agnosco," 346-7).[37] The sequence of deaths does not correspond to the order in which they perish but are rearranged so that Amphiaraus' death, the one of great concern to the seer himself and having the most immediate dramatic impact, is revealed last. This ἀναγνώρισις has a palpable effect. Unlike the others Amphiaraus at this moment learns that he will perish in the conflict against Thebes; everything he does from this point forward will be weighed against the foreknowledge that he and all but Adrastus are doomed.[38] In order for Statius to make full use of the knowledge that has been imparted he inversely reorganizes the sequence of deaths.

During the last major scene of *Thebaid* 3 Amphiaraus, horrified by what he has learned during the augury, shuts himself within his home (3.574). Meanwhile, the people have already begun the preparations for war. In part, this is attributed to Jove's commandment (3.575ff.). Despite the divine influence, Statius describes the people as "laeti" ("happy") as they prepare themselves and their weapons (3.578ff.). This indicates a relationship between divine influence and mortal predisposition. It is difficult to point to one or the other as a cause for the suffering and tragic events to come at Thebes. What is particularly important to notice here is the eagerness to go to war: the Argives have not heard what Amphiaraus has to report, yet ready themselves while he is shut away. They, like the ghost of Laius, "jump the gun." The Argives show no particular concern to know what path the gods would direct them toward anyway. An inquiry was made apropos their fated destiny that was unfavorable; however, the eagerness for war concludes that this inquiry is irrelevant. No one would listen, the people want war: "bella animis, bella ore fremunt" (3.593).

After three days of Amphiaraus being cloistered away, Capaneus, restless for war, derides the prophet: "unus ut e siluis Pholoes habitator opacae | inter et Aetnaeos aequus consurgere fratres" (3.604-5). He accuses Amphiaraus of cowardice, "quae tanta ignauia" (3.607), and jeers him out of his home. Amphiaraus emerges and relates his direful caution to which Capaneus responds with godless indifference[39] and successfully rouses public opinion for war (3.640ff.). The scene plays out a polarity of religious piety against impiety; the fervor for war augmented by a rousing speech triumphs over signs of certain disaster for the Argives.[40]

Notably, the model for this internal conflict between Amphiaraus and Capaneus comes from Aeschylus' *Septem*; however, the antagonist of the prophet in that play is not Capaneus, who seems the most natural choice to badger the seer, but Tydeus. In the *Septem*, the messenger relates how Tydeus rails against Amphiaraus for revealing unpropitious and unfavorable omens (*Septem* 377-83). Statius also favors the contrasting tensions of piety and impiety; Amphiaraus embodies the former, and Capaneus, not Tydeus as in Aeschylus' drama, embodies the latter. Indeed, the impiety of the seven seems to be distributed among them in Aeschylus' drama, instead of concentrated in a particular individual, like Capaneus.[41] In this way, Aeschylus can develop more fully the godlessness of the invading army, a matter for which Statius has little interest. Still, tension and infighting reveal the disorganization and incivility of the opposing army in Aeschylus' *Septem*, also an attractive theme for Statius. Amphiaraus is portrayed as a noble person, and Eteocles does not wish to send a champion strong in haughty boasts against him (568-9). Aeschylus revisits the hostility between the pious seer and Tydeus once more at 573-5 where Amphiaraus exchanges insults with Tydeus. Statius' *Thebaid*, however, takes the tension in the Aeschylean Tydeus-Amphiaraus paradigm and replaces Tydeus with the more effective Capaneus. Statius explores Capaneus as a model figure of impiety. He appears to have been responsive to the suggestions of Aeschylus and Euripides in the treatment of the Capaneus legend. Statius develops the antithetical conflict between Capaneus and Amphiaraus by building on the platitude expressed in Eteocles' comments of Tydeus in Aeschylus' *Septem*:

φεῦ τοῦ ξυναλλάσσοντος ὄρνιθος βροτοῖς
δίκαιον ἄνδρα τοῖσι δυσσεβεστέροις.
ἐν παντὶ πράγει δ᾽ ἔσθ᾽ ὁμιλίας κακῆς
κάκιον οὐδέν, καρπὸς οὐ κομιστέος.

Septem 597–600

Woe for that mortal fortune that binds the pious man to the impious. Nothing can be worse than wicked companions, where no fruit is reaped.

Eventually, Capaneus goads Amphiaraus into coming out; however, Amphiaraus claims this is not why he comes forth to speak (3.621–2) and asks the people why they are so eager to rush into war (3.629–35). Though Amphiaraus acknowledges the likelihood of divine interference, he also points to personal motivations: the blame and the consequence of their eagerness for war rests squarely on them. He also suggests the Argives are aware the omens are unfavorable and that they know this ("nulla omina curae?" 3.632). At last, Amphiaraus presents in précis what he has witnessed (3.640–3). In the end, however, Amphiaraus acknowledges that any effort to curb their desire for war is in vain: "sed quid uana cano, quid fixos arceo casus? | ibimus" (3.646–7).[42] He reveals a clear desire to forestall the conflict despite knowing this is impossible. The people and their battle-lust take the blame, ultimately, and the consequences. Further, Amphiaraus takes on doubly dramatic qualities: he is painfully aware that he will die in the war against Thebes, but he also has Cassandra-like qualities.[43] He has warned the people about what is destined to happen, yet no one listens.

The Bacchant and the Necromancy

In addition to the augury and portentous events at Argos, Statius relates two interconnected events at Thebes. In the first, a Bacchant, strongly reminiscent of Lucan's, prophesies war and fratricide.[44] The Bacchant's prophecy makes direct reference to the fratricide and marks Eteocles as the worse ("peior") party. Her metaphoric description of the two brothers returns us to the yoked oxen simile

(1.131-8), yet in that instance the two conflicting oxen create confused furrows ("uario confundunt limite sulcus," 1.136). Here, however, they have become bulls and killed each other in contest, which gives a trajectory for their conflict.[45] The Bacchant also presents through side-shadowing an alternative outcome when she demands of Eteocles: "tu cede" (4.401). She also prophesies that another will eventually rule Thebes. This "alter dux" could be Creon; however, there is the strong sense of one already "dux," instead of someone to become so as Creon would. The qualification of "alter" suggests one who is "another" in the sense of "opposing," or, as I prefer, "neighboring." Since this prophecy is accurate, there is the possibility that she foresees Theseus as the final victor and successor. Since this prophecy is accurate, there is the possibility that she foresees Theseus as the final victor and successor. In keeping with the nature of prophetic utterance, her words, especially "alter," are expectedly ambiguous.[46] Notably, she accuses mortals, not gods, of the suffering to be endured, and her condemnation of Eteocles further vocalizes the civil complaints presented by the Anonymous Critic (1.186-88) and, silently, the mothers of Thebes (2.480-81).

Rather than attend someone who has accurately forecasted events, Eteocles, fearful and despairing, turns to Tiresias (4.406-9), who suggests that her lines of communication are not as clear as direct communication with the dead (4.409-14). At *Thebaid* 4.419, Eteocles, Tiresias, and Manto enter Latonia's grove.[47] After making preparations and searching through several ghosts, which allow Statius to describe some of the underworld's denizens, old and fresh in the case of the ambush party dispatched by Tydeus, Tiresias coaxes out Laius. The grandfather had already brought horrific visions to Eteocles, and now prophecies more accurately and more forcefully that war is coming (4.637-44). Comparatively, however, the Bacchant's predictions (and advice) were clearer. Nevertheless, Laius prophecies a dire and unpromising future but assures Thebes' victory.[48] After the ghost disappears the party remains baffled over what they have heard: "haec ubi fatus | labitur et flexa dubios ambage relinquit" (4.464-5). Their confusion humorously refers to Tiresias' former extolling of necromancy as the surest and most direct means of getting at the truth, which was already related by the Bacchant and rejected. Statius illustrates that one explanation, even a true explanation, is not enough for Eteocles. Even when the truth is presented, if one chooses not to listen, the portent can be dismissed and another preferred until favorable results are obtained. The amusement is that Tiresias discredits the Bacchant as a mad woman in favor of a necromancy that leaves the recipients baffled. For readers, however, the end of the *Thebaid* is decided and assured. Despite all presented alternatives it is toward war and the fratricide that the narrative continues. Notably, having presented promises of the same outcome over the course of four books, and heightened anticipation for that outcome, the direction next shifts to the Lemnian interlude.

There is a complex psychology toward which Statius is acutely sensitive. After Amphiaraus' ornithomancy closes, the poet concludes that prophecy and fortune telling are futile enterprises.[49] As he claims at 3.551–65, the need for knowledge of the future is no benefit and indeed sometimes makes matters worse: "hinc pallor et irae, | hinc scelus insidiaeque et nulla modestia uoti" (3.564–5). This statement is not merely an offhand remark to punctuate the disastrous augury of Amphiaraus. Since the seers received dire knowledge of the unfortunate future, Statius suggests that perhaps it would be better had they not inquired. Despite being immensely preoccupied throughout the *Thebaid* with portents and their value, Statius concludes that there is none—or at least no benefit for the characters. Indeed, the first four books of the *Thebaid*, where prophecies and omens are the most concentrated, offer an elaborate approbation to Lucan's Cato. Throughout the first four books, as events are being aligned to compel the conflict, Statius presents knowledge of the negative outcomes, while also alluding to or hinting at exits. This bifurcation of narrative is a fundamental strategy in the development of anticipation and suspense.[50] The benefit, ultimately, goes to the reader who enjoys through portentousness the anticipation of terror and misfortune without actually suffering it.

3

Hypsipyle and the Army at Nemea

As the previous chapter demonstrates, Statius dedicates considerable energy in the first books to creating a portentous atmosphere that anticipates the unfortunate outcome for the Theban expedition. The Nemean Episode, which runs from the Argives' desperate search for water in the drought struck plains to the conclusion of the games honoring the death of the infant Opheltes/ Archemorus (4.646–6.946), protracts the distance between the Thebans' eagerness for conflict and the inauguration of that conflict. Indeed, the Argives, as much as the audience, are so engaged with the events at Nemea that they lose sight of their martial ambitions. The forward momentum stalls until Jove sees the armies dallying in the games and commands that Mars move the conflict forward again. While scholars have long noted the "mora," or delay, motif of these books,[1] little attention has been paid to the strategies Statius employs to maintain this digressive sequence. In this chapter I argue that, on the one hand, the canonical events of the Nemea episode (e.g. a search for water, an encounter with Hypsipyle, the death of Opheltes, and the institution of games) constitute an anticipated sequence within the digression, events that need to be ticked off before the *Thebaid* can be reoriented toward the conflict. On the other hand, the compelling digression distracts attention away from the conflict. This is the balance that Statius maintains.

After the baffling prophecies delivered by the ghost of Laius, Statius turns attention to the Argive progress toward Thebes. He signals the coming delay with an editorial bridge:

> interea gelidam Nemeen et conscia laudis
> Herculeae dumeta uaga legione tenebant
> Inachidae; iam Sidonias auertere praedas,
> sternere, ferre domos ardent instantque. quis iras
> flexerit, unde morae, medius quis euntibus error,
> Phoebe, doce: nos rara manent exordia famae.
>
> *Theb.* 4.646–51

Meanwhile the sons of Inachus in wandering march gain cool Nemea and the scrub that once knew the renown of Hercules. Impatiently, they yearn to return with their Sidonian plunder, to raze and rape homes. Tell, Phoebus, who distracted their war frenzy, from whence came the delay, what error halted their march. Only scattered origins of the story remain.

"Interea" often marks a spatial, rather than a temporal, transition in concurrent, or nearly concurrent, action.[2] The use generally compensates for the linearity of narrative and the inability to describe simultaneous events.[3] Despite zeal for the conflict, the army is already, even at this early stage, in disarray ("uaga legione"), where "uaga" suggests "scattered." While this could indicate gaps that are likely to stagger among the files on a long march, or having progress impeded by dense brush,[4] suggestions of military disorder persist throughout the Nemea sequence, which makes the description here suggestive. Statius was in no way obligated to present the forces as halting and disordered; he could have, instead, followed the chorus of Euripides' *Hypsipyle* who describe the arrival at Nemea: ἀσ[τ]ράπ[τ]ει χαλκέο[ι]σιν ὅπλο[ις | Ἀργεῖον π[ε]δίον πᾶ[ν, ("All the plain burns with the Argive's bronze," 752f 30–31).

Despite the army's enthusiasm to plunder Thebes, Statius signals the imminent delay and asks who turns their anger, and whence the delay. The poet asks Apollo to teach the origins of these things since so little of the story is available.[5] Such a claim is somewhat rhetorical, as though to excuse the substantial narrative energy spent on Nemea. Parkes rightly points to a lack of treatment in Latin literature; however, Statius' audience was undoubtedly acquainted with the canonical events and dominant episodes. Hyginus *Fabulae* 74 provides a compact summary of the plot, which having been produced prior to Statius' *Thebaid*, offers a general indication of what Statius' audience might well have been expected to know of the Argives' delay. Another key text in reading the Nemea sequence, which would have been available before Statius' *Thebaid*, is the *Hypsipyle* of Euripides. As Soerink (2014) has demonstrated, though not without difficulty, the fragmented drama can be applied to the *Thebaid* with profit. Enough remains to understand the major scenes within the work, though much remains open to speculation.[6] It is uncertain, given the lack of strong correspondence, how influential Euripides' *Hypsipyle* was for Statius.[7] Nevertheless, I will make considerable reference to the play throughout this chapter. While it is highly likely that Statius' audience was familiar with the outline of the episode, as in Hyginus' *Fabulae*, there is evidence that the play was read at Rome, the consolation speech of Amphiaraus to Eurydice having been particularly well known.[8]

Hypsipyle's Lemnian Narrative

When Bacchus sees the dust from the contingent's march through the plains, he imposes a drought to slow their progress and provide his favored city with more time to prepare for the war. Only Langia, shaded in secrecy, retains her waters (4.717). The heat and drought weaken Adrastus' army; they can barely carry on (4.723–38).[9] Before the army fortuitously encounters Hypsiyple, who leads them to Langia's rushing waters (4.739–803), Statius delimits the coming sequence with an anticipatory prolepsis that generates a temporal gap between the army's arrival and the canonical events for which the Nemea is famed (4.718–22). Statius positions the first mention to Opheltes/Archemorus at the start of the Nemea sequence and controls the temporal presentation of information by establishing the "now" of the story, that is to say the "when" relative to the Argives' arrival at Nemea, and where that arrival fits/sits in relation to the biographies of Hypsipyle and Opheltes/Archemorus, indicating that a key events, the death of the infant, has not yet (4.718 "nondum") occurred. And he positions reader awareness prior to events that will eventually take place. The two adverbs "nondum" and "tamen" establish the present time of the narrative in relation to future events, with a tone in the prolepsis that suggests a familiarity among readers; either the audience knows, or should know, since the story is so famous. Where "not yet" suggests events that will occur, and "tamen" in the sense of "still" or "at this time" sets up the Nemea sequence before the events for which Hypisiplyle and Archemorus are best known: i.e. founding the games. There might also be a playful thematic reference anticipating Hypsipyle's Lemnian narrative. While "avia" characterizes Langia as "solitary" or "remote" in the way she protects the waters, there is also the theme of "off the path" or "straying" that feeds into the narrative development that is to take place. Statius identifies the two primary characters connected with the location, Opheltes and Hypsipyle, and posits their future associations with the Nemean games. Sad Hypsipyle, so defined only because some events must have made her so, and Opheltes/Archemorus "raptus," which has an ambiguous use here, since it anticipates his death by the swipe of the snake and subsequent dragging, or his modest apotheosis, especially where Opheltes/Archemorus is described as "sacrum."

After the army slakes its thirst, Hypsipyle dominates the Nemea sequence until Eurydice requests her removal from the funeral of Opheltes (4.746–6.180–4). She is a tragic figure: of divine and royal lineage (her grandfather is Dionysus), one time Queen of Lemnos, fallen to the status of servant in a foreign house where her former power and freedom are denied. The inset of Hypsipyle's Lemnian narrative was undoubtedly a surprising addition, in length if not content, to Statius' audience. Events that could have been conveniently summarized expand in a grand epic style.[10] The sequence has been pilloried as irrelevant and/or digressive.[11] Others find thematic parallels between Hypsipyle and her extended narrative on the Lemnian massacre and those narratives in Statius' epic predecessors.[12] More significantly, scholars treat Hypsipyle's digression of the Lemnian massacre as a parallel to the impending fratricide between Eteocles and Polynices.[13] Discussion often centers on attempts to explain the sequence (and its considerable length) within the narrative structure of the *Thebaid*.[14]

Hypsipyle's own tragic comportment contends with and against the *Thebaid*'s epic armature, derailing the forward advance of the narrative. Despite being a tragic figure,[15] Hypsipyle's misfortunes told in the *Thebaid* are made more appropriate to epic than to tragedy.[16] Vessey has demonstrated that the Lemnian narrative parallels the march on Thebes.[17] She is introduced at nearly the midpoint of the narrative and occupies considerable length with no direct service to the advancement of the plot. She does little to complicate the march on Thebes other than postpone its advance. This differs from Euripides' dramatic version of her affair with the Argives and the consequences of her neglect toward Opheltes. Hypsipyle's narrative, however, provides a tragic balance to the Theban plot. Epic concerns are with war, "reges et proelia" as *Eclogue* 6.3 has it, but tragedy highlights private grief and suffering. Hypsipyle offers a tale that falls in between.

In creating her paranarrative, where events do not fully align with the trajectory toward Thebes, digressive but not irrelevant, Statius creates anticipation for events that direct the reader's attention away from Thebes. In order to effect this Statius, through Talaus' son, creates a temporal gap between Hypsipyle's tragic present and the past events that must have brought her to thralldom. He asks her to recount her origin, home, and father.[18] In response to this invitation to tell her tale she constructs an inviting prelude. Hypsipyle groans and delays a short while with tears before a Virgilian reminiscence in which she claims: "inmania uulnera, rector, | integrare iubes" "Great wounds you are asking me to reopen" (5.29–30).[19] and then presents a tantalizing prolepsis of the horrific murders of the Lemnian men to bait her audience with possible events in her narrative: "Furias et Lemnon et artis | arma inserta toris debellatosque pudendo | ense mares" (5.30-2). She indicates the presence of Furies at Lemnos, murders in marital beds, and men utterly ruined.[20] Hypsipyle then enters a near vatic trance as she is overcome by the recollection: "redit ecce nefas et frigida cordi | Eumenis. o miserae, quibus hic furor additus! o nox! | o pater!," "Behold! Evil returns! A chill Fury takes my heart! O wretches, on whom this madness was heaped! O night! O my father!"²¹ After which she confesses that she was, as though the story were well known, the one who took and hid away her father.²² But then as this is about to be related Hypsipyle prematurely reneges:²³ "quid longa malis exordia necto?," "why do I knot such a long preface to my woes?" (5.36). She points out that the army has a war to get on with, and it is enough to say that she is Hypsipyle, a slave to Lycurgus. Who, truly, could walk away from that? Certainly she would be foolish to suppose that on hearing such tantalizing "escas"²⁴ her audience would lose interest, thank her for the guidance, and be on their way. Rather, she calculates her exordia, as a good poet as "uates" would, to draw readers into her story and so away from the march toward Thebes. Though humbly reluctant at first, she offers an abridged story of her identity that encourages the Argives to listen more greedily. And we see the narrative prolepsis that Hypsipyle uses to create anticipation for her story. Certainly the initial exordium is well performed since "cunctis tunc noscere casus | ortus amor," "then a love rose in all to know her story" (5.41–2). Adrastus presses her to tell more, and Hypsipyle indulges a talking cure: "dulce loqui miseris ueteresque reducere questus," "sweet it is for the miserable to talk and call to mind old sorrows" (5.48).²⁵

Hypsipyle accuses Venus of sowing the seeds of the massacre. Because the goddess was not properly honored she leaves Paphos, frees her Idalian doves, and changes her aspect to rouse the Lemnian women against their husbands.²⁶ Some of the women, presumably recounting the events of the massacre, describe how Venus "implicitis arcana domorum | anguibus et saeua formidine nupta replesset | limina nec fidi populum miserata mariti," "filled the private spaces of our homes with twisted snakes and wedding thresholds with savage fear, nor was she sympathetic to her husband's people, even faithful," (*Theb.* 5.67–9). This divine attack emphasizes Venus' infection of the most secret and private places; the women themselves are attacked in the night in their homes and bedchambers, just as their husbands would soon be. Venus' skulking adds to the sense of suspense in the story because it presents a threat against unknowing parties.²⁷ The audience is aware of the threat, but the women and their soon to be murdered husbands are not. Just as the women were unaware that they were being catalyzed for murder, the men later, will be unsuspecting of their fate.

Hypsipyle uses oblique reference to two Greek legends to define the character of Polyxo, thereby using external recollection to anticipate the coming massacre. These moves, which are used to develop the figure of the beldam Polyxo who takes on Venus' vengeful impetus, cast attention toward external literary instances of women murdering men. In the first instance, Hypsipyle compares Polyxo to a

Bacchant (5.92–4), the association of which recalls notions of enraptured madness and a mania that culminates in the vicious sparagmos of Pentheus at the hands of his mother Agave and the daughters of Cadmus. Polyxo then, acting as "hortatrix scelerum" (5.103) rouses the women, whom she ambiguously addresses as "uiduae," to strike against their sons, husbands, and fathers founded on promises from Venus that came to her in dreams (5.137–8).[28] The speech that she makes concludes with the vow that she will kill her own children: "in gremio, licet amplexu lacrimisque morentur, | transadigam ferro saniemque et uulnera fratrum | miscebo patremque super spiratibus addam," "in my lap, they may slow me with hugs and tears, I will stab them through with the sword, mixing the blood and wounds of brothers, and heap on to the still breathing slain the father their father" (*Theb.* 5.126–8). The notion of children pleading for their mother to spare their lives recalls Medea's chilling final resolve to kill her sons.[29] Polyxo's characterization depends heavily on the embodiment of two literary episodes in which female violence against male issue is perpetrated. In this way, the allusions signal fulfillment of the massacre, the anticipation of which is strengthened by her demands for a promise that the women will do what she swears to do, which poses an affirmative or negative response (5.127–9).

Where Polyxo's rousing speech concludes with her vow and the demand for other vows to slaughter the men, and the sudden sighting of the Lemnian fleet on the distant sea, the vows are consecrated with the murder of Charop's child in which all the women except Hypsipyle participate in stabbing the "mirantia pectora." The horrific death of the child mirrors Opheltes', but also provides a synecdoche for all the infants and children to be slain in the massacre.[30] Hypsipyle closes this scene with a simile in which the comparand captures her own state of suspense as wolves pursue a hind (5.165–79); however, she breaks the action off before the event can be resolved. The hind is pursued, but it is unknown if she is caught or finally escapes. The scene closes at the moment which creates the greatest state of suspense. The power of this shift in moment articulates the fear and anxiety on the part of the deer. Recall that Gerrig insists that where the brain is wired to respond to moment-to-moment situations, this temporary shift in attention away from Lemnos to a deer pursued by wolves in a woodland creates a new moment, the anxiety and fear illustrated here is then to be smuggled back into the Lemnian narrative and applied to Hypsipyle, for whom audiences have increased concern for how events will play out. This intensity overrides the knowledge that she will eventually arrive at the house of Lycus.

Early in her speech Polyxo comments, in support of her prophetic expectations, that the Lemnian fleet can already be seen at a distance and after the conclusion of her speech and the grim sacrifice of the infant to consecrate their oath, the fleet arrives. The child sacrifice demonstrates the willingness of the Lemnian women to go forward with the massacre which, for the audience, raises the probability that this massacre will occur. The men arrive not knowing, as the audience and the soon to be assassins do, what awaits them. The ignorance of the Lemnian men is further presented after a series of inauspicious omens, revealed through the sacrifices, that Hypsipyle rightly discerns. At this height of intensity, however, Jupiter delays the looming expectation of misadventure, much the way Bacchus protracts the march to Thebes. The night is, against the will of the Fates, prolonged (5.178–80). Yet we should note that what is presented as a temporal delay within the narrative, and thus prolongs the massacre for the Lemnian men, elides for the audience the intervening time between their welcome and their murders, thus hastening the narrative's progress.

Once the Lemnian men have had their fill of feasting and love games ("ludo licenti," 5.195), the emphasis on a trivial, perhaps even light-hearted, approach to love further underscores the ignorance of the men. The women prepare for murder after sleep overcomes the men, a moment Hypsipyle describes with foreboding and a commonplace juxtaposition of Sleep with Death:

> cum consanguinei mixtus caligine Leti
> rore madens Stygio morituram amplectitur urbem
> Somnus et implacido fundit grauia otia cornu
> secernitque uiros.
>
> *Theb.* 5.197–200

Mixed with the darkness and dripping with the Stygian dew of his brother Death, Sleep embraces the condemned city, heavy leisure he pours from his restless horn, and sorts the men.

The allegorized Sleep nearly oversteps his authority as he assumes the mantle of his brother Death. Sleep surrounds the city, an image coextensive with night, and with the sense of embrace that suggests encircling or enclosing to entrap, especially where "morituram" provides a concise prolepsis of the impending massacre. Sleep also chooses the men that will perish, where "secernitque uiros" has the sense of "sorting" or "setting apart." Both of these activities are more appropriate to Sleep's brother Death, a motif that has a strong presence throughout Statius' *Thebaid*. Hypsipyle makes Sleep and Death indistinguishable, which underscores anticipation for the murders. This conflation of the two brothers collapses the temporal distance between the present, in which the men have had their fill of merriment, to contrast and heighten expectation for the future, in which they will be slain. As an anthropomorphic presence in the event and accomplice alongside Venus and the Furies, Sleep augments the supernatural support behind the event and increases confidence that events will play out as suggested. As the men sleep, however, their mothers, wives, and daughters remain awake and prepare (5.200–01). The "Sorores" merrily ("hilares") sharpen the weapons for the murderesses. "Sorores" could refer to the Erinys, since there is one to patron the heart of each woman (5.203), but this seems needlessly redundant. The Fates, however, appear apt and would further compound the supernatural abetment.

The massacre itself, like any epic undertaking, poses a considerable narrative burden for Hypsipyle. As she suggests, certainly in a bid to keep the momentum going, there is simply too much available story to tell (5.206–7). Hypsipyle isolates Gorges' attack on Elymus to trim the range of material (5.207–17) and offer a synecdoche, where one murder is made to stand in as typical of several.[31] This synecdoche strategically prunes the material to be covered, and allows Hypsipyle to present the gore and horror of the massacre while retaining a fairly brisk narrative pace as she moves toward the most notable scene, for her personal story at least, in the safe absconding of her father, Thoas. Hypsipyle narrows the scope from the entire group of male Lemnians to those of her most immediate concern, her family. After recounting Gorges' attack Hypsipyle assures the Argives that she will not recount the deaths of everyone, though the stories are undoubtedly worth telling, replete with horror ("quamquam crudelia," 5.219). Instead, she isolates those nearest to her, her family, and she swiftly recounts the ends of Cydon, Crenaeus, Gyas, Epopsus, and Cydmus. When Hypsipyle sees Alcmide carrying the severed head of her father, she recalls her own father Thoas and the contribution to Polyxo's pact she will be expected to make as his executioner. Hypsipyle rushes to Thoas anxiously recounting the night's events. Father and daughter take flight in the aftermath, and Hypsipyle recounts several scenes of carnage; analeptic references to the night's horrors (5.252–61). In search of a means for escape, they meet Thyoneus who reiterates the grave situation and advises Hypsipyle by which route she might save her father, then he vanishes, lending a sense of the fantastic to the scene.

Anticipation for Hypsipyle's safety replaces concerns for Thoas. When she returns to Lemnos after securing her father and surveying the damage the other women have inflicted, she builds a false pyre to deceive her compeers into believing that she killed her father. At this point, Hypsipyle's anxieties become two-fold: she worries that her faux-pyre portends her father ill and that her deception will be discovered. Both of these become future possibilities. Hypsipyle and her audience know the truth, but who else might? For her supposed patricide the other women elect her Queen of Lemnos, a promotion that has faint reminiscences of Oedipus' story, where the truth behind the royal position waits to be discovered. Meanwhile, in their regret the women turn against Polyxo (326-7), but the Argo's arrival suspends any outcome.

The timid gynomachy and the interpretation of their arrival as a fulfillment of Polyxo's prophecy suspends the discovery of Hypsipyle's deceit and seemingly resolves the possibility of turning against Polyxo. Yet, Hypsipyle's anxiousness keeps the possibility of an unfavorable outcome against her in play since she claims to worry that the Argo was sent as a punishment (5.359-60). After the feeble skirmish between the women and the Argonauts, the heroes are invited in and love, with some reluctance and effort, takes root, though Hypsipyle asserts her innocence and unwillingness (5.445-58). The threat of discovery becomes less immediate, but Hypsipyle briskly elides her remaining story. Lemnos is repopulated and the Argo departs; soon thereafter rumor circulates that Thoas is alive and rules with his brother. As a mob forms against Hypsipyle, she wanders off to the shore where she is abducted by pirates, providing another deviation from an expected outcome (5.486-98).

This concludes her backstory, one that appears to create sympathy toward her and which she is eager to tell. The comments of Hypsipyle's loquaciousness in the *Thebaid* point to a connection with a Euripidean model who is similarly over-nostalgic. Indeed, one of the defining characteristics of Hypsipyle is her connection to the past and her eagerness to share it. As she goes about her menial work in Euripides' *Hypsipyle* she sings a lullaby to Opheltes rather than a Lemnian song: οὐ τάδε πήνας, οὐ τάδε κερκίδος | ἱστοτόνου παραμύθια Λήμνια (9-10). Indeed, songs and reminiscences of her lost Lemnos and the Argo would be more typical,[32] as the chorus counters:

ἦ τὰν Ἀργὼ τὰν διὰ σοῦ
στόματος ἀεὶ κληζομέναν
πεντηκόντερον ᾄδεις
ἢ τὸ χρυσεόμαλλον
ἱερὸν δέρος ὃ περὶ δρυὸς
ὄζοις ὄμμα δράκοντος
φρουρεῖ, μναμοσύνα δέ σοι
τᾶς ἀγχιάλοιο Λήμνου,
τὰν Αἰγαῖος ἐλί[ς]σων
κυμοκτύπος ἀχεῖ;

Hyp. 752f 19-28

Singing the Argo? Her fifty oars celebrated in your song? Or the Golden Fleece perhaps? That sacred skin and the boughs of oak around which the serpent twined and watched? Or do you reminisce of sea-girt Lemnos, bounded by the Aegena's sounding waves?

Statius' Hypsipyle is similarly chatty as Lycurgus accuses before he attempts to kill her (5.568–60). Lycurgus has heard these stories before, as have Eurydice (6.149–50) and Opheltes (5.615–18), and we should suppose that they are told often, to anyone willing to listen, since she repeats them for the Argives ("iterat," 5.499).³³ Indeed, I am not beyond the conclusion that her Lemnian narrative in Statius' *Thebaid* is a playful exaggeration of a characteristic nostalgia manifest in the Hypsipyle tradition.³⁴ Such melancholy remembrance easily engenders sympathy for one who had become a slave and certainly Statius' iteration fully realizes this feature. Indeed, Statius' Hypsipyle appears to offer the epic song her Euripidean counterpart requests in a plaintive lyric:

τὰ δ' ἐμὰ πάθε[α
τίς ἂν ἢ γόος ἢ μέλος ἢ κιθάρας
ἐπὶ δάκρυσι μοῦσ' ἀνοδυρομένα
μετὰ Καλλιόπας
ἐπὶ πόνους ἂν ἔλθοι;

Hyp. 752h 5–9

What about my sorrows? What cry, what song, what lyre's sweetness will accompany my tears and join with Calliope to lament my sorrows?

Statius' Hypsipyle responds to this call herself; her accomplishment is to set in epic verse the great song of her past.³⁵ And indeed, Hypsipyle is stuck in the past; even where she receives no punishment for the death of Opheltes and is reunited with her sons, no future is expressed. Outside of anything related to her own story she is speechless.

The Death and Funeral of Opheltes

On completion of her backstory, Statius develops the second phase of the Nemea episode. Recall that at the start Statius describes the aetiology of the games "tristem Hypsipylen ducibus sudatus Achaeis | ludus et atra sacrum recolet trieteris Opheltem" (4.721–2). The description of Hypsipyle as "tristem" at the outset of the Nemea sequence creates an informational gap, a portion of which is closed with her backstory. The origin of the games, however, pairs Hypsipyle and Opheltes and anticipates her involvement in the death of her nursling. On the last presentation of the child, Hypsipyle had set him down in order to show the way to Langia for the soldiers, "sic Parcae volvere" (4.787). Opheltes busies himself with flowers and sweet boohoos ("floribus aggestis et amico murmure dulces | solatur lacrimas," 4.788–90), and is described as moving about oblivious of the dangers that surround him, and which the audience anticipates will soon kill him (4.793–800).[36] While Hypsipyle tells—actually retells ("iterat," 5.499)— her story she is, by the will of the gods, forgetful ("immemor," 5.501) of Opheltes, who in a prefiguration of his death, has fallen asleep nearby (5.502-4). The scene shifts to the serpent, whose great size offers the possibility of a savage death scene in which the monster could attack Opheltes in the manner of Laocoon's sons, or in which he is gruesomely eaten ("exedit") as at Hyginus *Fabulae* 74. Instead, the serpent merely grazes the baby with a large and indifferent tail (5.538–9). Searching for him after his scream is heard, Hypsipyle finds the body the way a bird finds a destroyed nest of birdlings (5.599–604), which emphasizes discontinuity in both her "nursing" generative capacities, as well as her own continued survival. In retaliation the Argives slay the serpent (5.554–82).[37]

Worry defines Hypsipyle's character. When she initially meets the Argives she worries that she will seem a poor guide and so puts Opheltes on the ground so that he does not slow her. When she saves her father and deceives the Lemnian women with the false funeral she worries that she will be discovered. When the Argo arrives at Lemnos she worries that it is a divine punishment (5.357–60). And naturally she worries about her lost sons (5.465–7). Hypsipyle's continual anxiousness for negative future outcomes allows the narrative to project reader attention forward. After the snake kills Opheltes, then, Hypsipyle worries about the outcome that will follow from her negligence; however, her future projection is misleading. Her worry anticipates a future that will not develop as she fears what will happen from the household. Hypsipyle is considerably anxious over the possible punishment that will be directed against her. She anticipates being condemned by Lycurgus, though this will not in fact occur. Her speech upon finding the child confesses that she was negligent, attempting to take the blame instead of assigning it entirely to the gods or fate or the Argives. Instead of face Opheltes' parents, Hypsipyle would prefer to be delivered to the snake herself, cut down by the army then and there, or have the ground open and swallow her alive (5.623–35).[38]

In addition to fearing the reprisal of Opheltes' mother and father, it is possible that she fears her eventual manumission for service is also lost. This possibility becomes more pronounced when some of the speculations on Euripides' *Hypispyle* are considered. To be sure, Euripides likely develops the relationship between Hypsipyle and Opheltes to maximize the dramatic effect of his Opheltes' death. Fr. 752f draws attention to Hypsipyle's role as wet nurse and care giver, i.e. where she claims αὔξημα τὸ σὸν (5). This is comparable to her role with the child in the *Thebaid* (5.617-9). As Bond suggests, Hypsipyle is responsible for the child's physical growth.[39] Opheltes is present in Hypsipyle's prologue speech, the two fragments of which demonstrate her situation and her strong feelings toward the child.[40] But if Hypsipyle had invested hopes for freedom in Opheltes, his death would have affected her in three ways: she would have lost the child that she seems in every respect to care for, she would have suffered for negligence under the family she served, and she would have lost her only hope of being free from her servitude. The likelihood of this hope and investment is further supported by Hypsipyle's claims during what was most likely a defense speech. In fr. 32, the speaker, most certainly Hypsipyle, describes placing Opheltes in the meadow.[41] This fragment may be either her account of what happened to the infant or, as Bond suggests, a portion of a plea she is making to Eurydice on her true feelings for Opheltes. Hypsiplye twice repeats ἀγκάλαις (*Hyps.* 757.841 and 754c.16). The action and the exact context of ἀγκάλαις is uncertain. Certainly, dramatic gesticulations are not inadmissible. The repetition returns us to the embrace Hypsipyle suggests at line 5 and reinforces the emotional closeness she feels for Opheltes, which is revealed through description of her physical actions. Just before the arrival of Amphiaraus, Hypsipyle pleads with Eurydice to spare her, stressing how she held the child. Granted, she might exaggerate her affections if this is part of a defense speech, but it is unlikely that her feelings of loss are being unduly exaggerated. Even if, and this seems most unlikely, Hypsipyle did not have a great affection for Opheltes and only wished to gain freedom through him, it is unreasonable to assume carelessness in her duties would gain her that freedom. The death of Opheltes would unquestionably mark the end of those hopes for manumission in her mind.

In addition to Hypsipyle's eagerness to bear the fault of Opheltes' death, there is also an underlying sense that the army shoulders some of the blame. Statius twice focuses attention on the army's role in Opheltes' death, after Hypsipyle completes her lament for the boy and, while she does not say so aloud, she assigns some blame directly to them and their need for the water: "tacite maerentibus imputat undas" (5.637).[42] Quite possibly the fault she imputes to the Argives is an attempt to reassign, or spread, the blame. During the funeral, however, Hypsipyle was not attempting to reassign blame or find company: "sensere Pelagi inuidiam et lacrimis excusant crimen obortis," "The Pelasgi feel her accusations, her crime they pardon with tears" (6.43-4).

After the death of the infant, Lycurgus returns home. Ill omens had conveyed to him the news (5.640-9). When the father returns to his palace and discovers what has happened he approaches Hypsipyle, prepared to kill her, raging with ready sword: "ibat letumque inferre parabat | ense furens rapto" (5.660-1). Tydeus stops Lycurgus declaring: "siste hunc, uesane, furorem" (5.663). Capaneus, Hippomedon, and Parthenopaeus draw swords against him. This point marks the beginning of Lycurgus' powerlessness to demand justice or to try Hypsipyle. Granted, little justice could be found in his outright execution of Hypsipyle. His grief and anger are, nevertheless, understandable. It is not unreasonable to assume, especially with the intervention of Adrastus, that a resolution could be reached. Amphiaraus pleads: "absistite ferro" (5.669) but Tydeus is "non sedato pectore" (5.671). The contingent's leaders have imposed their favor for Hypsipyle on Lycurgus. Neither of Opheltes' parents has any retributive power, as they do in Euripides' *Hypsipyle*. Lycurgus is aware of this when he pronounces: "si uilem, tanti premerent cum pectora luctus, | in famulam ius esse ratus dominoque ducique" (5.686-7). At this moment Hypsipyle is free (or could be free) from her servitude in the palace. Much like the powerless Thyestes, Lycurgus can only pronounce that the gods will have their due.[43]

Nevertheless, the Argive assault on Lycurgus' palace demonstrates that neither the Argives nor Hypsipyle have anything in the way of repercussion to fear. As Adrastus attempts to diffuse this tense situation, Rumor spreads among the soldiers that Hypsipyle has been condemned and that she is already dead. Immediately, and under no authority save their own, the armies attack Lycurgus' palace (6.690-8). Adrastus must intervene, showing the mob Hypsipyle, in order to curb the destruction to Lycurgus' home (701ff.). Evidently, Hypsipyle will not receive punishment from Lycurgus without the consent of the army. The army acts without command, and the inability of the leaders, who are already embroiled in conflict, are unable to effectively command. Indeed, Adrastus needs Hypsipyle to control the armies rather than command with his own bearing. Here the armies lost their order just as at Langia, which anticipates their ultimate failure. Notably, there seems to be no underlying cause for this kind of military instability, Statius never remarks that it is fated, or the fault of some god. Yet, an uncomfortable, damning, and anticipatory disorder lurks within the Argive forces.

The Argives, especially Amphiaraus, play some role in preventing Hypsipyle's execution in the Euripidean drama. Her execution appears certain. Without an advocate and feeling that she is being unjustly punished she declares: ἄγετε, φίλων γὰρ οὐδέν' εἰσορῶ πέλας | ὅστις με σώσει (*Hyps*. 757.851-2). Amphiaraus suddenly appears and Hypsipyle begs him to intervene claiming: [ῥ]ῦσαί με· διὰ γὰρ σὴν ἀπόλλυμαι χάριν (859). Surely, the execution would have been carried out had Amphiaraus not intervened. In 758.6, Hypsipyle with another declaration of σῶσαι, appears to request through a simile of good helmsmanship, further assistance, though for what end is uncertain. Whether Hypsipyle's fate is determined through an exchange between Opheltes' grieving parents and the persuasion petition of Amphiaraus in Euripides' *Hypsipyle*, or through the express commands of her divine grandfather Dionysus, this reveals how characteristically different Statius is in his pursuit. The death of Opheltes is a catalyst for further suffering in both versions; Hypsipyle moves quickly from a low and unhappy situation as slave and wet-nurse to one that is worse. The space given by Euripides to the loss of the child and the grief of the parents is uncertain. But it is clear that in order for Hypsipyle to become a tragic figure and fill the reader with pity and horror, the death of Opheltes is necessary. In Euripides' *Hypsipyle* the Argive presence, focused in the character of Amphiaraus, has a civilizing and rationalizing effect on the passionate urge to execute Hypsipyle. Amphiaraus declares: ἥκ[ω] δ' ἀρήξων συμφοραῖσι ταῖσι σαῖς, | τὸ μ[ὲ]ν βίαιον οὐκ ἔχων, τὸ δ' εὐσεβές, ("I come to defend you in your plight, bearing not strength but piety," 757.870-1). This is not unique in Greek drama; the Athenian show of justice is a motif frequently visited. In Statius, however, what the army brings to Lycurgus and Hypsipyle are those things that Amphiaraus claims not to bring in Euripides' version: strength and the threat of violence (βίαιον). It is an undeniable reality for Lycurgus that he is powerless before the contingent. Their show of tears, consolations, and Adrastus' exploration of sympathetic platitudes at 6.45-53 are tissue-thin and distressing masks for their domination over the situation. The key difference between Statius and Euripides, however, is that with the support of the army behind her the tragic complication of Opheltes' death becomes a windfall for her.

Funeral Consolations

Statius employs contingency to heighten pathos for the dead child; essentially, he creates a future that cannot be anticipated, a contingent future that proceeds from death through a great life, a kind of aristeia in reverse. This is developed through descriptions of Opheltes' toys and training aids.[44] It is clear from the passage that the toys have a physical reality for the child and his nurse. For

Statius, Opheltes' playthings take on a very different quality as they form a focus of grief as they are added to his funeral pyre.

> namque illi et pharetras breuioraque tela dicarat
> festinus uoti pater insontes sagittas;
> iam tunc et nota stabuli de gente probatos
> in nomen pascebat equos cinctusque sonantes
> armaque maiores expectatura lacertos.
>
> *Theb.* 6.74–8

And so to him his impatient father dedicated quivers and small darts and harmless arrows, and groomed in his name horses from a famed breed to be ready in his stables, and armor and belts that clattered as they awaited his larger limbs.

The pathos of his death is increased by drawing attention to the future that is not realized, but presented nonetheless. The imagery is striking. The "toys" are presumably for training. Once the child is old enough, he can practice with small javelins and arrows that have had their tips removed.[45] Lycurgus is described as "festinus," "impatient." He likely anticipated the earliest possible day for Opheltes to take up his harmless arms. The image moves to the horses pastured for the boy in anticipation of his youth when he has the physical strength to manage "equos sonantes." Finally, "maiores lacertos" provide the image of a full-grown man capable of wearing and using his "arma," which contrasts with the earlier descriptions of the boy's mangled limbs at 5.596–8, and where Hypsipyle presents the "laceras exequias" to Eurydice (5.650–1). Lycurgus' expectations provide in rough outline the growth and maturity that are lost when Opheltes dies. It is not unreasonable to punctuate this development with the gnomic declaration: "spes avidae!" This would underscore the father's lack of awareness and caution for life's uncertainties.[46] Lycurgus' wealth provided, and could provide, much for his son; however, it could not provide the fulfillment of Lycurgus' own expectations. The devastating loss that Lycurgus feels is well established by Statius. The parents' inability to punish Hypsipyle heightens the sense of frustration. Ultimately, Lycurgus comes to blame the snake and renounces his relationship with Jupiter. Eurydice, however, blames Hypsipyle. In either case, because the army now defends her, the parents are powerless to put forward any form of justice.[47] In this way, the emphasis on an impossible future sustains the pathos of the present scene.

This proud but ultimately impossible future is the sole consolation to Lycurgus and Eurydice. All they have now is what could have been, and this too is lost on the pyre. Certainly, Adrastus' soothing platitudes are not sufficient to soothe Lycurgus

(6.45-53).⁴⁸ Indeed, even the funeral and the establishment of the games, a generous token toward the grieving parents, is not for the child as much as for Argive forces: "quo Martia bellis | praesudare paret seseque accendere uirtus" (*Theb.* 6.3-4). As Eurydice comes to understand, there is no recourse for her loss. Hypsipyle attends the funeral with not a meager retinue: "nec Hypsipyle raro subit agmine" (6.132). The logic of recent events and the martial flavor of "agmen" suggests her attendants consist of Argive soldiers. She is now under protection of the army, which likely differs from the lost end of Euripides' *Hypsipyle*. The conclusion of Euripides' *Hypsipyle* and the final fate of its titular character is much in doubt. The games established in honor of Opheltes, now Archemorus, played some part in the drama since at fr. 64, she appears to have been reunited with her sons. Bond prefers a dark ending to the play and is reluctant to end with a simple pardon after Amphiaraus' speech. He argues that there is too much missing to have the main complications resolved at that point. Undoubtedly, Amphiaraus' defense of Hypsipyle is a pivotal moment; it rescues her from execution. Yet, five hundred or so lines remain in which to further complicate the drama. Bond suggests that Eurydice is moved by Amphiaraus to suspend the penalty of execution but decides instead to imprison her.⁴⁹ If this is the case, the essential prevailing tragedy of Euripides' *Hypsipyle* is that all avenues of gaining her freedom are finally and forever lost. Worse still, she has fallen from a place of royalty to servitude and at the end of the play falls farther still as a prisoner. The imprisonment theory, while satisfying and consistent with Hypsipyle's behavior, would provide a complicated and sorrowful end; however, without further evidence it must remain conjectural. Indeed, Bond is not much followed in his speculation and the majority of readings favor that Hypsipyle is reunited with her sons and restored to Lemnos, most likely through the intervention of Bacchus.

Still, the question of a fitting end for Hypsipyle, especially in the matter of her culpability and of an appropriate punishment, while lost to us in Euripides' drama is left to be inferred in Statius' *Thebaid*. With all avenues of justice or revenge closed, Eurydice can only plead: "prohibete, auferte supremis | invisam exequiis" (6.181-2) and attempt to deny Hypsipyle a presence at the funeral. Hypsipyle never pleads for her life in the *Thebaid* as she does in Euripides' version quite simply because she does not have to. Furthermore, it is unreasonable to suppose she will remain in Lycurgus' household after the contingent departs. She seems implicitly to gain her freedom as well as a reunion with her long lost sons; meeting the army and the death of Opheltes are the best things that could have happened to improve Hypsipyle's situation.

Often the anticipated end of a narrative is offset by expectations that differ from the projected outcome. As Ortony argues: "The mental preparation for or the forecasting of alternative possible events produces a kind of tension between alternative constructions that when resolved produces a more powerful effect than would have been the case without the suspense-inducing material."[50] Tragic inevitability and certainty are heightened through friction between likely and unlikely outcomes, and the *Thebaid* draws considerable momentum from developing or suggesting narrative outcomes that are in contradiction to, but nevertheless possible from, the anticipated and likely outcomes. Anticipated digressions force a shift in expectation such that what the reader formerly anticipates becomes misdirected toward unrelated, or not as strongly related, outcomes narrative. In the *Thebaid* we can distinguish two general types of misleading narrative and the anticipatory impact that they have on the reader. The *Thebaid*'s Hypsipyle sequence represents a unique interpretive problem because it anticipates endings that do not occur. Her fears and anxieties over what will happen when Lycurgus learns of Opheltes' death encourage us to predict an unhappy outcome for her, but one that, in fact, does not come to pass. Indeed, Statius is strangely unresolved on Hypsipyle's future after the funeral, though we can infer from the Argives' demonstrable concern for her well-being that, quite contrary to expectation, the death of Opheltes actually improves Hypsipyle's tragic situation. Statius does not provide a punishment for Hypsipyle, nor any form of resolution apart from the establishment of the Nemean games in the child's honor: a great consolation to Lycurgus and Eurydice to be sure. For this reason, it is difficult to view Hypsipyle as a strongly pathetic figure. Indeed, despite her tragedy and suffering, through the Argive military she is freed; one of the few instances in *Thebaid* in which the outcome is for the better. Statius does not go to any great length to construct her as a tragic figure; much of this is expressed through her narrative which is comparably less tragic than in the version of Euripides. This is largely the fault of the army who step in to defend Hypsipyle without regard for Lycurgus' household. The army is indebted to Hypsipyle. This is as true in Euripides as it is in Statius, but by degrees. The issue of Hypsipyle providing the army with water differs greatly. The water required by Amphiaraus seems to have been intended for a religious rite in Euripides' *Hypsipyle*. In Statius' *Thebaid* the lives of the army, rather than religious duty, are at stake. By leading the army to the Langia, Hypsipyle saves their lives. In both treatments, Hypsipyle builds sympathetic relationships between herself and others through the narration of her personal tragedy. If we were to assume that the army is not entirely pitiless, it could be argued they are further endeared to

Hypsipyle because of the suffering she relates in her very long personal narrative. Hypsipyle is under the protection of the army: "nec Hypsipyle raro subit agmine" (6.132).[51] A feature of the Nemean sequence is not only delay (*mora*) but also error.[52] This theme also occurs in Euripides' *Hypsipyle*. Amphiaraus, on first encountering Hypsipyle, complains of the difficulties of traveling, ἄπολις ἀνερμήνευτος ἀπορίαν ἔχων | ὅπῃ τράπηται· κἀμὲ γὰρ τὸ δ[υ]σχερὲς, ("Wandering, without guidance, and having difficulty; where does he turn? Such are my troubles," 752h.18–19). The Argives, forced to stray off course, encounter Hypsipyle who has also lost her way.

4

Jocasta

This chapter uses Statius' Jocasta as a lynchpin for discussion of her various roles and affective properties in antecedent story-versions. The mythic tradition reflected in Homer's *Odyssey* (11.271-9) and Sophocles' *Oedipus Tyrannus* 1223-530, as noted earlier, dispatches Jocasta through redemptive suicide shortly after realizing her participation in the incestuous union.[1] How Aeschylus features her in his lost Theban dramas is unknown, though a *Laios* or an *Oidopos* are difficult to imagine without her. Nevertheless, even if she survived the first two tragedies, he has her benched for the duration of the *Septem*.[2] The preference among Aeschylus' literary successors to develop a Jocasta fighting hopelessly against intractable fate implies that the tradition of early death was perceived as short-sighted, and did not fully realize her potential as a tragic figure. Why, after all, should she commit suicide for one generative sin, when if her miserable life is drawn out long enough, she can witness the wickedness she bore in two of her children as well? Quite likely Jocasta's attempts to forestall or deter the mutual fratricide of her sons is not as much a departure from the tradition deployed by Homer and Sophocles, as a return to an innovation explored by Stesichorus.[3] The Lille fragments, however, offer an incomplete picture of the poem's range and the mother figure is without name.[4]

Visual and literary art naturalized the canonical scene of her intermediation, which becomes inseparable from events leading up to the final duel. Pausanias (9.4.2) discusses the popularity of Jocasta's grief in painting and it was a familiar subject in Roman and Etruscan art.[5] In the *Satyrica*, Petronius (80.4), parodies effectively the scene in which Giton positions himself between his companions as *mediatrix*.[6] And this is how Jocasta's suffering was preferred. Curiously, however, Statius elides the canonical scene of her interposition; his Jocasta never gains sufficient advantage to stand between her sons.[7] Statius' occlusion of this scene plays against its anticipation in order to present the duel unexpectedly. The order in which Statius structures Jocasta's actions antagonizes expectations developed from familiar chronologies in antecedent story-versions. This chronological restructuring creates uncertainty and presents the duel with surprise within his overall strategy of delay: when further delay is expected the duel begins. In Statius' case, and perhaps in Euripides' as well, the creation of expectancy exploits Time and Event, two of the four constituent features of narrative presented by Bal.[8]

Tisiphone's Fears

At the start of *Thebaid* 11, Tisiphone calls her sister Megaera to help facilitate the final conflict.[9] Megaera "protinus abrupta terrarum mole sub astris | constitit," "forthwith sundering the earth in two, stands beneath the stars" (11.72-3). Her prompt arrival reveals an eagerness for destruction that she shares with her sister.[10] Tisiphone briefs her on their situation and the viability of success. She assures that the brothers are both ready: "ambo faciles nostrique" (11.102). But Tisiphone does express some concern. Hitherto, she has been a singular force of persuasion, keeping the fateful trajectory on track. The tactical summoning of Megaera, a second Fury with equal power, doubles the likelihood and certainty that the fratricide will take place. Yet, she confides:

> sed anceps
> uulgus et adfatus matris blandamque precatu
> Antigonen timeo, paulum ne nostra retardent
> consilia.
>
> *Theb.* 11.102-5

But the common lot are double-minded and I fear what the mother might say or Antigone, so persuasive in her entreaties, lest they hinder our plans somewhat.

Tisiphone does not doubt her eventual success, only its timely execution.[11] Statius' use of "retardent" merely suggests a delay consistent with the *Thebaid*'s overall strategy of delay/*mora*.[12] Tisiphone worries over the success of her plans because mortals are inconstant, mercurial, and liable to persuasion—a worry that is also seen in the Lille-papryrus mother and informs her judgment as well. Since the mother and sister could dissuade Eteocles and Polynices, they are a threat to Tisiphone's intention, and so the narrative's outcome. Jocasta and Antigone also threaten to delay the fratricidal scene because of their potential ability to resolve or forestall the conflict. Tisiphone has specific goals in mind, and Jocasta (and to a lesser degree, Antigone) conflict with this outcome.[13] As the family member taking the most active role in trying to prevent the fratricide, Jocasta operates as a counterpoint to Fury.[14]

The efforts of Jocasta threaten to delay the outcome, and resolve the conflict. Such possible but unlikely outcomes can be categorized as "disnarrated" events, which define hoped for, feared, or otherwise contrary outcomes and circumstances that a character might anticipate but always pass unrealized. The projection of these events "institute an antimodel."[15] Often these unrealized events antagonize outcomes in ways that create uncertainty or anticipation, such vacillation being dependent on what the spectator is conditioned to expect. These contrary expectations heighten suspense, especially in cases where sympathy is present for a character anticipated to meet an unpleasant outcome, and lay the groundwork for surprise endings. As Ortony maintains: "The mental preparation for or the forecasting of alternative possible events produces a kind of tension between alternative constructions that when resolved produces a more powerful effect than would have been the case without the suspense-inducing material."[16] The possibility of divergence destabilizes the expected course of events, which creates uncertainty. Throughout the *Thebaid* the most likely event to occur, the one several proleptic cues, anticipatory seeds, and past references posit as a near inevitability, is the fratricidal duel between Eteocles and Polynices. The more inevitable the fratricide becomes, the more hopeless Jocasta's cause, and the more certain her suffering. Tisiphone's needless fear, as it contrasts with Jocasta's baseless hope, enables Statius to create a misleading beat in the reader's expectations.

Jocasta and Polynices

As Statius steers readers toward the first sally between Argives and Thebans, the camp's liminal position—both physically along the walls, and temporally at the edge of the long-awaited war—becomes a critical space in which Jocasta's desired outcome for peace threatens Tisiphone's plans for mayhem. At the intersection between a peaceful resolution and war, both are rivals for sway over the combatants. Situated at the periphery of both sides, only Jocasta and the Fury have the freedom to cross lines. Tisiphone's concerns expressed in consultation with Megaera are not unwarranted. The first efforts at intercession are sandwiched between two scenes in which Tisiphone exercises influence over the brothers and their armies: her nocturnal skulking through both camps (7.466–8), and her opportune stirring of Bacchus' erstwhile peaceful tigers to kick-start the first conflict between contingents (7.579-81). Such physical and temporal proximity to Jocasta, and the near derailment of the war, which Tydeus redresses, provide a firm base on which Tisiphone should feel wary of the mother and sister.

At daybreak, Jocasta approaches the Argive camp with a frightful determination and force unnatural for her advanced years (7.474-8). Statius compares the sight of her to a most ancient Fury: "Eumenidum uelut antiquissima" (7.477). The simile misleads into supposing that a Fury's power emanates from the mother and falsely anticipates that the outcome of her embassy will be in proportion to the promise of such a great display of will. Moreover, such a description suggestively positions Jocasta within Tisiphone's sphere of power and influence.[17] Indeed, the superlative hints at a figure more august and influential than Tisiphone.[18] Readers cannot help but expect Jocasta to rival the Fury, as the *Thebaid* sets, or would seem to set, two powerful figures with irreconcilable designs against each other. This characterizing simile also responds to the uncertain soliloquy of Seneca's Jocasta, who asks what force will carry her to the battle lines.[19] Statius answers with power that comes from within, rather than an evil without. Jocasta's command and presence, as she demands the way be unbarred to her in the *Thebaid*, frightens the guards (7.485). The mother's ability to instill fear in men, which is also demonstrated in her embassy to Eteocles, arouses the misleading expectation that she may manage to veer the conflict from its trajectory.[20] Jocasta's entrance to the camp is guided by soldiers giving her way through their swords: "mediosque per ensis | dant iter" (7.487-8). This is either a passing nod to the tradition Statius chooses not to follow in his development of Jocasta's intercession, or an empty tease. It is surprising, after such an intense display of initial power that Jocasta will, in the end, be run off by Tydeus, not unlike Pietas by Tisiphone, or Atalanta run off the field by Mars.

When Polynices enters Thebes at the opening of Euripides' *Phoenissae*, he does so under an agreed upon truce that Jocasta mediated at a chronologically prior point (*Phoen.* 81-2). This analeptic detail in the narrative's prior reach allows Eteocles and Polynices to come together with their mother and reconstitute the second most canonical scene of the myth. When Jocasta enters the Argive camp she intends to advance the *Thebaid* to the point at which Euripides' *Phoenissae* begins and compete with her Attic counterpart to effect similar results. She makes her pleas in a two-pronged effort appealing first to Polynices (7.497-519), then addressing the armies as a whole (7.519-527).

Jocasta first addresses Polynices, whose lachrymose embraces reveal his strong familial attachment. He embraces his mother with emphatic and repetitious declarations: "matrem | matrem" (7.494-5), and is reunited with his sisters, who are also persuasive. Jocasta is angry, but much like her Senecan counterpart, she attempts to persuade through admonishment and scolding.[21] Polynices' emotional display does not exonerate or ease her judgment against him. But this emotional display offers a more sympathetic view of Polynices than anything seen in Eteocles. Because the focus is somuch on his due, we are likely to forget that Polynices' exile prevents contact with his family.[22] Nevertheless, Jocasta sharply rebukes her son and attempts to impede his actions with scolding, which further exacerbates the instability. Euripides' Jocasta, on the other hand, appears to side by a slight degree with Polynices when she asks Eteocles directly why he refuses his brother his share (Eur. *Phoen.* 546-8), but nevertheless remains sensible and reasoned in her approach to mediation. She makes her appeals through justice (452), wisdom (460), and reconciliation (461-9), and she is clearly superior in debate to her sons.[23] Similarly, Seneca's Jocasta puts forward sensible, though somewhat unrealistic, alternatives. She asks Polynices to consider being a king with new and honorable conquests (622), live a lie and suppose that Oedipus still rules (616-17), cautions that winning is not certain (632-3), and asks him to leave the curse for Eteocles to suffer (650-1), which reveals a slight preference for Polynices.[24] The maternal remonstrance of Statius' Jocasta, however, does little more than inflect her powerlessness. Clearly, her disnarrated terminus, the narrative point that she hopes to, but will not, achieve is to bring the brothers together under her arbitration, and recreate a scene equal to that of her predecessors' successes: "i mecum ... regnum iam me sub iudice posce," "come with me ... seek rule now under my judgment" (*Theb.* 7.507-9).

Jocasta's role as "iudex," however, is self-appointed. Outside her own maternity there is little to legitimate her authority, a fact on which Tydeus will quickly pounce. Indeed, she incautiously oversteps her purview as self-appointed spokesperson for all Thebes when she declares that if Polynices will persist they will give him triumph and his sisters bound in chains (7.516-19). As Augoustakis notes, "maternity is the case [Jocasta] makes."[25] She enters the camp "pectore nudo," "with chest bared" (7.481), which recalls Hecuba and Hector at *Il.* 22.79; she calls herself "impia belli | mater," "mother to an impious war" (7.483). Furthermore, "in his aliquod ius execrabile castris | huic utero est," "within this camp this womb holds law, abominable law" (7.484-5); "nupsi equidem peperique nefas," "I wed and bore sin" (7.514),[26] "sua credite, matri | viscera!," "believe a mother's flesh!" (7.521-2); "quo deinde redibit uictor? in hosne sinus?," "To what will the winner return? To these embraces?" (11.332-3); and "haec tibi canities, haec sunt calcanda, nefande, | ubera, perque uterum sonipes hic matris agendusa," "these breasts, you wicked man, must be trampled, drive horses through your mother's womb" (11.341–2). Such maternal pleadings contrast with the thanatopic drives of her sons.[27] Indeed, Statius' Jocasta lacks much of the sensibility and judiciousness present in her predecessors. It is to her sorrow that, try as she might, she remains non-generative of good; she can only bear *nefas*.

Jocasta furthers her plea through the Argive army. In her rebuke she flatters Polynices by noting the force that he commands: "quem non permoveas? longae tea iussa cohortes | expectant, multoque latus praefulgurat ense," "whom do you not command? Long lines of soldiers wait your orders, your side flashes with many swords" (7.501–2). Who, she implies, could ask for more? Though acknowledging the *cohortes* as his to lead, Jocasta usurps their martial ambition and Polynices' command by redirecting their attention back toward their homes and families. By appealing to their shame ("pudorem," 7.519), Jocasta opposes the command of her son. When Statius surveys the response to Jocasta's rhetoric the imminent conflict seems less likely: "tumidas frangebant dicta cohortes, | nutantesque virum galeas et sparsa videres | fletibus arma piis," "her speech softens the proud cohorts, you would have seen the helmets of troops nodding and arms sprinkled with pious tears" (7.527–9). The remorseful men are brought into a parallel description with a simile of subdued lions whose appeased hunger equals the Argives' now tamed lust for violence. We may now doubt Polynices' resolve, who forgets his claim as he embraces Ismene and listens to Antigone's more persuasive entreaties ("flebiliora precantis," 7.535), who might now pursue peace before battle with his brother, and giving rise to delay. Statius, in fact, finds the narrative strategy serviceable enough to reuse in *Thebaid* 11, but as a compliment to the anticipation of the duel, not as a redundancy. Hitherto, given the scene of her entrance as the oldest Fury, and so most worthy of respect, and the persuasive dexterity of her rhetoric, success for a brief truce appears to be Jocasta's to have. Clearly, she has proven here the potential to counter Tisiphone's *furor*. But her success is short, as Tydeus calls to mind his embassy to Eteocles and the ambush. He further argues that Jocasta, in fact, has no substantial authority over Eteocles and would ultimately betray Polynices to him (7.542–6). With this last argument Jocasta carelessly served the opposition in her pleadings (7.511–2). Instead, he suggests, let Eteocles come to the camp. Through Tydeus the army realize the mother's insubstantial power. His misgivings are justified, and it is unsettling to see how easily swayed the army and its leaders appear; "anceps uulgus," indeed. After trouncing Jocasta's argument, the forces reorient again toward war.

Jocasta and Eteocles

Jocasta and Antigone's efforts at *Thebaid* 7, despite being ineffective, demonstrate that they are capable of hindering Tisiphone's plans. The Fury's statement of "timeo" at the start of *Thebaid* 11 looks both temporally rear-ward to the near success in *Thebaid* 7, as well as forward to her second attempt to suspend the hostilities between her sons. Efforts at *Thebaid* 11.315-53 to prevail against Eteocles, after Creon chides him into facing Polynices (11.269-96), are markedly more heightened and anxious compared to her attempts with Polynices; however, it is somewhat formulaic (she appears disheveled, is possessed of unnatural strength and energy, and her presence causes fear among the soldiers).[28] Jocasta's dramatic entrance at 11.315 is similar to that at 7.470, but instead of drawing a comparison to a Fury, she is likened to Pentheus' mother Agave. Emotional desperation and physical deterioration mark her entrance (11.315-20). Jocasta again attempts to persuade through emotional appeal, asking Eteocles to consider the outcome and threatens that he will first have to trample her to face Polynices (11.339-42).[29] She closes her speech with the question, a very critical question to our understanding of how Statius attempts to make the arrival of a well-known scene uncertain: "tu limina avita deosque | linquis et a nostris in fratrem amplexibus exis?," "would you go forth from your ancestral home, and gods, from our embraces, to face your brother?" (11.352-3). Statius then abruptly shifts the scene, and Jocasta's question goes unanswered for the time being.

During her confrontation with Eteocles, Jocasta explains that Polynices demands combat only because he does not have a mother or sister ("non mater..., non...ulla soror") to allay him; only Adrastus dissuades, or possibly encourages, him (11.349-52). After she asks Eteocles if he will really go from her embraces to meet Polynices, Statius leaves the question unanswered and abruptly shifts the scene to Antigone who takes a position on the walls and finds Polynices. Statius suspends the outcome of Jocasta's plea. Antigone informs Polynices: "illum gemitu iam supplice mater | frangit et exertum dimittere dicitur ensem," "even now our mother softens him with supplicating tears, and he is said to be letting his drawn sword fall" (11.375-76). She tells him that Eteocles has been won over by Jocasta. And because of the break in scene, the possibility exists that this may have occurred; we cannot be certain how Eteocles responds to Jocasta in that intervening gap. Is Antigone telling the truth? Is she being deceptive? In any case, Polynices is persuaded; his battle spirit flags: "his paulum furor elanguescere dictis | coeperat, obstreperet quamquam atque obstaret Erinys," "at these words his anger weakened somewhat, though the Fury loudly rails" (11.382-3).[30] When

Polynices' sword drops, shame and regret overtake him. His repeated reluctance to engage in the conflict becomes exploitable within Statius' narrative designs. Statius focuses on him here and as he does so we are likely to wonder at what point the fratricide will take place. Polynices' commitment has waned, and Antigone offers assurances that Jocasta has done the same for Eteocles. At this point the narrative trajectory best indicates that the scene of mediation between the two will now take place, but just then, quite suddenly and contrary to expectation, Eteocles thrusts his mother aside and charges his brother.

Chronology and Suspense

The *terminus ad quem* for Eteocles and Polynices is their mutual slaughter. Jocasta's scene in narrative re-tellings as intermediary (excepting Aeschylus) markedly heightens suspense and anticipation as events lead to the fratricide.[31] Her role in the narrative's overall trajectory as she attempts to forestall or prevent the conflict between her sons is consistently presented with subtle variations in surviving versions.[32] Her actantial role within these story-versions, however, varies little: her purpose is to delay and discourage. It is for others, like Tisiphone, to hasten and persuade. Since her efforts to counter the inevitable are fundamental to story-versions that use her, the anticipation of her efforts and their chronological ordering does vary the urgency of the conflict. Seneca's *Phoenissae*, for instance, breaks off before their duel can be accomplished, but when Jocasta stands between her sons we are quite close to the moment of absolute crisis. And we should not assume that Seneca would have failed to deliver a similar scene.[33] The urgency is more intense, and this holds true for Euripides and Statius as well. A scene of intercession before the duel is outside the Lille papyrus' surviving fragments; however, the ominous force of the curse rests in the mutual slaughter as a looming possibility. Moreover, Stesichorus' configuration of her early intermediation leaves open the possibility of a conclusion in which she realizes that her intervention was either for naught, or worse, that she unknowingly hastened or encouraged the conflict between her sons. The placement of the intercession in the Lille-papyrus is not yet at a critical point.[34] But it does lay the foundation for an anticipatory gap between the present reality and the most assured outcome that runs counter to the Lille-mother's expectations.[35] The closer Jocasta's efforts are to the duel, the greater the expectancy and the urgency of the situation.[36] So Statius, like Euripides, brings Jocasta's efforts right up to moments before the duel. Indeed, Statius' Jocasta is still trying to prevent the conflict when the duel begins as she is holding Eteocles' arm in an effort to restrain him.

In order to best understand what Statius is doing with Jocasta's second effort, it is helpful to look at Euripides' *Phoenissae*, in the comparison of which we find critical permutations in her temporal and spatial location. Jocasta's Euripidean counterpart likewise is seen making two efforts to prevent or forestall the fratricide, which makes it our closest analog to the action sequences developed in the *Thebaid*. In the *Phoenissae*, Jocasta's efforts to mediate begin with Polynices just as they do in Statius' *Thebaid*. After Eteocles enters the brothers reveal their intractable positions and her efforts to negotiate peace, sensible as they are, break down. After the Menoeceus sequence, a messenger from Eteocles' loyal retinue, returns with news from the field. Jocasta anxious for news about her sons presses the messenger who misleadingly puts forward that all is well with Thebes (1085). Then judging the present situation safe, asks him to recount how Thebes has come to be safe so she can inform Oedipus (1086–9). The messenger describes how the Argives were slain and routed (1090–1199); throughout, of course, the looming duel and deaths of Eteocles and Polynices hang in the background.[37] Jocasta is relieved and feeling that only Creon has taken the worst of the conflict with the death of Menoeceus, asks the messenger to explain what her sons did afterward (1202–8). Here the messenger says something quite interesting: ἔα τὰ λοιπά· δεῦρ' ἀεὶ γὰρ εὐτυχεῖς, "let go of the rest: for here you are always fortunate" (1209), thus pinpointing the temporal juncture at which Jocasta's fortunes are liable to turn, positing an impossible (as Jocasta notes) vicinity in which her future unhappiness need not come to be. Suspense rises as the messenger tries to extricate himself and return to the field without revealing that Eteocles and Polynices have arrayed themselves for a decisive duel. But after giving in, the messenger urges Jocasta to go to them and attempt to intercede, noting: ὡς ὁ κίνδυνος μέγας (1261). Jocasta calls for Antigone, and they exit, while the chorus proleptically declares that their efforts will be fruitless (1304–6).[38] Euripides then shifts the scene to Creon who has come in search of Jocasta to tend Menoeceus' corpse. This break essentially establishes a cliff-hanger in which we do not know how the arrival of Jocasta and Antigone will play into the outcome. A messenger arrives and recounts to Creon the deaths of Eteocles and Polynices, Jocasta's too late arrival, and her suicide (1335–1424).

As we see from Jocasta's efforts at *Thebaid* 11, Statius follows Euripides in using abrupt scene shifts to suspend the outcome, and heighten anticipation before the duel. These shifts release the reader from the kind of immediacy that would inhibit thinking about what will happen next. In the intervening pause an audience has the opportunity to consider the probable vectors and the shape of future scenes based on what they know from other treatments and the internal logic of events as revealed in the work at hand. This strategy of cliffhangers and suspended outcomes works counter to the immediacy of occurrences and "anomalous suspense" sponsored by Richard Gerrig because the intervening lapse of time allows, and may possibly encourage, speculation on what will happen next.[39]

Strategies of Elision

What about Jocasta's great scene of mediation in the *Thebaid*? It is so nimbly elided that we hardly notice that its time has passed. Statius' treatment of her intercession is unique because he does not include a scene in which Jocasta actually stands with or between both of her two sons. Bal, and other theorists, suggest narrative has four constituent parts—Time, Event, Location and Characters — all of which we see varied by limited degrees in the reconstitution of *fabula*.[40] In Statius' case, and perhaps in Euripides' as well, the creation of expectancy exploits Time and Event, which we can combine under the notion of chronology, in order to create a narrative gap, and the uncertainty, needed to generate suspense. The end of the brothers in mutual fratricide is understood, and the events leading up to their conflict have been consistent. But the scene of Jocasta's intervention, the truce to reject terms opens a possibility. Readers do not know on first reading that Eteocles will reject his mother's pleas. They do not know that she has failed in persuading him. And they are left hanging on possibility, in a state of expectancy.

At the end of her speech to Eteocles, Statius abruptly cuts to Antigone's attempts to dissuade Polynices. In this way, he suspends the outcome of Jocasta's effort. The fratricide will take place, but Statius provides a misleading beat. Antigone pleads with Polynices and suggests that Jocasta's speech may have persuaded their brother. Because of the break in scene, the possibility exists for the reader that this might have occurred and the delay—however long in coming—that will bring them together only to reject terms seems possible. Antigone relates: "illum gemitu iam supplice mater | frangit et exertum dimittere dicitur ensem," "even now, they say, our mother subdues him with suppliant pleas and sheathes his drawn sword" (11.375-6). Polynices is persuaded, but just then Eteocles arrives and Statius narrates the duel. The division of Jocasta's efforts to intercede elides the point at which the brothers are seen together. The expectation of a key event that never arrives allows Statius to present the duel with surprise. The space of confusion, the alternative direction that Antigone forces on us, only lasts for a small space, a mere 5.5 lines, that feature Polynices' simpering and sorrow, but it is just enough to bring on the expected duel in an unexpected way. If we take Jocasta's intercession as a canonical set piece, then the scene could be anticipated as part of the reader's operative script. Logically, the next major episode would be Eteocles and Polynices squaring off, with Jocasta between them. Statius defies this expectation by cutting the scene entirely. But doesn't it seem odd that Statius, so keen to engage his predecessors and capable of such extraordinary virtuosity and excess, would shy from such a canonical scene? What is the advantage here?

By eliding this scene, Statius disrupts the reader's script. Familiarity with previous treatments leads the reader to project the possibility that Jocasta and her sons can still meet under truce, provided what Antigone tells Polynices is true. This would seem to be the only way to put the narrative back on track. As the audience recollects their Euripides or their Seneca or whomever to anticipate the next turn of events, Statius omits the most likely scene and moves quickly to the duel. The invitation to restyle this conventional scene is discreetly set aside. In a swoop Euripides, Seneca, and any similarly patterned narratives become useless to predict future action. And for the creation of a compelling narrative, Statius demonstrates that they are unnecessary. The trajectory between Antigone's persuasive pleadings and Eteocles' arrival is so short and seamless that we are actually liable to overlook that the moment of Jocasta's dramatic intercession has lapsed. But based on Tisiphone's remarks to Megaera discussed at the beginning of this paper, we are likely to have anticipated something more. Given that this was such a canonical set piece and especially having Euripides or Seneca or some other work in mind, at some point the famous moment needs to be arrived at, which Statius chooses rather to ignore. This breach of one of the most canonical scenes in the Theban narrative invalidates the anticipation of events the reader would enjoy from familiarity with the story's plot, their scripted notion of events and their sequential development in the way they are most likely and expected to happen. This invalidation creates the uncertainty needed for suspense through the forced anticipation of an alternative outcome, and may reveal the unreliability of previous versions. Bremer suggestirs that "instead of forcing his hand in an effort to resume, and improve upon, a scene already done three times with such impressive results, Statius preferred to elaborate a scene which was not presented in the texts of his predecessors, only alluded to by Euripides."[41] Bremer assumes that because Statius inherited at least three effective treatments of the scene, he abandons any hope of producing a rival version. Again, what Statius presents are the efforts of Jocasta that would have led up to the dramatic sequences presented by his predecessors. Then, quite contrary to expectation, he completely writes out of existence what would surely have been an eagerly anticipated moment where Jocasta stands between her sons with drawn swords. In this way, Statius rivals his predecessors, not by trying to imitate them, but by simply ignoring them. Essentially, the *Thebaid* demonstrates a competitive authorial occlusion where a famous scene is discreetly set aside and the power of its recollection and utility of prediction rendered impotent.

In addition to slighting its literary predecessors, this chronological maneuver heightens two features of the conflict: the enmity between the brothers, and Jocasta's failure. Statius never brings Eteocles and Polynices together until they are ready to kill one another at *Thebaid* 11.387–579. This delay in bringing them together heightens suspense.[42] But the distance also increases the enmity between them. When the two are brought together under some semblance of truce their willingness, no matter how reluctant, undercuts the hatred between them. Granted, when they are together there are staging directions that try to demonstrate their enmity through failure to physically connect.[43] Statius goes one better by not letting them come together at all. Throughout the epic they are separated, never seeing or coming into direct contact; but we can suspect that at some point they will come together. Statius' deft occlusion of this conventional scene intensifies the distance and enmity between them, and compounds Jocasta's powerlessness and failure. The Jocasta of both Euripides and Seneca have sufficient sway to bring them together, even if it is only once to refuse terms. But in the *Thebaid* the situation is markedly more hopeless, and the failure that much more acute. In drama, the agreement to meet would have obvious staging advantages, though this is not exclusive to drama as the Lille papyrus also appears to have the mother together with her sons. Audiences can take in at a glance the maternal suite for peace and the overriding obstinacy or hatred of one or both sons. The presence of both brothers before their mother also demonstrates an attempt at reconciliation and the dramatic heightening of conflict and tension as the two reveal their inability to come to an agreement and destroy, once and for all, Jocasta's hopes for peace. Statius, however, denies Jocasta even the smallest success in order to amplify her failure and frustration. Her efforts to open negotiations, positioned chronologically prior to Statius' forebears, are thwarted and there is never an agreement that brings her sons together.

Jocasta's Hope and Death

Where audiences might condemn the claims and subsequent actions of Eteocles and Polynices, and indeed there is no great challenge in faulting either, the same cannot be said of Jocasta. To be sure, audiences anticipate the fratricide, but there is also the secondary, and perhaps equally important, anticipation of fallout from the conflict. This has its flashpoint with Jocasta, and radiates outward to such episodes as Creon's assumption of power, the regret and banishment of Oedipus, the burial of the dead and Antigone's violation, petition to Theseus, and so on. Jocasta is the first respondent to carry the emotional interest because maternal and emotional investment in forestalling the conflict is something on which she is willing to wager her own life. Jocasta is critical to the creation of suspense not only in her chronological placement, but in her hopes and fears as well. One of the ways in which suspense appears to work is through the spectators' emotional regard, perhaps even attachment, to key characters. Suspense, like hope, fear, and dread, are prospect-based emotions. When a character identifies a future outcome to be hoped for or feared, provided sufficient concern presents, our own suspense can be roused by the expectation of that outcome as well. This is particularly true of Jocasta's situation. In the end, Jocasta must witness the mutual murder of her sons and die owning that she was the origin for so much wickedness, and powerless to stop it. In the *Phoenissae*, she commits suicide after their final duel, which provides Oedipus with a great lament. In fact, he offers a greater lament for his wife-mother than for his sons, which betrays his remorselessness for the curse he set upon them. In the *Thebaid*, Jocasta is in her chambers and stabs herself with Laius' sword after hearing the shouts that follow the duel outside. Statius provides the foundations for her suicide, cited as complaints: "multaque cum superis et diro questa cubili | et nati furiis et primi coniugis umbris" (11.637–8). The sense is that her attempt to mediate and reconcile the conflict between her sons was a final effort; the suicide punctuates her failure. Try as she might, Jocasta could not achieve a familial stability and the death of her sons by actions they willed against each other is directly responsible for her death. In a roundabout way, the brothers are also responsible for matricide. The action of her final scene is reminiscent of Dido's suicide and Anna's care as she dies, though the intertextual associations are less developed and not boldly striking.

For Aristotle the impact of tragedy is to arouse pity and terror, when events occur "because of one another but contrary to expectation" (*Poet.* 9.145a3–4). This closely resembles the notion of surprise, where events are incongruous or unexpected from the predicted pattern. Yet, it seems relatively self-evident that as familiarity with story-versions increases, affective states of suspense and surprise will be increasingly difficult to achieve, but in no way is the pressure diminished to present familiar material in novel ways. Throughout this chapter I have attempted to demonstrate Jocasta's integral role in the creation of suspense, anticipation, uncertainty, and possibly even surprise through her various reifications. Her chronological positioning is critical in this regard. In the Lille-fragments the duel, then but a prophetic abstraction on which the ambiguous feature seems to barely hang, gives us only a looming possibility, but a portentous ill-ease, just the same. Euripides positions Jocasta further along the time line, bringing her into the conflict early enough in the *Phoenissae* to present what was likely a canonical feature of the *fabula*, but delayed by a reluctant messenger. She arrives in the end too late and must make good on her promise to die (by her own hand) alongside her sons.

Suspense, as we see particularly in this instance, can be developed through the continual threat to undo the anticipated outcome.[44] The *Thebaid* achieves a certain amount of suspense and anticipation through the frequent threat of having the anticipated narrative derailed or subverted by oppositional events. The war against Thebes, the duel between Polynices and Eteocles, these are canonical events without which the narrative would likely fail. The competition between Tisiphone and Jocasta, becomes broadly allegorical. One should hesitate to say a contest between good and evil, as the *Thebaid* does not yield to such easy generalization. But certainly there is an *agon* between peace and war, with *furor* and irrationality on both sides, and short of that, a mother's deep concern to prevent what mortal and immortal worlds are hell-bent upon. Jocasta's role in the *Thebaid* can create suspense, because her desires construct a hopeful, but impossible, *telos* that, as much as she or even we might wish otherwise, cannot come to pass. The story demands two brothers die; anything less, in any reprisal, is a cheat. We need only look to the "end" of Seneca's treatment to realize how necessary the fratricide is to the outcome. The fact that the brothers only engage in rhetorical salvos at the close of Seneca's *Phoenissae* seems strong evidence that the drama is incomplete. Yet, in order to make the narrative trajectory more engaging there are repeated hints, suggestive efforts to derail, to prevent the horrible conclusion. Statius uses Jocasta for the creation of suspense and anticipation in the *Thebaid* by manipulating the temporal ordering of events, particularly in the use of a "cliff-hanger." Essentially, the elision of the canonical moment of Jocasta's intercession—her standing between her sons—provides a deft slip. As Gerrig and others have demonstrated, suspense can be experienced in cases of recidivism, where the outcome is already known. This appears to be generally caused when the reader is so caught up with the immediacy of the situation that access to the knowledge of the outcome is suppressed, and because the human mind is wired to respond to moment-to-moment situations. But the use of sudden scene shifts unbind attachment to the immediacy of suspenseful situations. I find it quite interesting that neither Euripides nor Statius depend on immediacy, but rather in breaking their scenes would encourage spectators and readers to draw a breath and consider what may happen next. How might the anticipated end be arrived at?

The most likely objection to the claims made here is that we do not know if Statius was modeling some other work in cutting out this scene and I would like to address this. It is quite true that many treatments of the story are lost. So yes, it is possible that Statius modeled his strategy on one or more of these. But if this were the case, then Statius could still find an advantage among competing versions. It is conceivable that readers could function with a kind of divergent or bifurcated script. At the point of Antigone's feint maybe they do not know which way the narrative is headed. The elision is still effective; mainly because, of all the works in antiquity treating the legend, Euripides' *Phoenissae* would still likely be the most familiar. The impact of the elision, admittedly, would not be as strong. As someone willing to err on the side of uniqueness, I find this a disappointing possibility, but cannot dismiss it. The more satisfying position, and what I have tried to show here, is that there was pressure to create novelty within tradition. And that Statius and Euripides can manipulate certain constituent features of narrative to achieve this novelty. Time, or rather temporal sequence (chronology), as events lead toward expected conclusions, is key. If Statius had followed any one model too closely, it would have been more likely to meet with dismissal rather than the success for which it was known.

5

iam pater est

Despite the array of characters within the Theban legend, the saga turns on the life of Oedipus.¹ The conflict between Eteocles and Polynices emanates from the crimes and pollution of their father; they are, as Jupiter observes, a "fatal offspring" ("exitiale genus," 1.243). Yet poets often suppress Oedipus' presence in their treatments of the myth. His curse over his sons looms large, for instance, in Aeschylus' *Septem*, but Oedipus himself is only present in the utterances and fears of other characters. Euripides affords the pariah a concluding part after the drama's key players (Polynices, Eteocles, and Jocasta) are dead, where he reminds Creon and the audience of everything he once was (*Phoen.* 1595–1620). Seneca's incomplete (or the poorly conjoined fragments of two plays) *Phoenissae* offers Oedipus a role, but in this dramatic iteration he prefers to watch from the sidelines and does not participate at all (350–62). Not surprisingly, Statius' epic treatment presents Oedipus on only a few occasions: he inaugurates the poem's action by means of the curse against Polynices and Eteocles (*Theb.* 1.46–87); he emerges from his gloomy world to banquet among his fellow Thebans in hopeful anticipation of success in the war and in expectation of Eteocles' ruin (8.240–58); and in the aftermath of the fratricide in which he grieves over the deaths of his sons (11.580–633), after which Creon banishes him from Thebes (11.673–756). There are also two notable mentions when Jupiter ratifies Oedipus' curse (1.239–40) and during Tisiphone's council with Megaera she claims that Oedipus, through the course of the conflict, has become a father once again (*Theb.* 11.105–8).² Yet, while few, these scenes provide an internal trajectory that manipulates audience expectations for grief at the end.

The Curse

Statius' *Thebaid* seems to open twice. As discussed in Chapter 1, the proem (1–45) establishes the epic within its mythic tradition and surveys, in brief, the ground Statius' version will cover, promising two cities depleted by alternating deaths ("egestas alternis mortibus urbes," 1.37) and fatal to both its contesting rulers ("geminis sceptrum exitiale tyrannis," 1.34). Such an authorial declaration offers a contract between the narrator and the audience that *this* epic aims toward *this* ending. The second opening is a quasi-prologic and theatrical curse delivered by Oedipus that also reinforces the expectation that Eteocles and Polynices will slay each other in the end.

Where the proem establishes the end, Oedipus' curse establishes the beginning. The lack of temporal frame in the omniscient prologue positions the narrator outside the story's time, which better facilitates his command of past and future. Until Oedipus provides a focus, there is no present, nor has the story really begun. Oedipus' curse initiates the sequence of events that will conclude with the fratricidal conflict. Indeed, all activity after the curse traces back to this flashpoint, which motivates the conflict.[3] When the prologue ends Statius shifts from the broad view of past and future moments to focus on Oedipus, not without some graphic intensity:

> impia iam merita scrutatus lumina dextra
> merserat aeterna damnatum nocte pudorem
> Oedipodes longaque animam sub morte trahebat.
> illum indulgentem tenebris imaeque recessu
> sedis inaspectos caelo radiisque penates
> seruantem tamen adsiduis circumuolat alis
> saeua dies animi, scelerumque in pectore Dirae.
>
> *Theb.*1.46–53

Already has Oedipus probed his deserving eyes with worthy hands and submerged his shame in everlasting night, his life is drawing out a long death. He devotes himself to darkness, dwelling in the deep shadows of his home, unseen by heaven's gaze. A fearsome day of the mind flies ceaselessly around him, Furies of his misdeeds in his heart.

The temporal quality of *iam* stabilizes the prophetic narrator's rapid and elliptical roving through Thebes' past and future to situate the reader in a "present." Where we read *iam* as "already" the sense governs a brief reference to Oedipus' violent self-blinding,[4] which is recounted through analepses to reveal what has been missed prior to this point in time.[5] Hidden away in darkness, straddling life and death ("longaque animam sub morte trahebat"), near madness ("saeua dies animi"),[6] and with torment ("Dirae") in his heart, the reader's gaze, a "lumina" in itself, violates his private damnation, a space which even the rays of the sun are unable to reach. The scene situates readers within Thebes' history and calamities. Oedipus tracks pollution between his past and his sons' future; as he was cursed, so he curses. He is a pitiable and repulsive figure for the misfortunes he has endured, and this will prove important for Statius to improve on the final scene of Oedipus' regret.[7] The appearance of this accursed man, as Moreland notes, "at once establishes an aura of darkness and agony."[8]

Readers now know when, so to speak, they are in Thebes' history. Oedipus has "already" wrenched out his eyes. As he prepares to make his prayer we learn that the sockets of his eyes are empty and his hands are blood stained through the act:

> tunc uacuos orbes, crudum ac miserabile uitae
> supplicium, ostentat caelo manibusque cruentis
> pulsat inane solum saeuaque ita uoce precatur:
>
> *Theb.* 1.53–55

Then to the heavens he shows empty orbs, his life's raw wretched, and with bloody fists he beats upon the empty earth, praying with voice enraged:

These visual presentations of Oedipus' tragic past as he prepares to act in the present moment hint at the persistence of his pollution.[9] In raising his hands and empty eye-sockets to heaven, Oedipus demonstrates a conventional posture for prayer.[10] Unlike his predecessors, however, Oedipus directs his prayer downward, and his blood-stained hands strike the empty earth ("pulsat inane solum") to direct his petition to the gods below. Here we have another instance of Oedipus between spheres. Oedipus wants the Olympian gods, who have hitherto shown him no mercy or justice and generally failed him, to observe his petition to Tisiphone.[11] He appears seemingly certain that he has nothing to lose, and only satisfaction at his insulted honor to gain, which will increase the sense of pathos for his final regret.

Oedipus begins his prayer with the misleadingly broad and inclusive address to "Di."[12] The intended recipients of his prayer, however, are not Olympian gods, but Chthonic deities, specifically Tisiphone. Oedipus calls on her with the formulaic conditional used when Chryses calls on Apollo at *Iliad* 1.37–42 for divine advocacy.[13] Oedipus revels in the perversity of his request as he acknowledges: "adnue, Tisiphone, peruersaque uota secunda," (1.59).[14] He intimately identifies with Tisiphone, who stood alongside him throughout the grim moments of his life after he fell from his mother's womb. Tisiphone is to be his avenger and the satisfier of his hopes. She will, he anticipates, provide the satisfaction for which he hopes (1.79–80). Indeed, she is family, seeming to

Oedipus as surrogate mother and divine patroness, suggesting that Eteocles and Polynices are her sons as well (1.70). This initial scene shows Oedipus frustrated in his powerlessness. The scene of the curse presents the inner nature of Oedipus, who here participates more actively in the development of Statius' Theban narrative than in surviving antecedent versions. This act of Oedipus' provides markedly more substance and immediacy to the curse, and its direct answer by Tisiphone, than the vague and nebulous background in the *Thebaid*'s antecedents. It is much less abstracted than in Euripides' *Phoenissae* and has a privileged place in initializing the action of the poem. Statius' Oedipus calls the curse down on his sons and summons Tisiphone, who embodies the epic's *furor*. Until the deaths of Oedipus' sons she will remain the foremost guiding influence and motivating spirit.[15]

The curse undergirds the narrative development in all complete extant treatments, is deeply rooted in the earliest known sources of the myth and is one of its most canonical features in the tradition. In preceding versions, however, its presentation does not yield the same degree of portentousness and urgency that we find at the start of Statius' *Thebaid*. Undoubtedly, the family curse is a pervasive canonical feature and two fragments from the cyclic *Thebais* present Oedipus' curse against his sons. In fragment 2, preserved in Athenaeus' *Deipnosophistae* (11.14.21–30), Polynices serves his father with Laius' possessions (a silver table and golden goblet filled with wine), which outrages Oedipus:

αὐτὰρ ὅ γ' ὡς φράσθη παρακείμενα πατρὸς ἑοῖο
τιμήεντα γέρα, μέγα οἱ κακὸν ἔμπεσε θυμῷ,
αἶψα δὲ παισὶν ἑοῖσι μετ' ἀμφοτέροισιν ἐπαρὰς
ἀργαλέας ἠρᾶτο (θεῶν δ' οὐ λάνθαν' Ἐρινύν),
ὡς οὔ οἱ πατρώϊ' ἐνηέι <ἐν> φιλότητι
Δάσσαιντ,' ἀμφοτέροισι δ' αἰεὶ πόλεμοί τε μάχαι τε ...

Thebais fr. 2.5–10

But realizing that his father's dear possessions had been spread before him, an evil welled in his heart. Straightaway, he called hard curses down on his sons, and these did not remain hidden from the Fury's notice. They would not divide their inheritance as brothers, but between them there would always be battles, and always conflict.

Similarly, in fragment 3, after he realizes that his sons served him the inferior portion of meat (ἰσχίον), he curses them: εὔκτο Διὶ βασιλῆι καὶ ἄλλοις ἀθανάτοισι, | χερσὶν ὑπ'ἀλλήλων καταβήμεναι Ἄϊδος εἴσω ("to Zeus and the other immortal gods he prays that they go to Hell each by the hand of the other," *Thebais* fr. 3.3–4). Since the cause of the curse differs between fragments they do not likely come from the same narrative. Moreover, fragment 2 emphasizes a demand for protracted torment and suffering, but not necessarily their mutual deaths. The Oedipus of fragment 3, however, wants his sons dead. It is also interesting that in fr. 2 Oedipus receives the evil, in the sense of being attacked, and his curse does not escape the notice of the Erinys. Both conditions open the possibility of grief and lament later when Oedipus' twisted hopes might be realized, but it is unknown whether this was explored in either of these two versions. What is notable about Statius' *Thebaid* is that Oedipus cites no specific crime. The crime itself is irrelevant because the tradition inveighs against the sons as guilty, no matter the details.[16] So though Statius was familiar with antecedent versions of the story, ones that specified the wrongdoings of Eteocles and Polynices, their import is slight.[17] This becomes a deeply embedded function of the myth for which the narrative need not expressly account.[18]

While Statius distributes the number of participants who hope to bring Thebes to ruin, he distils the act of cursing Eteocles and Polynices into the first introductory scene. Jocasta's prologue in *Phoenissae* traces the misfortunes at Thebes from Cadmus' arrival to the present contentions between her sons. She indicates a two-part prophecy from Apollo as one source of misery: εἰ γὰρ τεκνώσεις παῖδ,' ἀποκτενεῖ σ' ὁ φύς, | καὶ πᾶς σὸς οἶκος βήσεται δι' αἵματος ("if you have a child it will kill you and all your household will be bathed in blood," *Phoen.* 19–20). The first portion of this prophecy is satisfied when she recounts the conflict at the forked road to Pholkis. The second portion, however, that his house will be bathed in blood, is reinvigorated when Oedipus curses his sons. Once Eteocles and Polynices reached maturity they came together in mutual accord to hide Oedipus away, employing, perhaps, several deceitful measures to keep him hidden.[19] In response to their filial impiety Oedipus, living in this way, curses his sons:

ζῶν δ' ἔστ' ἐν οἴκοις·ἰκρὸς δὲ τῆς τύχης νοσῶν
ἀρὰς ἀρᾶται παισὶν ἀνοσιωτάτας,
θηκτῶι σιδήρωι δῶμα διαλαχεῖν τόδε.

Phoen. 66–8

He lives within, warped by his fate, he calls hateful curses down on his sons, praying that they might divide their inheritance with sharpened blades.

Jocasta's recounting of this episode captures the general tenor of the myth, especially where the entire genetic line appears cursed, but the brevity of the scene minimizes its potency. Certainly, the act of cursing his sons reveals his anger toward them and demonstrates his powerlessness to act in any other way, but within Euripides' drama Oedipus is not alone in this attitude. Indeed, we find the curse diffused throughout the play. Jocasta, for instance, vainly calls her own curse against the misfortune of her house, and spreads the blame:

ὄλοιτο τάδ' εἴτε σίδαρος
εἴτ' Ἔρις εἴτε πατὴρ ὁ σὸς αἴτιος,
εἴτε τὸ δαιμόνιον κατεκώμασε
δώμασιν Οἰδιπόδα·

Phoen. 350–53

This destruction, whether by swords, Eris, or the father, deserves blame, or perhaps some demon besets Oedipus' house.

Jocasta's multiplication of possible causes discourages reading Oedipus' curse as the prevailing cause.[20] The repetition of εἴτε suggests her reluctance or inability to identify the source. Later, the chorus perceives that "some god" has brought the events to ruin: τὰς σὰς δ' ἀρὰς ἔοικεν ἐκπλῆσαι θεός, "it seems some god has fulfilled your curses," (*Phoen*. 1426). Likewise, Antigone perceives that the present miseries have been brought to completion by "some god:" ὦ πάτερ, ἀμετέροισιν ἄχη | μελάθροις θεὸς ὃς τάδ' ἐκτελευτᾷ, "O father, the god that brings to pass these things brings now sorrow into our home," (*Phoen*.1580–1). Throughout the play, characters like Antigone and Iocasta show awareness that a curse is unfolding, or that a divine force has brought the curse to pass. Oedipus himself looks to the ancestral accursedness of Laius' descendants: παῖδάς τ' ἀδελφοὺς ἔτεκον, οὓς ἀπώλεσα, ἀρὰς | παραλαβὼν Λαΐου καὶ παισὶ δούς, "children, fathered as though my brothers, whom I ruin, passing from Laius and giving it to you my children, this curse" (Eur. *Phoen*. 1610–11).[21] Thus the forces that participants suspect control the conflict between the brothers appear abstracted and distant. Euripides, much like Aeschylus, has the curse(s) developing into fulfillment. For Statius, however, the curse offers a dramatic point of entry into the *Thebaid*, and also gives an initial characterization of Oedipus. Certainly, while the curse stands out as a canonical feature of the *Septem* mythos, Statius develops the scene to heighten anticipation for the eventual fratricidal conflict.

Oedipus' initial scene can also be said to double as an *ersatz* dramatic prologue.[22] His imprecations reveal to the reader his character as it relates explicitly to his sons and implicitly toward the gods. Oedipus takes on features similar to those of a Fury prologue in Seneca's *Thyestes*, which urges the ghost of

Tantalus to sow enmity and discord: "Perge, detestabilis | umbra, et penates impios furiis age," "On, cruel shade, whip your wicked house into frenzy," (*Thy.* 23–24).²³ The fury of Thyestes wishes for an excess in rivalry, passion, and sin, with swords drawn against each other (Sen. *Thy.* 25–66). As Richard Tarrant notes, this is a powerful piece of rhetoric, initializing the catastrophes to come.²⁴ Oedipus' prologue in Statius' *Thebaid* and Seneca's Fury press for a similar series of destructive events and initiate a palpable sense of inevitable doom. Oedipus does not indulge the long sequence of causality like Euripides' Jocasta; he is more like the Fury of *Thyestes* and develops not the problem but the mood: *furor* and its consequences. Statius uses Oedipus as a catalyst for the strife between the brothers.²⁵ While Oedipus strongly resembles the Fury of Thyestes, a critical prototype was likely provided in the figure of Calchas, the priest who is rudely mistreated and dishonored by Agamemnon in *Iliad* 1. He too cries out to the gods in powerlessness, lacking strength or authority to impose his will. And Apollo, like Tisiphone, delivers misery and suffering in vengeance.

Oedipus' powerlessness and frail authority can be set against prevailing notions of *patria potestas*, which notionally creates a stable social order.²⁶ The house of Oedipus, however, is a "confusa domus" (1.17), in which paternal power structures (and much else besides) have been up-ended. In his fall, Oedipus lost his crown and his authority, especially over his sons.²⁷ His lack of control anticipates unfortunate ends. Indeed, Jupiter puts Oedipus' case quite poignantly as he justifies the conflict between Argos and Thebes and remarks of Eteocles and Polynices that they "cadentes | calcavere oculos" ("trampled [Oedipus'] eyes as they fell" 1.238–9), which offers a metaphor for castration and Oedipus' impotent paternal authority.²⁸ At that point the sons had not only dishonored their father but usurped his power as well. Moreover, the filial usurpation of parental authority feeds into the Roman fascination with parricide and paternal dominance, in theory as well as practice.²⁹ Oedipus' fall allows his sons the opportunity to claim their inheritance early, whereas had he retained control they would otherwise have had to wait. This position, of course, takes as a given that Roman norms could be reflected in Greek myth.³⁰

Anticipation

After the initial curse that opens the *Thebaid*, Oedipus, apart from a few brief mentions, disappears from view. Then as the conflict gets underway, Oedipus indulges his wrath and bitterness, and anticipates satisfaction. As Statius describes the mounting chaos and tension at Thebes he writes:

> it geminum excutiens anguem et bacchatur utrisque
> Tisiphone castris; fratrem huic, fratrem ingerit illi,
> aut utrique patrem: procul ille penatibus imis
> excitus implorat Furias oculosque reposcit.
>
> *Theb.* 7.466–9

> Shaking twin serpents, Tisiphone riots through both camps. She jostles brother against brother, or father against both. Far off and in the palace's depths Oedipus rejoices, calls for the Furies, demands his eyes.

Tisiphone's influence extends to Oedipus as well, who calls on the Furies to further the mayhem, and wishes he had his eyes in order to observe the conflict. This moment establishes a shift that brings him in-line with his Senecan predecessor. At 8.240–58, however, he emerges, both within the narrative and from his own "dira sede" to interact with the Theban people and listen to news of the conflict's progress. Statius describes him:

> ... uultuque sereno
> canitiem nigram squalore et sordida fusis
> ora comis laxasse manu sociumque benignos
> affatus et abacta prius solacia passum.
>
> *Theb.* 8.242–4

> ... his face is serene and he has cleaned from his hoary hair and its tangled untidy locks the foul grime; he tolerates his people's greetings and their good wishes once disdained.

Oedipus' serene countenance and equanimity present a perverse and disturbing stoicism; in essence, he finds well-being and satisfaction in Thebes' progress toward war.[31] He is groomed, has washed his face, and cleaned his eyes of gore: "insiccatumque cruorem | deiecisse genis" (8.246–7).[32] Outwardly, the Thebans' success pleases him; however, privately he hopes Eteocles falls. Here at the outset of the conflict, Oedipus' desire for revenge and anticipation of its fulfillment perversely cheer and improve him. A sense of imminent death and coming catastrophe delights and cheers him; he is happy. It is unclear whether the hope for Eteocles' ruin extends to Polynices, but as conflict suggests that Polynices may be harmed, and with no specific suggestion of preference, his hopes for destruction are likely directed at both sons. He despises them as his own father despised him and he perpetuates the intergenerational legacy of paternal contempt by seeking their mutual destruction.

Oedipus' pitiable state when he pronounces the curse creates pathos and empathy in readers. It would be difficult to not feel some swell of sympathy for this unfortunate man who unknowingly committed heinous crimes, but atoned for them (as Jupiter notes in 1.236–7). Nevertheless, and this is quite important, when Oedipus emerges here in a state of hopeful anticipation for the conflict, the reader's expectations for a grieving father, like that of Euripides' are subverted, and with them the moral sympathy for Oedipus. The scene forces out of focus the ability to anticipate a response from Oedipus, based on Euripides' *Phoenissae*; it is no longer a helpful guide to anticipating Oedipus' reactions to the outcome he initiated. This brief scene also turns against Oedipus because he can no longer be sympathized with or pitied. The reader is suddenly confronted with the possibility that he will not lament but rejoice when the fratricide occurs. Put another way, the joy he hopes to find in the ruin of his son(s) suspends sympathy, the ability to be affectively disposed toward him until the conclusion of the fratricide: will he rejoice over their corpses, obdurate and unforgiving, as Seneca's Oedipus seems positioned to have done, or will he lament their deaths, as Euripides has him do?

Oedipus is ignorant of himself. This scene of satisfaction allows Statius to extend Oedipus' tragic flaw and the governing theme of his unfortunate existence: he lacks self-knowledge. Like Seneca's Oedipus, as J. P. Poe describes him, Statius' Oedipus "is bound to a universe whose process is destructive."[33] His ignorance stirs sympathy within the audience because the consequences of his actions are already known to readers. We observe that the tragedy of Oedipus in Statius' *Thebaid* is that his persistent *ira* prevents him from anticipating the regret he will, as we suppose he should, feel for his dead sons. Sophocles makes Oedipus' inability to identify himself as a possible fault in the blight that overruns Thebes apparent in his great proclamation after the citizens of Thebes have made their propitiations. At the start of Sophocles' *Oedipus Tyrannus* the titular hero calls down a curse on the person responsible for the plague and affliction (246–51). Granted, it may be too much to expect Oedipus to think himself the murderer, but then it seems convenient on his own part to be unmindful of the fact that he did once kill a man. Nevertheless, Oedipus cannot conceive of himself as a source of miasma, and he fails to count himself among the possible culprits. Examinations of Sophocles' Oedipus and his relation to himself, the *politai*, and the gods are extensive, and I have nothing new to add to that discussion, I wish only to reiterate that at the core of Oedipus' tragic life, the persistent issue is a lack of self-knowledge. The power of Sophocles' drama rests in Oedipus' realization of who he is. While Statius' Oedipus is not unaware of his identity, he does not know how to respond when tragic events conclude because he is so consumed by his own anger. Statius thus extends Oedipus' self-ignorance further into his biography. Audiences and readers familiar with Oedipus' biography will know him, at critical points, often better than he is able to know himself. His overall trajectory engenders considerable pathos as audiences anticipate the unfortunate occurrences that await him. He does not know that he will regret this gleeful anticipation and sponsorship of the conflict; however, audiences do, or may at least feel that he should. How Oedipus responds to the outcome of the war, and certainly to the fratricide, is critical to closing the story. While Oedipus only appears briefly over the course of the *Thebaid*'s narrative, these points display a tragic trajectory in which the first two events, utterance of the curse (*Theb.* 1) and hopeful anticipation of conflict (*Theb.* 8), anticipate the final scene of Oedipus' regret (*Theb.* 11). Audiences thus await his reaction to the loss of his sons because it is only through his response that a moral judgment of his character can be decided. Until the closing scene any sense of empathy or pity for Oedipus must be suspended.[34] Statius' strategy here is consistent with the problem of self-knowledge that dogs the character in Sophocles' *Oedipus Tyrannus*, but where in the latter Oedipus does not know who he is, in the former he does not know who he will be. Statius develops an Oedipus who curses his sons in a fit of extreme anger and in seeing Oedipus rejoicing at having his heart's perverse desire, readers can only speculate on whether or not he will regret that wish. And so we wait for Oedipus to fall again.

Oedipus' petition for supernatural aid to punish the offspring that dishonor him attempts to exercise power where he has none. Indeed, the curse underscores his own powerlessness to bring retribution or punishment against his sons. Consider the characterization of Seneca's Oedipus in *Phoenissae*. In Seneca's version of the story, Oedipus does not curse his sons, nor is there any sense that there is a curse in effect. The sorrows of his house are generally attributed to fate and bad luck.[35] The motivation for the conflict develops through the sons' inherently defective characters, rather than through a supernatural cause.[36] Thus, with the divine machinery removed, Seneca foregrounds the fault of character as sufficient for their mutual destruction.[37] This also makes Seneca's Oedipus a stronger character than his Statian counterpart. When the messenger arrives at *Phoenissae* 320–27 seeking Oedipus' help, he pleads: "prohibe pariter et bellum et scelus" (327). Oedipus condemns his sons and ironically urges the conflict. Here, then, Oedipus has a choice. The power to intercede and prevent the fratricide is his, and he chooses not to exercise it. The suggestion by the messenger is that Oedipus, and not the gods or fate, can halt the conflict between Eteocles and

Polynices. This affords him a degree of control, especially over the outcome, that he does not possess in Statius' *Thebaid*. His hopeful anticipation of a tragic outcome in which one or both of the sons is slain anticipates his satisfaction once the fratricide is fulfilled. At the close of the first fragment, Antigone petitions her father to prevail upon her brothers: "auctorque placidae liberis pacis veni" (*Phoen*. 349).[38] Oedipus' rhetorically charged response indicates that he is not of any mind for calm and peace, rather:

> tumet animus ira, feruet immensum dolor,
> maiusque quam quod casus et iuuenum furor
> conatur aliquid cupio. non satis est adhuc
> ciuile bellum: frater in fratrem ruat.
> nec hoc sat est: quod debet, ut fiat nefas
> de more nostro, quod meos deceat toros:
> date arma matri.
>
> *Phoen*. 352-58

My heart swells with rage! Boundless burning woe! I want more than that impulsive fury which youth tries. Civil War is not enough: I want brother spurred against brother! Nay, even that is not enough—what should be must be an evil in my fashion, what suits my marriage: give arms even to your mother!

Here we find Seneca's Oedipus eagerly desiring to find satisfaction in the event much in the same way Statius' Oedipus does. He expresses a hopeful anticipation that continually escalates in *nefas*. Civil war is not enough, fratricide is not enough. The event needs to exceed his own story. Oedipus then hides himself among the cliffs, caves, and brush to await news. Because Seneca's *Phoenissae* is incomplete it is unknown how (or even if) the fratricide would have affected him. Nevertheless, it is clear that Seneca developed his Oedipus along a different track than that of Euripides. The potential for a father pleased over the deaths of his sons, rather than lamenting his hardness toward them, held an attraction for Statius' development of the father.

Outcome

After Megaera joins Tisiphone at *Thebaid* 11 to ensure the fratricide takes place, news of Oedipus' attitude toward his sons is brought to the reader's attention. At the height of the battle, just before the fratricidal duel between Eteocles and Polynices, the Fury summarizes her achievements in a speech of swelling satisfaction (11.76–112); however, she lists the possible impediments to her goals. She notes especially what has become of Oedipus:

> ... ipse etiam, qui nos lassare precando
> suetus et ultrices oculorum exposcere Diras,
> iam pater est: coetu fertur iam solus ab omni
> flere sibi.
>
> *Theb.* 11.105–8

Even that one exasperating us with his prayer upon prayer and demand we Furies be avengers for his eyes decides now to become a father; they say he weeps by himself, alone, apart from all else.

Oedipus' view on the conflict has undergone a shift. Tisiphone's tone is uncertain as the comments could be tinged with sarcasm, irritation, annoyance, irony. The remark is slight; however, she reveals here the seeds of Oedipus' regret, but in such a way as to put forth a few future anticipations.

Because the mention of Oedipus' present state follows Tisiphone's list of possible impediments to the fratricide, she may fear (and therefore we may anticipate) that Oedipus might attempt to intervene, performing the duty that the messenger pleads of him in Seneca's *Phoenissae*: "prohibe partier et bellum et scelus" ("forbid both war and wickedness," *Phoen.* 327). Such a possibility threatens the canonical episode in which Jocasta acts as intercessor between her sons. This information also presents the possibility of a scene in which he regrets his anger, thus anticipating that Oedipus might behave as a father when he sees Eteocles and Polynices dead. At some unidentifiable point in the development of the conflict a change has occurred within Oedipus. But Tisiphone here only plants a seed that anticipates how attempting to take on a paternal role will affect him.

Now consider what Statius does: when the pariah emerged to banquet among the people he was cleaned. After his sons are dead, however, Oedipus returns to the same disordered and tragic appearance with which Statius began the *Thebaid*:

> ... saeuoque in limine profert
> mortem imperfectam: ueteri stat sordida tabo
> utraque canities, et durus sanguine crinis
> obnubit furiale caput; procul ora genaeque
> intus et effossae squalent uestigia lucis.
>
> *Theb.* 11.581–85

At the fierce limit he reveals his unfinished death. His gray hair covers his mad head, stiff and grimy with old gore and flattened with blood. The sockets of his eyes sink deep revealing foulness where the light was dug out.

The two descriptions of *Thebaid* 1 and 11 fit neatly together by the suggested infection around Oedipus' eyes. During the banquet Oedipus is happy, or perhaps overcome with a misguided anticipation of happiness, as he waits to hear the clash of swords that will signal fulfillment of the duel between Eteocles and Polynices. However at a point unwitnessed, but related by Tisiphone (11.107), Oedipus realizes the consequences of his dark hopes and is brought to an even lower emotional state.[39] Oedipus' foul outer appearance reveals how he has reverted to his tragic position.

The scene in Statius' *Thebaid* in which Oedipus encounters the corpses of his sons revisits Euripides' *Phoenissae* (1539–1702). At Euripides' *Phoenissae* 1693–1701, Oedipus asks Antigone to lead him to the bodies of Jocasta, who had committed suicide earlier, and his sons. After she presses his hand to the faces of his sons, Oedipus shares in their misfortune claiming: ὦ φίλα πεσήματ' ἄθλι' ἀθλίου πατρός ("o, sweet dead, cursed sons of a cursed father," 1701). Oedipus is oddly reconciled in this way to the deaths of his sons. The father does not mention or imply the effect of his curse. Instead, he asks by what fate these things occurred: ποίᾳ μοίρᾳ | πῶς ἔλιπον φάος; ("by what fates, how did their light leave?" 1552–53). Antigone identifies: ... σὸς ἀλάστωρ | ξίφεσιν βρίθων | καὶ πυρὶ καὶ σχετλίαισι μάχαις ἐπὶ παῖδας ἔβα σούς, | ὦ πάτερ, ὤμοι, "your vengeful spirit, weighted with swords and fires and woeful battles, has fallen upon your sons, alas, O father" 1556–69). Thus, Oedipus has some part in the outcome of these events.[40] Certainly there are clear staging advantages in allowing Oedipus to grieve over his sons and Jocasta in the way Euripides presents it. Statius' development of the scene excludes Jocasta, who commits suicide after he completes his lament over the bodies of his sons. This forms a convenient shift in scene before Oedipus' banishment. Statius' separation of Jocasta from the brothers allows a greater emphasis to be placed on his role and subsequent grief as their father.

In Statius' treatment, Oedipus presents awareness of his curse's power when he proclaims:

heu dolor, heu iusto magis exaudita parentis
uota malaeque preces! quisnam fuit ille deorum,
qui stetit orantem iuxta praereptaque uerba
dictavit Fatis?

Theb. 11.616–7

> Oh, grief! Oh, a parent's wishes and evil prayers overheard! Which one of the gods stood beside me as I prayed, snatched my words up and conveyed them to the Fates?

Oedipus quickly scatters the blame across other parties and agencies as he declares: "Furor illa et mouit Erinys | et pater et genetrix et regna oculique cadentes" ("it was madness that caused it, and a Fury, and my father and mother, and a throne, and falling eyes," 11.619-20). With this claim, Oedipus identifies a conspiracy of fate against his sons.[41] When Oedipus declares *nil ego* (11.621), he acknowledges the end of his dynasty.[42] With the death of his sons, there will be no further succession. Oedipus is now truly nothing. At this moment he acknowledges the irrevocability and finality of the tragedy, even if the degree to which he might personally be thought responsible (e.g. through the curse) is somewhat ambiguous.[43] Statius maintains a close awareness of Oedipus' tragic development as it relates to the outcome of his curse; his Oedipus is intended to live on in sorrow and regret.[44]

Oedipus concludes his speech over the corpses with the all too late lament that he now becomes an intercessor ("medium nunc saltem admittite patrem," 11.626), the role of arbitration that Oedipus rejects in Seneca's *Phoenissae* (328-47). He then makes an attempt at suicide (11.627-33).[45] As he mourns over the corpses of his sons he begins to feel around for a blade presumably to throw himself upon but Antigone secretly has hidden the swords of her brothers.[46] Even death as a possible relief from his grief is denied to him. For the purpose of Statius' epic narrative this is a marked advance on the character that Euripides and Seneca had developed in their *Phoenissae*. They do not afford him, for whatever reason, a similar series of moments that culminate in an image of such extreme misery. And it is this scene, this portrait of his misery that had been promised from the first book. Once Oedipus mourns the loss of Eteocles and Polynices, he completes the proleptic utterance made by Jupiter when he ratifies Oedipus' "perversa uota: iam iam rata vota tulisti, | dire senex," ("now, now, you will suffer the prayer's approval, sad old man," 1.239-40). While we find here, from the mouth of the supreme cosmocrator, the anticipation of this final scene, it is important to keep in mind that this prophetic utterance is not so straightforward as might have been expected. Certainly, the canonical scene does arrive, but Statius creates a trajectory that threatens to subvert that initial assurance, at least for a short span.

Statius sets the development of Oedipus within a highly established tradition freighted with certain critical expectations, chiefly regret. I have demonstrated how Statius develops Oedipus' narrative arc to work within but also against that tradition. A few additional points are crucial here. The first is that the pronouncement of the curse against his sons, which in the *Thebaid* contributes directly (but not exclusively) to the fratricide and loss of Oedipus' hereditary line, establishes the expectation for a concluding scene in which Oedipus grieves over the loss of his sons. The second point is that Statius subverts the expectation of this scene by suggesting a contingent outcome. Because there are assurances from the tradition (as informed by Euripides' *Phoenissae*) that Oedipus will grieve over the loss of his sons. When, however, Oedipus appears to gloat over and enjoy the prospect of his sons' death, somewhat like the Oedipus of Seneca's *Phoenissae*, or to a lesser degree like that of Sophocles' *Oedipus at Colonus*, it overturns the readers' expectations for the anticipated ending of Oedipus mourning his sons. Initial pity for Oedipus fades in light of the satisfaction and the delight in *nefas* that he later anticipates. Insofar as Oedipus experiences the escalation toward war with great serenity and contentment it becomes increasingly difficult to sympathize with him further. Vessey suggests that the philosophical characterization of dominant figures forces "oversimplification" and "there is little room for ambivalence or ambiguity,"[47] but this seems not to be so. His *furor* and desire for retributive justice are strikingly human and it is not so difficult to identify with him. Moreover, there is considerable ambiguity in the realization that with regard to fate, Oedipus, the most powerless figure within the epic, and Jupiter, arguably the most powerful, both attain the same goal. Contrary to expectation, the character of Oedipus, who holds the least power and authority in the *Thebaid*, manages with a simple prayer to be among its most influential.

6

Portentous Ends

The *Thebaid* aims toward death. This brings an irrevocability and finality that, except under the most fantastical circumstances, cannot be changed. It is an end that the dramatist Agathon best expresses when he writes: μόνου γὰρ αὐτοῦ καὶ θεὸς στερίσκεται, | ἀγένητα ποιεῖν ἅσσ' ἂν ᾖ πεπραγμένα, "For even this is deprived of god, to undo that which has already been done" (Fr. 5.1–2). As we see in the preceding discussion, portentousness occupies the first half of the *Thebaid*. A number of the major scenes prefigure and render as inevitable the destruction presented in the second half of the epic. The final books, in turn, have as their predominant concern the deaths of the heroes, which as anticipatory readers, we are primed to witness. This chapter concerns the deaths of the primary heroes (excepting Polynices who is discussed alongside Eteocles in the next chapter) and the narrative maneuvers used to continue the foreshadowing of and anticipation for these ends. I am primarily concerned with the cues that create anticipation for the aristeia, with the games of *Thebaid* 6 figuring prominently into the discussion. Indeed, the games are peculiar in that the heroes are each victorious; however, their victory prefigures their defeat and death.[1] Games—a stock feature of heroic epic—offer a place "quo Martia bellis | praesudare paret seseque accendere uirtus," "in which military virtue sweats and burns in preparation for war" (6.3–4). The games also serve as a prelude to the coming war.[2] The honor attached to Opheltes recedes in light of this. Even the civilizing aspect of the games reduces to the savagery of war: "pax nulla fidesque. | bella geri ferro leuius, bella horrida, credas" (6.456–7). Generally speaking, Statius' depiction of the epic games has strong affinities with those presented in the *Iliad* and the *Aeneid*. Legras[3] notes that the sequence of sporting events corresponds roughly to the order in which the heroes are slain in subsequent books[4] with the number of contests varied from eight in the *Iliad* and five in the *Aeneid*, to seven to match the number of heroes participating in the expedition:[5] a chariot race, a foot race, the discus, a boxing match, a wrestling match, a sword fight (almost), and an archery shoot.

Amphiaraus

Amphiaraus knows from the augury that he is fated to die, that five of the leaders in the campaign will die, and that the war will be disastrous. Statius frames the experience of Amphiaraus' foreknowledge in very emotional terms.[6] Where the seer is deeply aware of the likelihood and outcome of war Statius writes: "... iam bella tubaeque | comminus, absentesque fremunt sub pectore Thebae," "Already war trumpets openly, and distant Thebes rages in his heart" (3.568-9).[7] Despite knowing that the omens are unfavorable ("nullisque secundus in extis | pallet et armatis simulat sperare sacerdos," "and the priest, who finds no promise in the entrails, pretends hope for the men in arms," 4.14-15), Amphiaraus begrudgingly goes along and feigns hope. After the death of Archemorus, Statius reminds us that Amphiaraus bears the burden of knowing the unavoidable truth: "hic luctus abolere nouique | funeris auspicium uates, quamquam omina sentit | uera, iubet," "Here, the prophet ends the mourning and the portents of grief, though he knows the omens true" (6.221-3). Developing Amphiaraus' trajectory in this way isolates him from the conflict as a whole, and his knowledge, which we share with him, rouses our sympathy. His death is one that we anticipate. He is preserved from the stain of "nefas" and thus we go into the sequence of deaths knowing that Statius will present each thereafter in a way that supersedes wickedness.

Amphiaraus' victory in the chariot race foreshadows his own end. Just as Apollo will provide his seer an immaculate death, during the chariot race Apollo provides Amphiaraus an immaculate victory. The contest itself does a double duty since it both prefigures the death of the prophet,[8] and also emphasizes the character of Polynices, showcasing his inability to control the steed Arion or attend Adrastus' advice, which further prefigures Adrastus' final plea to Polynices before his duel with Eteocles. The intervention of Apollo presents the snake-haired image of a monster ("anguicomam monstri effigiem," 6.695) that frightens Arion. The horse comes in first, but without Polynices, so Amphiaraus is declared victor and receives as his prize a "catera."[9] The irregularity and confusion of this event anticipates further instances throughout the games of misfortune, cheating, and, of course, ominous presage. In particular, for Amphiaraus who is destined to be swallowed alive by a chasm in the earth, anticipation for and a reminder of this event is seeded in his victory. At the moment that his win in the race is assured the earth becomes eager to receive him and groans in anticipation, "dat gemitum tellus" (6.527).

Later, as the initial battles at Thebes begin, Statius surveys the initial confrontations of each hero, until focusing on Amphiaraus, who is "prominent above the rest" ("eminet ante alios," 7.690). This initiates Amphiaraus' *aristeia*. While the conflict between Thebes and Argos is only just beginning, madness and war fury have already begun to overtake the men. Not even Amphiaraus, second only to Adrastus in mildness of temper, can avoid being infected by savage bloodlust.[10] There occurs an unexpected shift in his character: "ardet inexpleto saeui Mauortis amore | et fruitur dextra atque anima flagrante superbit," "He burns with depthless desire for savage war, delights in his right hand, takes pride in his burning soul" (7.703-4). Statius draws attention to the surprise he intends, where he distinguishes his Amphiaraus from tradition, but explaining: "quantum subito diversus," "How suddenly different" (7.706). Amphiaraus will not die by human hands;[11] however, his immaculate end does not detract from his gleeful savagery just before he is swallowed into Hell. Amphiaraus knows that he will die and he glories in it (7.697ff.). He is the first of the seven heroes to perish and the first, it should be remarked, to be overcome by the frenzy in war that will visit each of them. In this way, Amphiaraus offers a prelude to the savagery that reaches its pitch in the fratricide of Eteocles and Polynices. Of all the heroes, the one who is least expected to behave madly, succumbs to blood lust, such is the potency of "ira" and "furor" in Statius' *Thebaid*.[12]

Statius presses further the foreshadowing of Amphiaraus' death and the final scene. As the chariot becomes bloody with gore and the wheels clogged with the dead some remain conscious "at illi | uulnere semineces (nec devitare facultas) | uenturum super ora vident," "But these men, half-dead from wounds unable to avoid it, see the wheel about to roll over their faces" (7.763-5). Similarly, Amphiaraus has seen his death coming and like these "semineces" has no power to alter his destiny. Further, anticipation comes shortly after as Statius describes how the ghosts howl in pursuit of Amphiaraus' chariot, understanding that they and the chariot will soon enter the underworld: "strident animae currumque sequuntur" (7.770). Finally, hurrying things along in seeming impatience, Apollo reveals himself to his devoted seer, and Amphiaraus asks: "How long do you slow my appointed death? I already hear the swiftly purling Sytx, Dis' dark rivers, the treble gape of the pitiless guardian," "instantes quonam usque morabere manes? | audio iam rapidae cursum Stygis atraque Ditis | flumina tergeminosque mali custodis hiatus" (7.781-3). And as Apollo alights from the chariot, the car groans (790) and a simile punctuates anticipation of the scene that describes a ship's knowledge that it will perish when it sails under Helen's star (791-3).

Amphiaraus remains faithful to his god even in the end, which is consistent with the piety of his character and contrasts with the disassociation and rupture between gods and mortals that continues to grow throughout the death scenes. Indeed, there is a positive affinity between the two that offers an inverse reflection of Oedipus and Tisiphone. His final words to Apollo are a reasonable appeal for justice against the betrayal of his wife:

> ... nunc uoce suprema,
> si qua recessuro debetur gratia uati,
> deceptum tibi, Phoebe, larem poenasque nefandae
> coniugis et pulchrum nati commendo furorem.
>
> *Theb.* 7.785–8

Now with final word, if any the receding prophet deserve any grace, Phoebus, I leave to you my deceived home as well as my treacherous wife and the lovely madness of my son.

Not one to let opportunity pass, Amphiaraus makes a similar plea to Dis after he crashes into the underworld from above: "si quando nefanda | huc aderit coniunx, illi funesta reserua | supplicia: illa tua, rector bone, dignior ira," "If someday my wicked wife arrives here, save your direst punishments for her. She, good ruler, warrants your anger more" (8.120–2). For Amphiaraus, his wife deserves hell and its torments. He asks nothing more and accepts his end. And so Amphiaraus' final wish evokes an event outside and beyond the scope of Statius' *Thebaid*.[13]

Tydeus

As Statius relates early in the *Thebaid*, in anticipation of his later scene of homophagy, that Tydeus is more daring in every deed: "cunctis Tydeus audentior actis" (2.175). He is the warrior of excess, the greatest hero, and yet also the perpetrator of one of the greatest atrocities. There are traditional problems with the presentation of the cannibalism scene.[14] Nevertheless, Statius makes us aware quite early on, by hints at his character, that he will present the masticating Tydeus. After the defeat of Eteocles' ambush party, Statius develops a simile where Tydeus is described as a lion:

> ut leo, qui campis longe custode fugato
> Massylas depastus oues, ubi sanguine multo
> luxuriata fames ceruixque et tabe grauatae
> consedere iubae, mediis in caedibus astat

aeger, hians, uictusque cibis; nec iam amplius irae
crudescunt: tantum uacuis ferit aera malis
molliaque eiecta delambit uellera lingua.

Theb. 2.675-81

As a lion, who has routed a shepherd far from his field, and sates himself on Massylian sheep, his hunger has enjoyed abundant blood and his neck and mane are matted with gore, he then rises sick amongst his kill, panting so full of food. His fury no longer swells. He just snaps at the air with empty maw and laps his softened coat with a long tongue.

This simile foreshadows the gory death scene and offers a kind of mental profile of Tydeus. The suggestion is that only weariness can stop him; though his taste for blood is difficult to sate. Notably too, Athena, Tydeus' patron, imparts wise council to her favorite in a scene strongly reminiscent of her visitation to Achilles at *Iliad* 1.206-22 and encourages him to set a limit: "iam pone modum" (2.688); a suggestion that will prove ominous. Tydeus will not, he cannot.

The wrestling match provides a scene in which Tydeus grapples with excess. The contest also builds on the unequal pairings seen in the discus contest and the boxing match. Tydeus steps forward to wrestle Agylleus, son of Hercules. Tydeus is short in stature but wiry (6.845-6) and, as evinced by his confrontation with Polynices at Adrastus' palace and then during his monomachy in the ambush, capable. Agylleus, though having bulk, lacks his fathers' honed musculature. Instead, he spreads out like a blob: "sed non ille rigor patriumque in corpore robur: | luxuriant artus, effusaque sanguine laxo | membra natant," "but he lacks rigor, the strength of his father's body. His limbs luxuriate, they spread and swim, slack in their vigor" (6.840-2). Tydeus, however, is more like Hercules: "Oenidae superare parem" (6.843) in muscle and might, if not height. This parallel is reinforced by the clear analog to Hercules' defeat of Antaeus when Tydeus lifts his opponent off the ground (6.893-6).[15] By demonstrating how like Tydeus is to Hercules, we are reminded of how unlike Hercules Tydeus will be in the end. As Vessey notes, Tydeus' death fails to attain the same immortality and divinity that graced Hercules.[16]

Tydeus' *aristeia* breaks into two sections within the narrative, where a teasing *mora* is employed by the poet. First, Tydeus fights against Haemon, urged on by Athena: "saevum sed Tydea contra | Pallas agit" (8.499-500). Haemon is supported by Heracles. The two gods reach an accord. Favor is dispensed to Tydeus. Haemon feels the god leave him (8.519), just as Tydeus will eventually feel the divine spark leave him (8.733), and he retreats. Tydeus aims his spear to strike Haemon in the neck but misses. His foe remains alive. This prefigures Tydeus' later failure to kill Eteocles. Tydeus next attacks Prothus (536ff.). He strikes and both horse and rider fall; however, Prothus is trampled by the horse. He does not exactly die at the hands of Tydeus. Atys then taunts Tydeus, and presumes that because of his stature he is an easy mark (8.578-8). Atys hurls a spear with all his might but Tydeus, assured of Atys' death, will not deign to make such an easy kill. Statius concludes the first part of Tydeus' heroic finale with another lion simile:

> innumeris ueluti leo forte potitus
> caedibus imbelles uitulos mollesque iuuencas
> transmittit: magno furor est in sanguine mergi
> nec nisi regnantis ceruice recumbere tauri.
>
> *Theb.* 8.593-6

> As a lion having enjoyed innumerable kills passes unwarlike calves and soft heifers: he rages to wallow in great blood and set himself on nothing other than the neck of a reigning bull.

Tydeus has an overwhelming taste for blood but he wants a victim worthy of his effort. Thus, Statius leaves off tracking Tydeus presumably until the raging warrior can find a fitting adversary. There follows a brief interlude between Antigone and Ismene over the cause of all the suffering before Statius returns to Tydeus.

In the second part of Tydeus' *aristeia*, we find him searching out Eteocles. When he finds the king, he calls him out. Eteocles replies by hurling a spear and Tydeus charges (8.695). Tydeus attempts to make his way to the king, paying little regard to the men in the line; although he maims and injures few. Finally, Melanippus hurls the fatal spear and Tydeus with his last bit of strength manages to slay Melanippus in turn. Tydeus' comrades pull the hero from the fray despite his eagerness to fight on (8.727-30). As the great hero lies propped amid shields, he feels death claiming him: "et ipse recedere caelum | ingentesque animos extremo frigore labi | sensit," "But he perceives that the sky recedes and his mighty heart fails in that last chill" (8.733-5).

The hero asks to see the head of Melanippus and his comrades oblige. Tydeus is described as "amens | laetitiaque iraque," "mad with joy and anger" (8.751) when he sees them dragging his foe toward him and he asks for the head to be removed. At this point, Tydeus appears content but Tisiphone urges for more: "infelix contentus erat: plus exigit ultrix | Tisiphone" (8.757-8). When Athena arrives to bestow on him "decus immortal," she finds Tydeus eating Melanippus' brains out of his skull and she flees. Divine immortality is lost to him.

What we find in Tydeus is an emphasis on limits; a character with immense power and ability that cannot control his battle lust and savagery, like Capaneus later. To be sure, we could dismiss his savage homophagy as the work of Tisiphone who possesses him. Yet, Athena cannot excuse the act and his comrades feel that he goes too far (9.1-4). So Statius' audience would have been unlikely to condone, or even excuse, his cannibalism.[17] Statius has steadily built Tydeus to be consistent with this moment of violent excess.

Hippomedon

Hippomedon, along with Capaneus, are the impious and contentious counterpoints to Amphiaraus. His victory during the games, like that of Amphiaraus, is something of a disappointment. Hippomedon hurls the discus and beats the other contestants well. His only true rival is Phlegyas of Pisa who delights in the sport and is viewed by the spectators as "promissa" (669).[18] Fortune, however, intervenes and the discus slips and falls at Phlegyas' feet. As Lovatt points out, Hippomedon takes the prize with no one to stand against him as rival.[19] The man-giant hurls the discus like Polyphemus hurling the rock at Ulysses' ship (716-18) and wins a tiger skin.[20] Since no mere mortal can oppose him, this opens the way for divine opposition, and anticipates his confrontation with the river Ismenos.

For his impiety, it seems likely that he, like Capaneus later, will die by the direct intervention of a god. Statius twice provides portentous moments that prefigure Hippomedon's great battle with the river Ismenos.[21] At *Thebaid* 7.424ff. Hippomedon eagerly fords the stream before all others. He is later described in battle as being like a rock that withstands the barrage of waves:

... ceu fluctibus obuia rupes,
cui neque de caelo metus et fracta aequora cedunt,
stat cunctis inmota minis, fugit ipse rigentem
pontus et ex alto miserae nouere carinae.

Theb. 9.91-4

As a rock cresting the waves: no fright from the sky, and the broken waters recede. It stands unmoved by any threat, even the sea flees the intransigent face and wretched ships among the depths know it well.

The simile anticipates the battle with Ismenos; the rock is successful, Hippomedon is not. The hero makes a valiant stand against the river god, fighting beyond mortal capacities. Yet, despite all his effort, he does not achieve a glorious death. He is overwhelmed by a god and then beset by opportunistic pests. As Statius asks: "quid faciat bellis obsessus et undis? | nec fuga iam misero, nec magnae copia mortis," "what shall he do, overwhelmed by battle and water? There is neither flight for the unfortunate, nor opportunity for noble death" (9.490–1).

Hippomedon's death scene recalls the speculations of Andromache on what will befall Hector when he falls in battle. During Hector's encounter with Andromache, the wife of the Trojan hero expresses her anxiety over her husband's bravery. She fears: τάχα γάρ σε κατακτανέουσιν Ἀχαιοί | πάντες ἐφορμηθέντες, "for swiftly the Achaians will rush together and kill you" (*Iliad* 6.409–10). Of course, this is not how Hector dies, but her speculation notes the inglorious and heroically dissatisfying ends of one outnumbered and slain by a mob. The death of Hippomedon studies tragically disappointing and inglorious ends. Dewar asserts that Statius' revision of the story provides a "totally original moral significance."[22] A high moral tone seems, however, undercut by the ignoble and unjust way that Hippomedon meets his end. Hippomedon slew Nomius, Mimas, Lichas, Lycetus, one of Thespis' sons, Gyas, Erginus, Herses, and Crethus. He boasted over them: "acerbat uulnera dictis" (9.302). He then slew Crenaeus, who provides a foretaste of Parthenopaeus' tragic death.[23] But no one can boast slaying Hippomedon and even Hypseus' pompous vaunting is rewarded with Capaneus' spear.[24] There may be a moral to Hippomedon's death, but it lacks the divine agency we might expect. Rather, like Tydeus, Hippomedon goes too far.[25] Even Hippomedon is pathetically aware that he does not deserve his fate as he prays to Mars (9.506–10). As Vessey points out, Hippomedon "does not see that death is common to all, whether warriors or herdsmen, and that it must be accepted in whatever form it comes."[26] Perhaps Vessey has in mind the sort of platitude put forth by Horace: "pallida Mors aequo pulsat pede pauperum tabernas | regumque turris," "Pale death strikes in equal measure the haunts of the poor, the towers of the rich" (*Carm.* 1.4.13–14). Statius' thinking, however, is probably closer to Otho's described by Tacitus: "mortem omnibus ex natura aequalem oblivione apud posteros vel gloria distingui; ac si nocentem innocentemque idem exitus maneat, acrioris viri esse merito perire," "Nature has made death for all, but afterward each death differs in whether it brings glory or oblivion; if all then meet in the same place it is the duty of the valorous man to deserve his fate" (*Hist.* 1.21). In any case, it is a despairing death, like the one

Andromache imagined would meet her husband. Merited or not, Hippomedon's final moments are strikingly unjust and surprise readers by defying expectations of heroic men dying heroic deaths.

Parthenopaeus

Until Parthenopaeus realizes his rash folly, he evokes very little sympathy or interest.[27] Unlike the others, and outside of his relationship with his mother, Atalanta, Parthenopaeus is not very compelling. Amphiaraus is betrayed by his wife and bears the burden of foreknowing the failure at Thebes. Tydeus is a devoted friend and brother-in-law to Polynices and despite his rancor and excess presents a degree of sensibility that Polynices lacks. Of course, he cannot restrain his "ira" and pushes the limits of heroism, not unlike Capaneus. Parthenopaeus' death aligns more closely with that of Hippomedon in that it strives to rouse pity—swarmed and slain by a mob who found an advantage. Parthenopaeus dies demonstrating the shortcomings of his youth: "a rudis annorum, tantum noua gloria suadet!" (4.247) and "audaces annos" (9.810). As his mother accuses, he is caught up in the ideas of glory: "cruda heu festinaque uirtus | suasit et hortatrix animosi gloria leti!" (9.716–17). The callous reader might point to his death as the logical result of youthful overreaching; unfortunate but not unwarranted. The boy appears, indeed, vain (4.251–3).[28] But it is not youth or eagerness, but strength and experience that win battles. The boy has neither of these. This is best illustrated in the impracticality of his battle dress. He presents himself in a "pallam" twice dyed in Oebalian purple and a tunic embroidered by his mother. His shield droops (693) and his sword is too heavy, "ense grauis nimio" (694). He is delighted by the "aurea fibula" and the sounds of his scabbard, the rattle of arrows in his quiver, and the clink of chains on his "conus."[29] The preoccupations with pomp and his idealized notions of glory anticipate his eventual fall, which is also anticipated during the foot-race.

During the games Parthenopaeus competes, to his glory, in the foot-race. The foot-race is the event best suited for those who are not prepared for war: essentially, youths in the intermediary stages of manhood.[30] And, as Statius notes, certainly good practice in battle, should one need to retreat, being "nec inutile bellis | subsidium, si dextra neget," "not useless in battle, should the right arm fail" (6.552–3). Nearing the finish line, Idas, the strongest competitor against Parthenopaeus, finds an opportunity to claim victory by yanking the younger racer back by his long flowing hair, which he grew from youth to be dedicated to

Trivia (6.607–617). This foul allows Idas to win the race. In battle, such treachery means the difference between life and death. Certainly, deceit during the fratricide will enable Eteocles to kill Polynices. Parthenopaeus is demonstrably unprepared for war. This is evident in his inability to perceive his long flowing hair as a weakness. His comeliness is his undoing. One thinks of the male peacock, whose tail-feathers, despite their beauty, are long, cumbersome, and make the bird easy prey. Idas' trick nearly ignites a war among the troops (6.618–21). Some of the soldiers, however, are pleased with the treachery. Adrastus does not know what to do.[31] As he recently experienced with the armies during the Hypsipyle episode, Adrastus knows that his power over the army is weak and in danger of quick change. He arrives at the most compromising solution: he declares neither victor and stages the race again. Despite the laudable civility of this decision, Parthenopaeus will not have the same referee judgment in battle. This scene demonstrates how far from the reality of war the games actually are. In the second run, Parthenopaeus emerges the clear victor, takes the palm, and wins a horse (6.642–4). Being neither a boy nor yet fully a man, his victory in the foot-race reminds us of how much potential is lost in his death.

Parthenopaeus also lacks the experience and forethought that would dispose him to protect himself: "ubi pugna | cassis anhela calet, resoluto uertice nudus | exoritu," "but when his panting helm warms from battle, he frees his head and proceeds bare" (9.699–701). Statius takes this opportunity to describe his handsomeness, but also notes that Parthenopaeus is unaccustomed to the discomfort of arms.[32] Though he is capable in battle, Amphion's insult fits: "proelia lude domi," "play at battles back home" (9.786). In response to Amphion's taunts, Parthenopaeus boasts of his lineage; he makes a grand speech. Meanwhile, Amphion hurls a spear that is noticed by Parthenopaeus' horse, but not by Parthenopaeus. The stead's quick reaction causes a wide miss. His horse is better prepared for battle.

Statius develops the tragic anticipation of Parthenopaeus' death through his mother, Atalanta. As the armies prepare to set forth on their march toward Thebes, Atlanta hears the news that her son will lead the Arcadians into the conflict. Like Jocasta when she attempts to intervene, Atalanta flies to the scene to make her protest. Through a series of questions she stresses her son's lack of preparedness to participate in the war and chides his inexperience in the kind of parent-child back and forth we see throughout the epic (e.g. Jocasta and sons, Adrastus and Polynices, Creon and Menoeceus). She further reveals that unfavorable omens foretell disaster:

> sunt omina uera:
> mirabar cur templa mihi tremuisse Dianae
> nuper et inferior uultu dea uisa, sacrisque
> exuuiae cecidere tholis
>
> *Theb.* 4.330-33

Omens speak truth: I wondered why the temple of Diana recently trembled before me and the goddess seemed in appearance hellish, and why spoils fell from her sacred rotunda

Parthenopaeus, however, dismisses her council and the other captains attempt to allay her fears. She has no other options but to assent.

In expectation of Parthenopaeus' death, Statius reveals that she frequently has prophetic dreams, and has recently been troubled in her sleep by them: "praecipuos sed enim illa metus portendere uisa est nox miserae totoque erexit pectore matrem," "But that night seemed to portend dangers to the poor woman and worried the mother in her whole heart" (9.583-4). She dreams of the Acadian oak to which spoils are consecrated dying and bloody (585-98) and prays for her son in Diana's temple. On her return she encounters Apollo who relates of Parthenopaeus' death that it is: "non hoc mutabile fatum," "fated, and not to be changed" (9.661). Despite the foreknowledge and presages of her sons' death, she tragically endures the inevitable and like Jocasta, Adrastus, and Creon, makes futile attempts to alter the course of events.

Despite his youthful optimism, Parthenopaeus realizes that his end is near, and he sees himself for who he is. The warrior Dryas, more seasoned in battle than the youth, approaches to slay Parthenopaeus, who is taken by sudden awareness of his doom. This is particularly effective in evoking pathos:

> ... urguent praesagia mille
> funeris, et nigrae praecedunt nubila mortis.
> iamque miser raros comites uerumque uidebat
> Dorcea, iam uires paulatim abscedere sensit,
> sentit et exhaustas umero leuiore pharetras;
> iam minus atque minus fert ira, puerque uidetur
> et sibi, cum torua clipei metuendus obarsit
> luce Dryas: tremor ora repens ac uiscera torsit
> Arcados
>
> *Theb.* 9.850-58

A thousand presages of ruin press on him, clouds of dark death go before him. And now he sees few beside him, sees the true Dorceus and feels his strength slowly fading, feels that his shoulders are lighter, and his quiver spent. Less and less easily he carries his arms and to himself even he seems like a boy—when the savage shield of hard Dryas flames before him. A sudden convulsion knots the Arcadian's face and bowels.

The flash of Dryas' shield recalls Parthenopaeus' vain pride in his arms and his own shield, which along with his sword was too heavy to carry, as he marched among and against men in battle. He met his end bravely, and he did not run. As the race demonstrates, he could have fled and saved himself but he stood his ground. The knowledge of this greatly complements the pathos developed in his death scene. Statius wrenchingly describes the young man as seeing himself as he truly is.[33] The pathos that begins with Parthenopaeus seeing himself as a boy carries into his dying words to Dorceus as he is carried off the battlefield. Nobly, he feels that the fault lies within himself: "merui, genetrix, poenas; inuita capesse: | arma puer rapui," "I deserve this, mother; punish me, though you be unwilling" (9.891–2).

Capaneus

Capaneus is a giant figure of outrageousness and uncontrollable volatility in the Thebic war.[34] Indeed, when embroiled in the thick of the war in Thebes that war does not satisfy him and he must lay siege to heaven. It is not enough that Capaneus burn and sack the city, but that he claims to do it whether the gods will it or no. Initially, we might be inclined to read Capaneus' death as the reasonable outcome of his contempt for the gods and his impiety.[35] Aeschylus' *Septem* relies on the threat of a foreign enemy of barbarians besieging the city for its dramatic mood. Here also Capaneus is a figure of godlessness described by the messenger:

ὁ κόμπος δ' οὐ κατ' ἄνθρωπον φρονεῖ,
πύργοις δ' ἀπειλεῖ δείν,' ἃ μὴ κραίνοι τύχη·
θεοῦ τε γὰρ θέλοντος ἐκπέρσειν πόλιν
καὶ μὴ θέλοντός φησιν, οὐδὲ τὴν Διὸς
† Ἔριν πέδοι σκήψασαν ἐμποδὼν σχεθεῖν
τὰς δ' ἀστραπάς τε καὶ κεραυνίους βολὰς
μεσημβρινοῖσι θάλπεσιν προσήκασεν·

Sept. 425–31

He hurls terrible threats at the towers, pray fate not fulfill them. And he says he will take this city, gods willing or no! And not even Zeus, who hurls lightning that slays giants at the earth can oppose him. He compares the flash and thunder to the easy warmth of noon.

He is a boaster, bold in the face of the gods. He does not speak as men, presumably men who are pious and civil, do. He strives neither for nor against the gods, but indifferently to their will and has no fear of Zeus. This attitude is consistent with that of Capaneus in Statius' *Thebaid*. Aeschylus' Capaneus embodies the godlessness and barbarian nature of the attacking army.

Eteocles' rejoinder to the messengers' description heightens the tension, and places increasing emphasis on Capaneus' impiety and the promise of justice from the shafts of Zeus' lightning bolts:

> Καπανεὺς δ' ἀπειλεῖ, δρᾶν παρεσκευασμένος,
> θεοὺς ἀτίζων, κἀπογυμνάζων στόμα
> χαρᾷ ματαίᾳ θνητὸς ὢν εἰς οὐρανὸν
> πέμπει γεγωνὰ Ζηνὶ κυμαίνοντ' ἔπη·
> πέποιθα δ' αὐτῷ ξὺν δίκῃ τὸν πυρφόρον
> ἥξειν κεραυνόν, οὐδὲν ἐξῃκασμένον
> μεσημβρινοῖσι θάλπεσιν τοῖς ἡλίου.
>
> Sept. 440-6

Kapaneus is prepared to act on his threats in disdain for the gods, boasting in vain joy, though mortal, he aims a scathing torrent of abuse at heaven, at Zeus! I believe a flame of torch and thunder will justly strike him, not as warm noon sun, but from the very sun itself.

The chorus seconds Eteocles' prophecy declaring: κεραυνοῦ δέ νιν βέλος ἐπισχέθο, "may the hurl of lightning stop him," (*Sept*. 453). The limited scope of the drama, however, prevents Aeschylus from developing this further. His death is never described beyond the fulfillment of this wish and promise, it is simply left for us to believe at the end of the *Septem* when the pyres for the dead are lit, that Capaneus received his due. In Euripides' *Phoenissae* 1172-86, which is closer to the treatment given by Statius, Capaneus ascends the battlements by means of a long-necked ladder and declares: μηδ' ἂν τὸ σεμνὸν πῦρ νιν εἰργαθεῖν Διὸς | τὸ μὴ οὐ κατ' ἄκρων περγάμων ἑλεῖν πόλιν, "neither the fires of Zeus will keep him from sacking the city from the topmost towers" (*Phoen*. 1175-6). In response to this proud boast, Zeus lets fly a bolt of lightning that blasts his hair to Olympus, his blood to the ground, and causes his limbs to whirl like the wheel of Ixion. The hero is reduced to cinders and falls to the ground a scorched corpse. Surely Euripides, if not Aeschylus as well, served as models for Statius, though the scene is considerably elaborated in the *Thebaid*.[36]

After the Argive captains slay the serpent that killed Opheltes, Jupiter prepares to strike down Capaneus, but holds back. Jupiter calls for his thunderbolts to strike down Capaneus for his railing impiety but he checks his wrath and Capaneus is "gravioraque tela mereri | servatus," "spared to deserve a heavier shot" (5.585–6). Jupiter thus preserves Capaneus for a greater scene, one that we eagerly anticipate because it promises to be bigger than what could have happened at this point.[37] Statius then ominously prefigures Capaneus' eventual death by a lightning blast when "moti tamen aura cucurrit | fulminis et summas libauit uertice cristas," "nevertheless, the wind of that readied bolt lapped the crested plumes on his head" (5.586–7). Such a moment conditions the reader to expect that Capaneus will be killed for his impiety against and contempt toward Jupiter.

When Adrastus calls to begin the boxing match he makes the comparison: "haec bellis et ferro proxima uirtus," "here valor is closest to battles and steel" (6.730). The boxing match demonstrates Capaneus' reliance on brute strength and the lengths that he will go for victory. Capaneus is savage, eager to kill Alcidamas and exceed the measure needed to secure a victory. Indeed,[38] he enters the contest calling for an Aonian to kill. While this might initially appear an arrogant exaggeration, his actions during the contest and the near bludgeoning to death of his opponent, demonstrate his eagerness to carry forward his intentions. His display demonstrates that victory in itself is not sufficient. He is haughty and much of what we experience in the games, beyond the prefiguration of their heroic actions, presents a glimpse of their character.[39]

The attitudes and capacities of the boxers Alcidamas and Capaneus indicate an instability that we find elsewhere in the match: Alcidamas is the more skilled and fights with his head, Capaneus is stronger but reckless.

> doctior hic differt animum metuensque futuri
> cunctatus uires dispensat: at ille nocendi
> prodigus incautusque sui ruit omnis et ambas
> consumit sine lege manus atque inrita frendit
> insurgens seque ipse premit.
>
> *Theb.* 6.765–9

This one, the more skilled, delays his instincts, lingers, guarding his strength and worries over what may come. The other, excessive in harm and without instinct for self-preservation, rushes out, both hands flying unrestrained, gnashing his teeth for no reason, pressing upon himself.

Statius describes Alcidamas as "doctior" (6.765) and "prouidus" (6.769), but in the end, and in accord with the spirit of the Theban conflict, brute savagery and unchecked rage win. This boxing event informs readers of Capaneus' character as he moves toward sheer uncontrolled rage against the gods. Adrastus acknowledges that Capaneus is out of his mind and must hurriedly be appeased. He declares:

> "ite, oro, socii, furit, ite, opponite dextras,
> festinate, furit, palmamque et praemia ferte!
> non prius, effracto quam misceat ossa cerebro,
> absistet, uideo; moriturum auferte Lacona."
>
> *Theb.* 6.809–12

"Go, please, friends, he's crazed! Go, oppose your right arms, quickly, he's crazed! Bring forth the palm and the prizes. He will not stop until he has brought bone together with shattered brain, I see this in him! Take the Laconian away or he surely dies!"

But even that is hardly enough to appease Capaneus, which further foreshadows the ferocity that leads to his death.[40] Tydeus and Hippomedon plead with Capaneus to calm down: "uincis, abi; pulchrum uitam donare minori. | noster et hic bellique comes," "you win, leave it. It is a fine thing to spare the loser's life" (6.816–17). Certainly, "pulchrum uitam donare minori" recalls Anchises' injunction that Aeneas should "parcere subiectis et debellare superbos," "spare the suppliant and war down the proud" (*Aen.* 6.853). The Laconians jeer at his further threats and Capaneus' violent strength is restrained (but not entirely controlled) by Adrastus and his comrades. Their intervention, however, just as we see with Parthenopaeus in the foot-race, cannot save him when he attempts his assault on Heaven.

Capaneus becomes a spectacle of downfall as he is blasted by Zeus in Statius' *Thebaid*. His affronts against the gods have been building for some time, so Statius informs: "diu tuto superum contemptor" (3.602). This suggests that divine grudges targeted against Capaneus are not recent. His impiety against the gods is established early in the poem, and Statius also begins early to anticipate his death by lightning. He uses Capaneus to explore godlessness because he is a fitting counterpoint to Amphiaraus whose piety has strong links with Aeschylus' *Septem*.[41] What is curious about Capaneus' death is that Jupiter does not actually blast him for impiety. The hero who exults in an unequal match (7.675) actually pleases the god. When Capaneus storms heaven, Jupiter actually laughs.[42] Based on the failure of Phlegra, he asks, without anticipation of a negative or positive response, if Capaneus must also be destroyed, knowing already that his hopes of storming heaven are in vain. The minor gods, however, pressure Zeus and express their fears and doubts: "mirantur taciti et dubio pro fulmine pallent," "silently, they wonder and pale before the wavering bolt" (10.920). Capaneus does not, however, ascend much higher than the *arces*, despite the noise and clamor he brings against Olympus. Jupiter destroys Capaneus but in a demonstration of might and power intended to restore (or preserve) confidence in his abilities for those who doubt him, not necessarily because Capaneus offends him.

Adrastus

At *Thebaid* 11.424–446 Adrastus hears that Polynices and Eteocles rush to duel one another. He hurries to set himself physically between them, a reminiscence of the scene Jocasta could not attain. Adrastus pleads with them and goes so far as to offer even his own kingdom if they will relent, though to no avail. He realizes the situation is lost and departs:

> ut periisse preces geminoque ad proelia fusos
> puluere cornipedes explorarique furentum
> in digitis ammenta uidet, fugit omnia linquens,
> castra, uiros, generum, Thebas, ac fata monentem
> conuersumque iugo propellit Ariona
>
> *Theb.* 11.439–43

After he realizes prayers are wasted and sees the horses in two dusty lines hurrying and the raging men pawing their javelin straps, he flees, leaving his camp, his men, his son-in-law, and Thebes, spurring Arion on, turning the yoke and warning fate.

This is the last we see of Adrastus: defeated and departing. As Vessey notes: "Statius says nothing more of him, for there is nothing more to tell. The gentlest of kings, through the harshness of destiny, has been utterly defeated."[43] Adrastus as the lone survivor of the seven who marched against Thebes was foreshadowed in the conclusion to the games, where Adrastus participates in a one-man contest of archery. The scene is essentially a distillation of the Virgilian event.[44] The overall purpose is to foreground the ominous sign that only one of the leaders will return from the battle against Thebes.[45] As Vessey notes, the archery event "makes it clear that the games are prefigurative."[46] The crowd encourages Adrastus to make some demonstration in order to place an honor of victory on each of the leaders and a final honor for the tomb of Opheltes. This supplies the final event in the games sequence. The king intends to shoot an arrow across the length of the circus and hit a designated ash-tree. The arrow travels the length of the field and strikes the tree, but— "horrendum visu"—ricochets back across the same field and lands near the opening of the quiver from which it was drawn. This omen is a clear indication that Adrastus, and only Adrastus, will return from Thebes. The cadre naturally develops explanations for such a fantastical occurrence, but of course, fails to grasp the truth.

Nevertheless, certain signs that indicate the strong likelihood of failure were evident from the earliest. To be sure, Adrastus carries the tremendous burden as leader to his people and the armies. His command over the heroes, however, is tenuous and uncertain. His age and ability still command respect, which Statius develops through a simile that compares him to an old bull:

> ipse annis sceptrisque subit uenerabilis aeque:
> ut possessa diu taurus meat arduus inter
> pascua iam laxa ceruice et inanibus armis,
> dux tamen: haud illum bello attemptare iuuencis
> sunt animi; nam trunca uident de uulnere multo
> cornua et ingentes plagarum in pectore nodos.
>
> *Theb.* 4.68–73

> He unites them himself, equally venerable in years and authority, like a bull who strides proud among his own pastures; but his neck sags and his limbs lax. Still, he is the leader; the steers don't have the grit to try him in contest, since they see his horns busted from many blows and the giant scars of his wounded chest.

There is something discomforting in the suggestion "dux tamen," Adrastus leads, but he is not the ideal leader, or the strongest leader, and throughout the *Thebaid* there are a number of scenes that reveal how weak his control appears to be. Nevertheless, the other bulls respect him and do not have the spirit to try him in combat. Adrastus has even the respect of Eteocles, who considers him formidable (10.31). Burgess' description of Adrastus is particularly apt: he is a "well-meaning" and "pacific leader."[47] His initial position in the catalog of *Thebaid* 4 suggests Adrastus holds a prime position among the leaders and their armies; however, the ultimate authority over the army remains unclear throughout the *Thebaid*. Indeed, confusion characterizes the development of Adrastus' army from its formation. Initially the leaders cannot speak with each other clearly after Adrastus breaks up the quarrel between Polynices and Tydeus: "haec passim turbatis uocis amarae | confudere sonis" (1.450–1). No doubt, these two verses portend a less than promising undertaking to Roman readers because in anger none are capable of effectively communicating with each other and anger is the motivating spirit behind the war against Thebes. An ethnically diverse contingent in the *Thebaid* would no doubt appear doomed to its readers. Disorder also characterizes the internal workings of foreign armies. Although the Boeotians, for instance, rally to support a people, they do not support the king: "tamen et Boeotis urbibus ultrix | adspirat ferri rabies, nec regis iniqui | subsidio quantum socia pro gente mouentur," "Nevertheless, the lust for vengeance and battle blows also over the cities of Boeotia; moved not as much to help an unjust king as to aid an allied people" (4.360–3). The ethnic diversity of the armies under Adrastus becomes a way in which Statius reveals military disorder and anticipates their eventual failure and routing at Thebes.[48]

In Statius' epic, prominent military figures lack the needed qualities of pietas and gravitas to lead armies or govern communities. Adrastus embraces Polynices as his son-in-law. He sees this as the fulfillment of the prophecy, and he cannot be greatly faulted for failing to realize the outcome of his support; after all, it was hidden from him. Nevertheless, Statius presents Adrastus as a flawed leader, unable to maintain and stabilize the army. Before Adrastus breaks up the brawl between Polynices and Tydeus he is described as: "magnis cui sobria curis | pendebat somno iam deteriore senectus," "an old man strained by poor sleep and sober with great concerns" (1.433–4). Indeed, Adrastus often appears worried and uncertain.[49] As his concerns grow for the likelihood of war, Adrastus advises that they leave some things to the gods and others in his care: "ista quidem superis curaeque medenda | linquite, quaeso, meae" (3.388–9).[50] His counsel, however, goes unheeded. This contrasts strongly with the view of authority put forward by Tacitus' Antonius, where a difference in attitude is to be maintained between soldiers and leaders: "sed divisa inter exercitum ducesque munia: militibus cupidinem pugnandi convenire, duces providendo, consultando, cunctatione saepius quam temeritate prodesse," "the officers or soldiers and leaders are divided: for soldiers there is the desire for fighting, leaders contribute with foresight, planning, and more often by delay than rashness" (*Hist.* 3.20).

The most decisive scene of disorder within Adrastus' army is the scene at the river Langia. After Bacchus catches sight of the Argive expedition, he causes a drought to retard their progress and provide the Thebans with more time to prepare for war. Only Langia retains her waters, but in shaded secrecy (4.717). The heat and drought weaken Adrastus' army to the point that they cannot continue (4.723–38) until they come across Hypsipyle and she leads them to the water (4.739–803). Hypsipyle's role in aiding the Argives is significantly amplified from Euripides' *Hypsipyle*. When Adrastus approaches her in the drama, he requests merely water to perform a sacrifice. In Statius' *Thebaid*, the search for water takes on far greater urgency. As the army nears the river, the marching order dissipates, some walk behind and others walk ahead of Hypsipyle as she guides them. This is prelude to the breakdown in hierarchy that is to come. Once the army sights water through the woods their ranks fail completely:

> incubuere uadis passim discrimine nullo
> turba simul primique, nequit secernere mixtos
> aequa sitis, frenata suis in curribus intrant
> armenta, et pleni dominis armisque feruntur
> quadripedes; hos turbo rapax, hos lubrica fallunt
> saxa, nec implicitos fluuio reuerentia reges
> proterere aut mersisse uado clamantis amici
> ora. fremunt undae, longusque a fontibus amnis
> diripitur; modo lene uirens et gurgite puro
> perspicuus, nunc sordet aquis egestus ab imis
> alueus; inde tori riparum et proruta turbant
> gramina; iam crassus caenoque et puluere torrens,
> quamquam expleta sitis, bibitur tamen. agmina bello
> decertare putes iustumque in gurgite Martem
> perfurere aut captam tolli uictoribus urbem.
>
> Theb. 4.816–30

Everywhere soldiers and officers dive without distinction into the river, a shared thirst does not distinguish the blended melee. Armed horses enter with their chariots, those full of riders and arms are carried along. Some are caught by the winding currents, others are deceived by slippery rocks. None hesitate to trample kings overcome by the torrent or drown the voice of a shouting companion. Waves sound and the long river is sundered. Initially, it was a placid green, glassy in its flow, but now its bed is polluted, its depths churned, the banks and uprooted grasses fall in. Now it flows thickened with mud and mire. Nevertheless, they drink, even though their thirst is quenched. You would have thought armies fought a raging battle in the flood or a conquered town were being despoiled by its conquerors.

There is no discrimination between prince and common soldier when the ranks are broken. Their thirst makes all equal to the degree that they will trample one another. The river even becomes a metaphor for the disorder as it becomes muddied and befouled (4.809–21).[51] Statius uses their thirst to highlight how quickly and easily military distinctions can be blurred and how little stability and control the leaders of the army, especially Adrastus, can effect in the men.[52] In fact, he notes that they must be restored to martial order. After the troops are refreshed, they are described: "dispositi in turmas rursus legemque seueri | ordinis ut cuique ante locus ductorque, monentur | instaurare uias," "Once more marshaled into their lines and under the hard rule of ranks, each takes his former place under his captain, and they are ordered to march on" (5.7–9). They must be organized according to the stern law of order. Military leadership here is an exercise in might and force, not in pietas, duty, or obligation. And this reorganization of order, which dimly recalls the upset of *Iliad* 2, proves to be short lived.[53] Statius condemns the Argives' military abilities to endure such disorder on the occasion of their first hardship; is it any wonder they will ultimately fail in battle?[54] We are encouraged to anticipate as much.

The scene of riot at Langia certainly invites comparison with a similar occurrence of thirsting armies in Lucan. During the march through the Syrtes, Cato's men suffer from dire thirst. At one point, a small and foul rivulet of water is found by a soldier who breaks from the ranks and scoops muddied water into his helmet. He offers it to Cato, who replies with a stern rebuke:

"Mene" inquit "degener unum
miles in hac turba uacuum uirtute putasti?
usque adeo mollis primisque caloribus inpar
sum uisus? quanto poena tu dignior ista es,
qui populo sitiente bibas!"

BC 9.505–9

"Do I really seem," Cato began, "a soldier in this outfit so weak and lacking in strength? Do I appear so feeble that I can't take a little sun? I'm almost inclined to make you drink this water as punishment, while the others go thirsty."

This reaction demonstrates Cato's ability to lead his soldiers and his willingness to suffer equally with them. The anonymous soldier's actions demonstrate his respect for the general. Cato, however, takes his offered respect as an insult to his military prowess. His response to the soldier further maintains the order and control established over his troops. As Lucan writes: "sic concitus ira | excussit galeam, suffecitque omnibus unda," "His anger thus roused, he dashed the helmet to the ground and there was enough water for all" (9.510).[55] This is very different from the discovery of water by Statius' Argives. Cato is a figure that casts Adrastus, and the other Argive leaders, in conspicuous negative relief. Cato is a leader they cannot (or do not) aspire to emulate. In this episode, Statius inverts rather than imitates Lucan's paragon of leadership in Cato. Where in Lucan we find a leader who commands order despite hardship, in Statius we find the absence of such a figure and their "aequa sitis" allows gross disorder and internal conflict. Indeed, such an event creates anticipation for and increases the likelihood of the army's inability to conduct a campaign against Thebes. Such an initial instability does not bode well or instill confidence in the army, or more especially its leaders, particularly Polynices who, among the leaders of the army, seeks to be King of Thebes. In an opportunity to stand out as a soldier among soldiers, it is a damning comment against the leaders, but mainly Polynices, that none do stand forth, no individual is named. Indeed, Statius preserves anonymity and lack of distinction when even after their thirsts have been slaked one of the princes ("aliquis regnum," 4.831) offers a paean to the waters.

While the disorder at Langia offers the most patent scene of lost authority, the theme persists throughout the *Thebaid* and builds to Adrastus' final failure to dissuade Polynices from the duel with his brother. When Lycurgus threatens Hypsipyle, the Argive soldiers riot over the possibility that she has been executed. Adrastus must stop the troops by showing them that she is unharmed; he cannot simply command them to desist (5.685ff.). When Polynices insists on driving the horse Arion, Adrastus offers "multa monens," "much advice" (6.317), but does not have the gravitas to make his son-in-law listen.[56] When Idas cheats in the footrace, pulling Parthenopaeus by the hair, the soldiers draw their weapons: "Arcades arma fremunt, armis defendere regem," "The Arcadians roar 'To arms,' with arms they hasten to defend their king" (6.618). Adrastus wavers on a course of action, "furit undique clamor | dissonus, ambiguumque senis cunctatur Adrasti | consilium," "on all sides discordant clamor rages, and the wavering counsel of old Adrastus is delayed" (6.625-7). He then declares that they rerun the race, instead of selecting a victor.[57] This decision allows him to sidestep a judgment between the two contestants that could provoke a riot. Moreover, it reveals his unfortunate need to compromise with the armies instead of command them.[58]

Within the military structure of the Argive forces under Adrastus, Statius also builds in an ongoing threat of inner dispute that suggests eventual failure. This kind of tenuous authority is revealed when Adrastus and the chiefs appoint Thiodamas to replace Amphiaraus. Thiodamas takes this position humbly, but with the concerns typical of uncertain power:

incerta formidine gaudia librat
an fidi proceres, ne pugnet uulgus habenis,
cui latus Euphratae, cui Caspia limina mandet;
sumere tunc arcus ipsumque onerare ueretur
patris equum uisusque sibi nec sceptra capaci
sustentare manu nec adhuc implere tiaran.

Theb. 8.288-93

Joy is balanced by uncertain dread: are his nobles loyal, will the people not fight the reins, to whom shall he entrust broad Euphrates' or the Caspian threshold? Then he dreads to take the bow and mount his father's horse, his hand seems to him too small to wield the scepter and his head to fill the diadem.

Thus, a foreboding possibility of a lack of control is again presented. The men of Elis, Lacedaemon, and Pylos will follow Thiodamas, though Statius comments: "necdum accessere regenti," "not yet have they taken him as leader" (8.366).

Finally, and most notably, when Adrastus attempts to prevent Polynices' duel with Eteocles (11.424ff.), he fails. His support of Polynices reveals some slipperiness and ambiguity. As McGuire notes, when Adrastus forbids the duel between Agreus and Polynices, he "tells the young men to preserve their desire for an opponent's blood for a later date, when there will be ample opportunity for slaughter; and he adroitly dodges the real issue here, which is that Polynices and Agreus are ready to shed allied blood."[59] All of these scenes culminate in his inability to command or persuade Polynices from his fratricidal duel. Thus, we see that Adrastus, although a venerable and respected leader contributes little to a stable and ordered military campaign.[60] Thus, Adrastus' commands and cautions cannot persuade others or change the course of events. In the end, he is ineffective, and it is through continual descriptions of his tenuous command over the army that readers anticipate his failure and that of the expedition against Thebes.

With Adrastus, Statius presents an ongoing preoccupation with the disordered marshaling of troops and the ineptitude of planning in conflict.[61] To be sure, Adrastus reluctantly agrees to war (4.38–40), and his reluctance inclines us to be sympathetic. Nevertheless, Statius repeatedly points out the tenuousness of his command and control over the armies. Adrastus does not lose his life in the conflict, but his decision to march against Thebes does not lead to a greater glory for his people. The war is an unequivocal failure. His hesitancy and vacillation reveal a lack of conviction, and weak command, that are contributing factors in the outcome of the expedition. Adrastus as a leader can be compared to Theseus only in so far as they are both leaders. The difference in the authority they have over their respective armies, however, is considerable. As Tacitus writes of Vitellius: "non iam imperator sed tantum belli causa erat" (*Hist*. 3.70). Or as Williams similarly remarks in Shakespeare's *King Henry* V 4.1: "Now, if these men do not die well, it | will be a black matter for the king that led them to | it." Leaders are always at fault. The absence of sound leadership in the preparation and waging of war is keenly felt throughout the *Thebaid*.

Menoeceus

While not one of the seven captains, Menoeceus, and his suicide, does warrant a brief discussion. At *Thebaid* 10.589, a desperate and fearful mob throng around the prophet Tiresias as suppliants and want to know if there is a way to save the city. The seer listens to Manto as she describes the flames. He interprets:

> audite, o sontes, extrema litamina diuum,
> Labdacidae: uenit alma salus, sed limite duro.
> Martius inferias et saeua efflagitat anguis
> sacra: cadat generis quicumque nouissimus extat
> uiperei, datur hoc tantum uictoria pacto.
> felix qui tanta lucem mercede relinquet.
>
> *Theb.* 10.610–15

Hear, guilty Labdacids, the god's last sacrifice. Nourishing salvation comes, but by a hard way. The serpent of Mars requires death and a harsh rite. Whoever is youngest of the serpentine race, he must fall. Only in this way is victory assured. Happy is he who departs this world for that exchange.

Creon is near the altar when Tiresias delivers the prophecy and identifies Menoeceus within the explanation (10.616–23).[62] A shared and common fate joins Creon to the people of Thebes. Before Tiresias reveals the prophecy, Statius indicates that Creon is like all the other Thebans looking to the seer for some hope of salvation. Creon's realization of the truth distances him emotionally and privately from his fellow citizens. Thebes finds salvation but Creon finds greater suffering. Statius images the emotional shock in moving martial terms, Creon becomes another victim in battle:

> ... grandem subiti cum fulminis ictum,
> non secus ac torta traiectus cuspide pectus,
> accipit exanimis sentitque Menoecea posci.
> monstrat enim suadetque timor; stupet anxius alto
> corda metu glaciante pater
>
> *Theb.* 10.618–22

... he then feels a heavy blow from a sudden thunderbolt, as though a flying javelin had transfixed his breast, and barely able to breathe, he knows Menoeceus is the one demanded, so fear shows and urges. The anxious father is stunned, his heart turned to ice with deep fear.

Against the backdrop of war, Statius foregrounds Creon as another fatality, another wounded troop. Creon shifts from being one among many who, while alive, hopes for the safety of the city, to one among the dead. The emotional limbo that he occupies is highlighted by the contradiction provided by "exanimis sentitque." Then, remarkably, Creon shifts to a position that is unexpected. He takes the posture of a suppliant: "nunc humilis genua amplectens, nunc ora canentis, | nequiquam reticere rogat," "now embracing his knees, now his mouth as he prophecies" (*Theb.* 625–6). This is well outside the character of Creon who more often appears headstrong and ill-tempered. The scene is similar to that of Euripides (*Phoen.* 923ff.). To take the knees of Tiresias delivers the full impact of his powerlessness in this situation. This further individualizes Creon and highlights his personal vulnerability as a father. It is not difficult to feel some sympathy toward him.

Menoeceus offers himself as a sacrifice to save Thebes. As Vessey notes, there are several significant parallels between the Statian and Euripidean treatments.[63] Approaches to the scene are varied[64] and, in some instances, short-sighted. Vessey, for instance, declares that Menoeceus "represents the summit of 'pietas' and 'virtus' and his death is to be forcibly contrasted with the degraded 'furor' that inflames the sons of Oedipus in Book 11."[65] But is it reasonable to suggest that his death was unselfish, insisting that his "leti amorem" is selfless and pure?[66] Does Menoeceus truly demonstrate a representative Virgilian "pietas?" It seems more reasonable to consider that both father and son present fractured, inverted, and fundamentally irreconcilable aspects of "pietas." The acme of "pietas" and "uirtus" is not Menoeceus, whose "pietas" is a one-sided fulfillment of personal ambition, motivated by personal glory over and above selflessness. The *Thebaid* uses the Menoeceus scene to strain competing notions of public and private "pietas:" where Menoeceus espouses the former, his father Creon argues the latter. Statius seems to be exploring the difficult tensions between obligations to the state and obligations to family in a time of crisis.

Disguised as Manto, Virtus finds Menoeceus among the fray and encourages him, claiming that his true glory lies in sacrificing himself to Ares. On his way to the wall, he is further encouraged by the people, hailed as "auctorem pacis seruatoremque deumque" (10.684) and filled with "ignibus honestis" (10.685). He hopes not to encounter his "miseros parentes" (10.687): an ambiguous phrase that could suggest contempt and a lack of familial piety but more likely looks ahead to the future, when they will be "unhappy" after he commits his self-sacrifice. Nevertheless, he meets Creon who wishes to know why he has withdrawn from the battle. Menoeceus lies and tells his father that Haemon is wounded.[67]

Euripides' *Phoenissae* 962–90 offers a simple scene between the two in which Creon urges his son, who was present during Tiresias' revelation of the prophecy, to flee before the city discovers that only he can save them. Menoeceus plays along asking: ποῖ δῆτα φεύγω; τίνα πόλιν; τίνα ξένων; "To where would I flee? To what city? To what ally?" (977). The boy insists on seeing Jocasta before going. Creon exits and Menoeceus declares his intentions to sacrifice himself (*Phoen.* 997–8). Creon's speech to Menoeceus in Statius' *Thebaid*, however, is particularly interesting and it differs from that of Euripides most strongly in the tug-of-war between father and son over what defines "pietas."[68] Rather than command Menoeceus, Creon provides the young man with reasonable advice and a very practical plea. The father suspects, by the look of his son, that he has heard Tiresias' words and insists the young man not take the prophecy at face value. He suggests that Eteocles might have influenced the prophecy in order to impede a possible threat to the throne. Now, because Creon demonstrated the reaction of a suppliant beseeching Tiresias to be silent, this seems a strong suggestion that he believes the prophecy. What he tells Menoeceus is either from some reconsideration or a lie. In any case, Creon casts some doubt on the validity of Tiresias' prophecy to his son, which fails. This tells us something about Menoeceus: he believes the prophecy. Creon also attempts to give his son advice; generally, the same advice that fathers often give children that goes unheeded (10.703–13).

Creon sets "pietas" within the private sphere when he claims: "haec pietas, hic uerus honos," "this is piety, this is honor!" (10.711). Creon[69] acts selfishly; however, this is his son. He takes sound advice but masks his own private aim for the preservation of Menoeceus. The advice would not, in another situation, be impractical but the situation at Thebes is dire. Menoeceus' longevity is central to Creon's argument; becoming a parent emphasizes familial continuity and most crucially emphasizes obligations to the household and the family, rather than the state. Statius' Creon, however, appears unconcerned that the people may demand Menoeceus as a sacrifice once the prophecy becomes more widely known. Instead, he simply encourages his son to return to the fighting. Further, Menoeceus' disregard of his father keeps with a theme routinely explored throughout the epic: disregard for practical advice.[70]

Another wrenching aspect of this scene is the rift that grows between a father and his son. To gain what they want, both are dishonest with one another. Where Creon places the private before the public in his attempts to change Menoeceus' mind, the son's actions demonstrate that he places the public (and his glory) before the private. The embrace of the two at 10.78ff. is a powerful moment in the scene. The value of the public over the private, however, is greatly enhanced by the glory that comes from his self-sacrifice and not, it should be added, a glory that Menoeceus thinks insignificant. As Statius indicates, he is filled with "ignibus honestis" and obviously motivated by the people as they encourage him.

After the young man has stabbed himself, Statius offers a surreal and touching description of the personifications of Pietas and Virtus catching his body as it falls from the battlements, bearing the corpse gently to the ground.[71] Because of the glory gained in this moment, it is too easy to permit Menoeceus' engagement with his father to recede and become something of a trivial point; however, it is important not to overlook that Menoeceus was dishonest with his father and served his own purpose. His act of public "gloria" grew from a moment which, because of the shade in meaning, can be regarded as "impietas;" as un-filial conduct. Whether Menoeceus bases his decision on a love of glory, or an honest compassion for his people, or both, is unclear. In the end, Menoeceus is described by Statius as "Pius Menoeceus" (10.756). What Statius presents in this scene is a competition, in which a young life is at stake, between two competing notions of piety. And these two notions become a suspenseful contest for the young man's life. Creon's response and concern are critical to arousing anticipation for Menoeceus' death. This marks a much richer and more emotionally demanding development from the presentation of Euripides.

7

hic imperat, ille minatur

The present chapter explores the characters of Polynices and Eteocles that anticipate their ruin and how Statius leads readers to conclude that, in addition to the *nefas* of a fraternal conflict, neither brother is a fit ruler. The reader anticipates the deaths of Eteocles and Polynices, but part of that anticipation is being assured that Thebes is the better for this loss. The analysis relies largely on the literary presentation of psychological interiority to elicit anticipation and suspense. Throughout the discussion which follows it can be helpful to bear in mind the Aristotelian notion of seriousness, or *spoudaios*. For Aristotle, *spoudaios* is a mark of dramatic tragedy, a notion to be sure, applicable to an epic narrative. Certainly the conflict between Polynices and Eteocles has as its terminus a woefully tragic outcome. According to Held there are teleological implications to be considered in this as well. The seriousness of a tragic narrative, he argues, "should be to some extent well directed at the end proper to man's nature, happiness."[1] The central action of the *Thebaid* is the respective bid of each brother to rule Thebes.[2] By this line of thinking, the tragedy that results from the conflict between Oedipus' sons is the pursuit of their individual happiness: Eteocles believes that happiness for himself and the polity is best maintained through his continued presence on the throne at Thebes as he maintains at *Theb.* 2.442-48; however, Polynices believes that his happiness can be achieved only through taking the throne as they had agreed.[3] These positions are irreconcilable and end in mutual destruction. Concern for the Theban people and their happiness emerges throughout the contest for power between the brothers. The ruler of Thebes directly impacts the stability of the people over whom he rules. Held's teleological view of seriousness motivated by happiness is particularly serviceable as we consider the relationship between Eteocles, Polynices, and the people of Thebes. After all, for as tragic (in the contemporary sense) as these events are, the mutual annihilation of the brothers benefits Thebes.

The Anonymous Critic

Statius defines the present state of Thebes under the compact of shared rule by introducing an anonymous critic. An embodiment of Theban grumbling, the *vox populi* expresses the suppressed discontent between the people and their alternating rulers, exaggerating slightly the circumstances at Thebes by way of a long-standing suffering that began in the distant past and continues up to the present time:

> "hancne Ogygiis," ait, "aspera rebus
> fata tulere uicem, totiens mutare timendos
> alternoque iugo dubitantia subdere colla?
> partiti uersant populorum fata manuque
> fortunam fecere leuem. semperne uicissim
> exulibus seruire dabor?"
>
> *Theb.* 1.173-96

"Has hard Fate given this share to Thebes" he begins, "to so frequently exchange them that we are afraid and must low our doubting necks to alternating yokes? Dividing us between each other they direct the lives of peoples and have made, by force, Fortune uncertain. Will I always be traded as a slave to exiles taking turns?"

The critic demonstrates a concern for the future based on past occurrence. The past, indeed, becomes thematic. His reference to the people of Thebes as "timendos" expresses an ongoing condition of fear, a state that will last into the future provided conditions do not change. Similarly, "dubitantia" reveals an expectation for future conditions. The two actions, "mutare" and "subdere" are connected to "totiens" which has an ongoing force. In truth this could not refer to a past action since, though the decision was made in the past, the critic can only anticipate this first change. What the critic anticipates is a protracted series of alternate rules and notably a deep distrust of exiles, which we must consider more fully with Polynices below.

After expressing concern over the present condition that is likely to persist into the future, the critic looks backward to the time of Cadmus (1.180-5) and the "uetus omen" that binds Thebes' present to its past. The critic speculates on a relationship between the sowing of the dragon seeds and the current state of strife at Thebes. The present is positioned in such a way as to seem that it has passed, that there is an ongoing exchange, which in fact Eteocles and Polynices have only now come to the end of their first year of alternating reign. The critic grumbles of Eteocles' power:

> cernis ut erectum torua sub fronte minetur
> saeuior adsurgens dempto consorte potestas.
> quas gerit ore minas, quanto premit omnia fastu!
> hicne umquam priuatus erit?
>
> *Theb.* 1.186–9

See how power cruelly swells when there is no one with whom to share it? What threats his expression reveals, and how his arrogance outdoes all! Will he ever become a private citizen?

Here "minetur" characterizes Eteocles just as "minatur" at 1.196 also typifies Polynices. On taking the throne, Eteocles grew savage, which suggests that a disposition toward cruelty was already within him before he ruled; moreover, it is evident to the critic that Eteocles has little intention of becoming a private citizen. Thus, Statius uses the voice of the people to begin his characterization of Eteocles as a cruel tyrant, whose interests in ruling are for his own sake and not for the good of Thebes. Notably, the critic also condemns the Theban people for the ease with which they are persuaded from one ruler to another. This description is consistent with the ease with which they will finally give themselves over to Theseus' army (*Theb.* 12.782–7). The role of the critic is to reveal the lack of political cohesion at Thebes. In his first year of rule Eteocles has failed to win over his people.[4]

The critic suggests that Eteocles governs poorly. Statius repeatedly bears this out when he relates that Eteocles has governed cruelly and remained beyond the agreed year (2.386). Statius further condemns Eteocles in later books. As Tydeus leaves Thebes the mothers accuse both the ambassador and Eteocles of sowing war and conflict (2.480–1). Statius condemns the king's ambush plot against Tydeus (2.488–91). Indeed, when Eteocles orders the ambush party against Tydeus, Statius comments that it is to be done with a silent sword ("tactioque inuadere ferro," 2.487). This may be merely synecdoche for the ambush party, but it seems coextensive with Eteocles' character. After Maeon's suicide the savage anger of the "ducis infandi" prevents the corpse from receiving cremation or burial (3.96–98). And when the relatives of the deceased ambush party come to find and collect the remains of their loved ones (3.114–217), the scene culminates in Aletes' speech, a harangue that offers consolation to the grieving parties through criticism of Eteocles (3.206–12). Thus, concern for Eteocles' use of power is very actual, very real. Having already endured a year of his reign, the critics' judgment is severe.[5] In the conclusion to his lament he states: "hic imperat, ille minatur," "this one rules while that one threatens to" (1.196). This Theban thus fears both

Eteocles and Polynices, the former for what he is and the latter for what he could be once in power. The concern over Polynices is for his potential; if he would be as heavy handed as his brother remains a matter of speculation, although the critic supposes he was milder, and suggests of the exiled brother: "tamen ille precanti | mitis et adfatu bonus et patientior aequi," "Nevertheless, the other treated the suppliant gently, he was good of speech, and more tolerant of justice" (1.189–90). The critic sets the brothers on a level plane, the difference is that one is a very real problem and the other is a potential problem.[6] A year of possessing the "sceptrum exitiale" and luxury has allowed Eteocles to be cruel and sluggish, while Polynices, as discussed below, is hardened, almost feral, in exile.

As the critic makes clear, the happiness of the Theban people is linked to their political situation. Thebes needs stability and order, its happiness depends on this, yet Statius underscores the seriousness of the Theban situation through the lack of a stabilizing figure. The contrastive narrative position is ordered against the anticipation of their ruin. If the Thebans, despite their fickleness, are to be happy, Eteocles should not continue to rule, but tragically the incumbent brother should not achieve the throne either. The reader is forced into a frustrating position of cheering for neither. Eteocles is given to fits of sloth, cruelty, and over-confidence. Polynices, on the other hand, has sympathetic qualities. Yet, the qualities that make him endearing are undermined by the reality that these would also make him a terrible ruler. Through these characterizations Statius reveals that Polynices' bid for Thebes must fail. His death, though unfortunate, is for the good of Thebes. The best possible situation, in fact, is the death of both brothers. Statius does not favor one brother over the other; they are both unbalanced, which makes both deficient.[7] Statius calls into question the power and effectiveness of the brothers to rule the kingdom that, in the end, neither will not should posses. If good for Thebes is to be achieved, neither brother can hold power.

The End of Polynices

The people of Thebes slightly favor Polynices. As Statius contrasts: "tacitumque a principe uulgus | dissidet, et, qui mos populis, uenturus amatur," "the people are silent, opposed to the prince, and, the one who would be prince, as is common among people, is adored" (1.169–70). Their praise, however, is based on his potential, something about which the critic appears to be suspicious nevertheless.[8] The critic's remarks are keyed to how this policy will impact the people. Statius offers four thematic demonstrations that suggest that Polynices would not likely be an effective king for Thebes. First, Statius repeatedly indicates that it would be better had Polynices never been born. Second, he is an exile, which makes him less civilized. Third, he expresses a disinterest in good council. And finally, he is not entirely committed to the course of action he has selected.

Statius frequently returns to the tragic trope that it would have been preferable had Polynices never been born, an adage that we can trace back to Theognis, but certainly indicative of a much older world-view. This perspective, as Steiner points out, "entails the view that human life *per se*, both ontologically and existentially, is an affliction. That non-existence or early extinction are urgent desiderata."[9] The fundamental tenet of this world-view is that life is not worth living and it conveniently aligns Polynices with his tragic father.[10] The sentiment first occurs when Polynices survives the throw from his chariot during the race, which allows Amphiaraus his easy victory:

> quis mortis, Thebane, locus, nisi dura negasset
> Tisiphone, quantum poteras dimittere bellum!
> te Thebe fraterque palam, te plangeret Argos,
> te Nemea, tibi Lerna comas Larisaque supplex
> poneret, Archemori maior colerere sepulcro.
>
> Theb. 6.513–7

What a point at which to die, Theban, had hard Tisiphone not denied it! How much war you would have been able to deter! Thebes, even your brother, Argos and Nemea would have wept for you openly. Lerna and Larisa would dutifully set their hair before you. Your grave would be more treasured than Archemorus.'

Polynices himself even expresses regret that he was not slain by Tydeus when they quarreled over the doorstep: "non me ense tuo tunc, maxime Tydeu, | (et poteras) nostri mactatum in limine Adrasti," "Why was I not slaughtered by your sword, Great Tydeus, you could have done it, on the threshold of our father Adrastus" (9.63–4). The sentiment is once more asserted by Phorbas in his lament to Antigone (7.365). Thus, Statius repeatedly reminds the reader that the events that unfold throughout the *Thebaid* could have been avoided had Polynices died before he could come against his brother.

Additionally, Polynices' exile frustrates his situation. This is evident when Polynices is first introduced. What he feels he is due as the alternate ruler of Thebes stretches away from him ("dilatus…honos," 1.165). He wanders in exile ("uagus exile…pererrat," 1.312–13) during a long year ("longum…annum," 1.315). He grumbles because he cannot control the tedious term of his exile ("tarda fugae dispendia," 320). His thoughts are singular ("recursans," 322) and do not progress beyond his anxious hope ("spes anxia," 322) and long prayer (323) to hold Thebes. Yet for all this anxiousness Polynices cannot affect the change he seeks, as an outsider and private citizen. His frustration continues until Argia perceives his sleeplessness and weeping and motivates her father for war on his behalf. The anguish of exile is keenly presented when he is reunited with his mother and sister and weeps to his mother (7.492–6). Yet for as powerless and pitiable as Polynices' exile makes him seem, it also makes him dangerous. The notion that each brother will, in his annual return, be an exile troubles the critic. Polynices is an exile, and so a character of some apprehension. After a year in exile, Thebans probably suspect that Polynices is made savage. No doubt Statius' Roman audience does. Romans were wary of exiles, and certainly one had to be hard to endure it. Since the brothers' agreement on alternate rule Polynices initially left in a spirit of *concordia*, where exile is taken up for the benefit of the community. Nevertheless, he remembers those whom he noted were pleased at his departure, as well as those who grieved (2.316–21). There is thus a strong likelihood of house-cleaning had Eteocles ceded or had Polynices triumphed. Polynices surely holds a grudge against those who favored, or that he suspected of favoring, his exile.[11] This raises the likelihood of civil unrest *post reditum*.

The trouble with exiles and the reason they are to be such an object of concern is that banishment could make them fierce. Otho, for instance, feared Piso because a long exile had made him savage (*Hist.* 1.21). Exile has either made, or exacerbated, Polynices' ferocity and mental disquiet. Note in his initial presentation how a storm augments the turbulence of his anxious and unsettled mind: "incertusque uiae per nigra silentia uastum | haurit iter; pulsat metus undique et undique frater," "Though uncertain of his way, he takes the open road through still darkness, terrified of meeting his brother at every turn" (1.368–9). There is a literary intertext here with Euripides' *Phoenissae* 263–4, but we should not be unmindful of the truth of Polynices' situation as it is expressed through Statius: under Domitian the threat of unexpected murder was particularly acute for exiles.[12]

More telling than his apprehension, however, are his actions, which are uncivilized and feral. This is revealed in the animalistic contest over the stoop between Polynices and Tydeus.[13] Additionally, we almost have a sword fight between Agreus and Polynices (*Theb.* 6.911–23). As Lovatt points out this event and that of Adrastus' archery shoot are peculiar for being non-contests.[14] After Tydeus' victory in the wrestling match some of the men are eager and would like to test themselves with bare swords. Agreus and Polynices stand ready and armed. Adrastus, however, steps in and forbids the contest. He declares:

> manet ingens copia leti,
> o iuuenes! seruate animos auidumque furorem.
> sanguinis aduersi. tuque o, quem propter auita
> iugera, dilectas cui desolauimus urbes,
> ne, precor, ante aciem ius tantum casibus esse
> fraternisque sinas (abigant hoc numina!) uotis.
>
> *Theb.* 6.914–9

An abundance of death remains, young men! Save your enthusiasm and eager furor for the blood of enemies. And you, for whom we left our family farms and abandoned the cities that delight us, do not, I beg you, don't permit such things to chance or to your brother's prayers (may the gods deny those!) before the battle begins.

There is a terrible irony here. Statius has already made it plain that it would have been far better if Polynices had died during the chariot race. Since he did not, he continues to march against his own brother. Adrastus here would not have him trust his fate to chance. Again, the better course, a premature death of Polynices, is thwarted. He is spared, like the unholy Capaneus as we saw, for another death, which will be more entertaining for readers than anything offered during a mere game.[15] Additionally, Polynices listens and obeys his father-in-law, which he fails to do when he confronts his brother. And of course, Adrastus' successful veto of the sword fight underscores the later failure to forbid the fratricidal duel, a time unlike in the games that most matters. In any case, the ferocity of Polynices' quarrel with Tydeus and his willingness, indeed eagerness, to contest with bare swords during the games evince a hardness and savagery consistent with his exile, taking on the features of barbarism and foreignness. Indeed, the most troubling aspect of Polynices' exile is his association with foreign leaders and armies, which are, if we trust Tacitus (*Hist.* 3.33), notoriously unstable and difficult to order. Thus, Polynices brings not only the promise of himself as a leader fierce in exile, but he brings with him a disordered, foreign force.

When Polynices prepares to take Arion's reins from Adrastus during the chariot race, his father-in-law attempts to impart advice. The scene allows Statius to draw parallels with Phaethon; the poet conveys as much when he signals the comparison:[16]

> sic ignea lora
> cum daret et rapido Sol natum imponeret axi,
> gaudentem lacrimans astra insidiosa docebat

nolentesque teri zonas mediamque polorum
temperiem: pius ille quidem et formidine cauta,
sed iuuenem durae prohibebant discere Parcae.

Theb. 6.320–5

As when the Sun gave to his child the reins, setting him in the swift chariot, weeping he instructed the joyful boy in adverse stars, and zones preferring to be left alone, and the choice places between the poles: he was thoughtful certainly and with cautious fear, but the harsh Fates forbid that the boy would pay attention.

The scene, however, conveys more than this. Or rather, there is more at stake here. Phaethon is a tragic young man whose reach exceeds his grasp. Polynices, however, designs to be a leader of men and a kingdom. The metaphor that develops of a young man failing to heed the wise and practical council of an elder has greater implications for Polynices as a future king than for Phaethon. Polynices is unfit and ill-prepared to take the role that he desires. He lacks control over "potestas" (note the recurrence of the theme and how this impacts reading Polynices). Phaethon died because he did not listen to his father. The implication that Polynices cannot effectively govern or learn how to, as metaphorically expressed through Arion, suggests unfortunate events for the people of Thebes should he take power. There was never accord between horse and driver. Indeed, Arion's tremendous initial speed is actually an effort to get away from Polynices (424–30). If we are forced to conclude that Polynices will be an ineffective and unstable ruler then the chances are quite likely that, as unfortunate as it may seem, his death is a good thing—for Thebes, at least.

Despite Polynices' inability to listen to sage council he can be swayed by emotional appeals. This too is a cause for concern, and we see this pliability revealed more strikingly in Polynices than any other character.[17] The ability to influence the decisions of rulers likely had unsettling resonances in the Roman mind. Emotion also makes it difficult to know whom to trust and to whom one should listen.[18] When Polynices reunites with Jocasta her pleas cast doubt in the hearts of all the troops (7.532–3). Polynices is so moved that he loses his ambition (7.536–7). Tydeus, however, cautious and mindful of Eteocles' cruelty, counters Jocasta and sets everyone back on track (7.539–59). There is clearly a power to emotional persuasion and this is, in fact, the one thing that Tisiphone fears will undo her plans (11.103–4). Tisiphone defines the Furys' power through counsel and persuasion, which is set against rival power in Jocasta and Antigone. Her concerns are not baseless: Jocasta was nearly successful and Antigone's winning words overcome Polynices. After her pleading speech, a last effort to prevent the fratricidal duel, Polynices is visibly moved.

> his paulum furor elanguescere dictis
> coeperat, obstreperet quamquam atque obstaret Erinys;
> iam summissa manus, lente iam flectit habenas,
> iam tacet; erumpunt gemitus, lacrimasque fatetur
> cassis; hebent irae, pariterque et abire nocentem
> et uenisse pudet....
>
> *Theb.* 11.382–387

With these words his furor weakens somewhat, even though the Fury opposes. His hand falls. He turns his horse less deliberately. He is silent. Groans emerge from his helmet, betraying his tears. His rage evaporates and he is as much ashamed to leave as he was to have come...

This reveals how easily Polynices can be persuaded. There is also a strong notion that if Eteocles had not suddenly arrived, a truce may have been managed. The characterization that develops, then, is one of a wavering and inconsistent man who is unwilling or incapable of doing the things needed to attain his desire, dark as it might seem. Such is the leadership Polynices offers Thebes and if his people are to be freed from cruelty and tyranny, Polynices must not rule. Therefore, as sympathetic as his situation is, the qualities necessary to effectively rule are not present, and Polynices is truly a threat to his own country even beyond his ambitions to hold power.

Polynices also carries a sense of entitlement and believes that he already rules Thebes. His pride carries him ("attollit flatus ducis"), and he imagines that Eteocles is already deposed and he alone sits on the throne: "sedisse suberbus | deiecto iam fratre putat" (1.321-2).[19] Polynices' optimism prevails when Argia expresses her concern for so many ominous presages (2.356-62). But he enters a conflict to which he cannot entirely commit. His enterprise is poorly planned and poorly executed because he is too ambitious for "nudas potestas" to abandon the expedition, yet he is not sufficiently monstrous to confront his own people. This comes out as reluctance. Consider how, swept up by the ache to rule Thebes, he hesitates to leave Argia:

> iam regnum matrisque sinus fidasque sorores
> spe uotisque tenet, tamen et de turre suprema
> attonitam totoque extantem corpore longe
> respicit Argian; haec mentem oculosque reducit
> coniugis et dulces auertit pectore Thebas.
>
> *Theb.* 4.88–92

He holds already, in his hope and prayers, Thebes, and embraces his mother and his faithful sisters. Yet, he looks back to Argia, still visible though far off. She grieves from the highest parapet. She draws her husband's eyes and his attention back to her, and turns sweet Thebes from his heart.

The scene is tender. Is it not still possible for Polynices to have a happy life? Abandon that which, in truth, is not worth having? The disnarration is implied in the choice Polynices is still making. Indeed, here there is some difficulty in reading Polynices. His ambition has flagged, which reveals a lack of commitment. He is emotionally held back by a tender affection for his wife.[20] Indeed, the Argive departure scene is in stark contrast to the quick kisses and brief embraces, "raptim … oscula natis | amplexusque breves" (12.640–41), that Theseus' men give their loved ones. Hippolyta is eager to lead her Amazons for Theseus though he insists she remain out of this conflict because she is pregnant. Polynices' affections for Argia make it difficult for him to maintain a ruthless singularity of intention. He is divided between two kingdoms. When the decisive moment comes, he shrinks and cannot attack his own countrymen: "nec segnem Argolicae sensere Eteoclea turmae, | parcior ad ciues Polynicis inhorruit ensis," "His comrades did not notice his hesitation, but Polynices' sword shudders to attack his former countrymen and is more sparing toward them" (7.688–9). His men do not perceive that he is slack, but we know that he is. Polynices' enemies are his kin, whom he clearly has qualms against attacking. Eteocles, on the other hand, unflinchingly strikes against Polynices' army because the Thebans who support the coup can be viewed as traitors. Polynices is obligated to the men who support him, and his lack of resolve is costly. The advantage here is to Eteocles. Indeed, the consequences of his pursuit reach a climax with the death of his brother-in-law. Polynices' tragic realization that he has wasted Tydeus ("Tydea consumpsi!" 9.60) may be that as the leader of an insurgency, he recognizes that he has "misspent" his best man.[21] The only compensation he can now offer is to die.[22]

The End of Eteocles

Polynices' furor contrasts with Eteocles' sloth. The reigning king of Thebes shows little to no interest in a potential conflict or concern for Polynices' return until Laius' ghost prompts him. Where impatience and atavism draw Polynices, torpor and sluggishness characterize his brother. Our first introduction to Eteocles shows him sleeping and at leisure:

> nox ea cum tacita uolucer Cyllenius aura
> regis Echionii stratis adlapsus, ubi ingens
> fuderat Assyriis extructa tapetibus alto
> membra toro. pro gnara nihil mortalia fati
> corda sui! capit ille dapes, habet ille soporem.
>
> *Theb.* 2.89–93

> When that night the fleet Cyllenian glided along silent airs to the Echonian king's bed, where he sprawls his great bulk on high beds, his limbs poured over Assyrian coverlets. Not knowing their fates, poor mortal hearts! He eats. He sleeps.

The use of "ingens" is evocative, but vague. The usage should be taken in an unheroic sense, one that suggests a physical rather than kingly or heroic stature.[23] Eteocles lives much at leisure and without care. In his appointed year, Eteocles has served only himself taking his fill of food and sleep. Thus, a polarity is explored between the brothers with an absence of middle ground. Exile has made one brother wild, luxury makes the other sluggish.[24]

A vital feature of the Theban mythos is the relationship between the ruler and the ruled, the anonymous masses, the subordinate ends of a power relationship. The regal but doomed house of Oedipus embodies the strength and salvation of the city and Statius, as well as his predecessors, plays with complications that arise from this. Indeed, Aeschylus' *Septem* presents a relationship between Eteocles and the lower positioned women of the city that form the chorus. Much that characterizes Eteocles in this play is developed through his responses to the chorus.[25] Yet, for as high-handed as he appears, there is a bond of trust. He defends Thebes. Yet, in order to defend it, he must do the unspeakable and combat his own brother. Trapped in this way between public and private and herded by fate to a fratricidal conflict, Aeschylus' Eteocles becomes a truly tragic figure. His efforts toward stability are a feature of Aeschylus' Eteocles that does not match Statius' Aeschylean successor. In fact, he is much closer to that of Euripides, especially in his lack of concern for those he leads.[26] Likewise, the chorus of Argive elders in *Thyestes* reveal that their livelihood hangs on the choices and decisions of their rulers. As Tarrant observes of the choral passages in *Thyestes* generally, they reveal "with powerful empathy the feelings of subjects whose lives are ruinously affected by events they are helpless to control."[27] The chorus of Seneca's *Thyestes* is confronted with a dire situation in the struggle between Atreus and Thyestes. The division between king and people is exaggerated by the lack of direct interaction. The chorus presents idealistic notions of kingship that are couched in the same Stoic terms used to define the blessings of anonymity; the detachment from passion and vanity compliments both king and person. This ideal, however, conflicts with the affairs of Atreus' house. The chorus assume that by maintaining an unobtrusive political position, and by embracing anonymity, they will remain untroubled:

> me dulcis saturet quies;
> obscuro positus loco
> leni perfruar otio,
> nullis nota Quiritibus
> aetas per tacitum fluat.
>
> Thyestes 393-7

> Let me be saturated with easy quiet, set in a humble place, enjoying a leisure unbothered, unknown to anyone, let my time flow silently.

They are, however, foolishly misled by their observations of the reconciliation between Thyestes and Atreus (558-62). In the end, they too will endure the woe and suffering to come from Atreus' crime, but remain baffled as to why (789-826). Remarkably, the divide between the cause of their suffering and its effects is reinforced by a resolution that highlights their ignorance of the situation:

> o nos dura sorte creatos,
> seu perdidimus solem miseri,
>   sive expulimus!
> abeant questus, discede timor:
> vitae est avidus quisquis non uult
> mundo secum pereunte mori.
>
> Thyestes 879-84

> Sigh for us wretches, created by hard lots, we lose the light or banish it! Away, grumblings, depart, Fear! He is covetous who would not die in a dying world with the rest.

The relationship between the person of great status and the "cives" appears much bleaker in Seneca's *Thyestes*, not only because the people suffer in consequence of the actions of the royal house, but because they also remain ignorant to the cause of their suffering. Statius is sensitive to the relationship between the citizens and the ruler. Unlike Seneca, however, in the *Thebaid* many who suffer are aware this is a consequence of a ruler's actions. This allows more pronounced expositions of grief and lament.

Statius' Eteocles similarly demonstrates an adverse relationship with the Theban community.[28] This is stressed during Tydeus' embassy to Thebes. Tydeus travels to Thebes as Polynices' ambassador in order to test Eteocles' willingness to cede the throne. Unfortunately, Tydeus is not the best choice of spokesperson,[29] though his deficiency as diplomat is unlikely to make much difference in Eteocles' eagerness to retain Thebes. Tydeus offers a fiery and declamatory harangue to Eteocles. In forming his response to Tydeus, Eteocles argues that a change in rule would be disadvantageous to the Theban people:

> iam pectora uulgi
> adsueuere iugo: pudet heu plebisque patrumque:
> ne totiens incerta ferant mutentque gementes
> imperia et dubio pigeat parere tyranno.
> non parcit populis regnum breue; respice quantus
> horror et attoniti nostro in discrimine ciues.
> hosne ego, quis certa est sub te duce poena, relinquam?
> iratus, germane, uenis.
>
> *Theb.* 2.442–9

> Now the hearts of the people know this yoke: Alas, I bear the blame for plebs and fathers. Should they really be forced to change so often and endure uncertainty and swear obedience to a changing lord? Brief reigns do not leave the state unharmed. Do you not see the horror, the dumbfounded citizens in our quarrel? Do I just hand over to you those who are certain to receive punishment? You come in anger, Brother.

The argument serves Eteocles, but it has already been established by the anonymous critic and the narrator's comments as Tydeus enters Thebes[30] that concern for the people is hardly uppermost in Eteocles' mind.[31] Eteocles later claims, in his speech to the "magnanimi reges" of his army, "meritas ira" (7.378) in response to the conflict and casts blame on Polynices: "cerne en ubicumque nefandus | excidium moliris auis," "You see, wicked one, wherever you be, planning the ruin of your forbears" (7.386-7). Though it seems also likely that he enjoys squandering Thebes' resources and banqueting. Eteocles suggests that Polynices should be thankful for Argia's dowry (2.430-2) and suggests that Thebes would not provide a quality and style of life to which Polynices' wife is already accustomed: "anne feret luxu consueta paterno | hunc regina larem?," "Could the queen accustomed to her father's wealth endure this home?" (2.438-9).

Eteocles' speech is, however, unconvincing, though there is reasonable speculation in the question: "hosne ego, quis certa est sub te duce poena, relinquam?" (2.448). Eteocles, despite the tyranny of his first year, has supporters who would likely be executed or sent into exile in the shift of reign to Polynices.

As a result, Eteocles likely has the support of pragmatic men at court, or at least the support of those with an interest in self-preservation, should they wish to avoid proscription. Eteocles is a tyrant and greedy to retain sole power; however, his motivation for retaining power could also be that he would not want to endure the possible threats to his life that Polynices would impose were he to take power. Suspicion may contribute as much to the brother's ruin as ambition. In any case, as Tydeus points out, war will be a misfortune to those people that Eteocles suggests he is protecting: "ast horum miseret, quos sanguine uiles | coniugibus natisque infanda ad proelia raptos | proicis excidio, bone rex," "but I pity these whose cheap blood, whom you rush to ruin, taken from wives and children and delivered into battle, my good king" (*Theb.* 2.458–60). And it is also worth noting that when Tydeus departs from Thebes, the mothers accuse both Tydeus and Eteocles of sowing war and conflict among them: "aspectant matres, saeuoque infanda precantur | Oenidae tacitoque simul sub pectore regi" (*Theb.* 2.480–1).

Statius condemns the ambush plot against Tydeus (2.488–91). Indeed, when Eteocles orders the ambush against Tydeus, Statius comments that it is to be done with a silent sword ("tactioque inuadere ferro," 2.487). This may be merely synecdoche for the ambush party, but is more probably meant to be taken as coextensive with Eteocles' deceptive nature, which is revealed in the way he responds to provocation and finally stabs Polynices. Eteocles refuses to surrender his authority and Tydeus reviles him for this. Before responding to the aggressive speech, Statius inserts a simile that characterizes Eteocles' psychological nature at that moment. In this first instance, Statius compares Eteocles to a snake that has been struck by a rock:

> ... ast illi tacito sub pectore dudum
> ignea corda fremunt, iacto uelut aspera saxo
> comminus erigitur serpens, cui subter inanes
> longa sitis latebras totumque agitata per artus
> conuocat in fauces et squamea colla uenenum
>
> *Theb.* 2.410–14

But Eteocles' fiery heart roars in his silent chest, as when a vicious snake, roused from the earth by thirst, rears up when a stone is thrown too near, and draws to his jaws every drop of venom in its body.

This simile revises Virgil's characterization of Androgeos who suddenly perceives that Aeneas and his small cadre are not from the Greek contingent (*Aen.* 2.378–82).[32] Whereas Virgil focuses on the hapless Androgeos' surprise and fright, Statius shifts the focus to the snake. Androgeos is like the hapless traveler; Eteocles like the provoked serpent. Eteocles swells with anger; of Androgeos recoils in fear. Moreover, "squamea colla uenenum" seems a very suggestive revision of "caerula colla tumentem." These two similes are also notable, though not unique, for the way in which they heighten tension. Both abruptly interrupt their primary narratives, which causes a frustrating delay, at the point where something could happen. Then, in order to heighten the tension in the primary narrative, the simile provides an incomplete episode that is interrupted without resolution. What happens? Does the snake bite him or not? We do not know. At the point where something could happen and resolve our expectations in the simile, the poet returns us to the primary narrative more anxious than we were before. The use of these two similes to create tension appears to be a close point of contact between them. In both instances, the simile breaks from the narrative—the scene of Androgeos' encounter and Tydeus' verbal assault—and heightens anticipation by bringing readers to the pivotal image where the snake is just about to strike, just before returning to the narrative. This sudden shift between situations heightens expectation in the primary situation by further evoking tension in a parallel narrative.

Eteocles' anger takes place "sub tacito pectore" (2.410). This may reveal an unsettling calm in his outward appearance, notable in his undisturbed breathing despite being upset. Eteocles does not easily or quickly reveal his anger. This recalls Calchas' fear of powerful rulers. When the seer petitions Achilles for safety before breaking the bad news to Agamemnon, he expresses serious concern for a leader who nurses his anger quietly (*Iliad* 1.80-3). Eteocles is the kind of ruler Calchas fears. The anxiety over being unable to read the inner nature of those in power by their outward actions or expressions lest they hold some grudge is something that we have moved beyond in our present age.[33] Statius expresses Eteocles' ability to control his anger through the simile of the snake. On the relationship between inward anger and its outward expression in Flavian epic. See McGuire.[34]

The epic simile associates two, occasionally more, unalike comparands at a point of similarity. With regard to narrative time, similes offer a "descriptive pause: text without story duration."[35] Statius draws attention to Eteocles' suppressed anger during exchanges with Tydeus, Maeon, and Creon. During each confrontation snake imagery is used to express his emotional state. In two of these instances—during the encounters with Tydeus and Creon—his wrath and its restraint are compared to snakes that have been disturbed. His reaction to Maeon, however, draws on a sibilant alliteration of a serpent-like hiss. Eteocles' emotional responses, and the suppression of his anger after these abusive harangues, reveal a pattern of frustrated and incomplete action. He does not attack Tydeus with his own hand, but instead sends an ambush party against him. Nor does Eteocles have opportunity to attack Maeon, who commits suicide after his speech. Eteocles nearly attacks Creon, but sheaths his sword instead. The possibility of attack, of actually striking out in anger, is continually frustrated. In fact, we never see Eteocles use his sword until he uses it against his brother, and it is noteworthy that when he does make the fatal blow against Polynices, the description recalls the same actions of the snakes used in similes that had earlier characterized him. Thus, the snake images connect both to the primary comparand (Eteocles) and the *Thebaid*'s narrative arc.[36]

Statius again connects Eteocles to a snake when, after the failed ambush, Maeon returns to Thebes. An earthquake, the ominous presage of misfortune, signals the doomed survivors' return. So the Elder Pliny claims: "nec vero simplex malum aut in ipso tantum motu periculum est, sed par aut maius ostento. numquam urbs Roma tremuit, ut non futuri eventus alicuius id praenuntium esset," "nor is the danger simple and does not amount to the earthquake alone, but is in itself an omen. Rome was never shaken without this being a portent that something was about to happen" (*HN* 2.200). Consider also the earth that groans to receive Amphiaraus, "dat gemitum tellus" (6.527). After Maeon's speech, Eteocles' psyche is presented in a line of hissing sibilance:[37] "iam mouerat iras | rex ferus, et tristes ignescunt sanguine uultus," "Now the hostile ruler's wrath is roused, and hot blood rushes to his face" (3.78-9).[38] Here it is difficult for Eteocles to conceal his emotions. Certainly, there is more outward indication than we saw with Tydeus.

When Creon confronts Eteocles we find yet another comparison to a snake and a suggestion that his anger almost, but has not quite yet, roused sufficient emotion to make him strike: "atque ensem, quem iam dabat ira, repressit," "but the sword that anger drew he put away" (11.309). This is the closest Eteocles comes to using his sword directly, though there is some suggestion that it has been used in battle (7.688-9). Direct focus here, however, is on the sluggishness of Polynices' sword. Eteocles is thought by the Argives to be "nec segnem," but we cannot be sure in what manner. In any case, taken with earlier passages there is the sense that a moment, the long anticipated moment in which Eteocles will draw his sword and strike, is close. The repeated suppression of his anger frustrates the expectation of readers. Statius crowns this particular encounter with another snake simile that is very similar to the one used during Tydeus' confrontation with the monarch:

> ictus ut incerto pastoris uulnere serpens
> erigitur gyro longumque e corpore toto
> uirus in ore legit; paulum si deuius hostis
> torsit iter, cecidere minae tumefactaque frustra
> colla sedent, irasque sui bibit ipse ueneni.
>
> *Theb.* 11.310–14

As a serpent, uncertain of its wounds after some shepherd strikes him, raises up from his coil and from its whole body calls poison to its throat, but if the enemy will sidestep, even just a little out of his way, the threat subsides, the throat swelled for no purpose settles, and he swallows down his own gall.

Where the serpent of the earlier simile was reared and about to strike, calling the venom forth, here the serpent swallows the venom, and relaxes the tension. And the anticipation that Eteocles will draw and use his sword is further delayed. In the duel against Polynices, we finally see Eteocles use his sword. An interesting feature of Statius' *Thebaid*, unlike Euripides' *Phoenissae*, is that the brothers are always kept at a distance from one another. They never come together until their final duel. The verb used to describe Eteocles' use of his sword corresponds to the description of the angered snakes. The verb *erigo, -ere* occurs several times in the *Thebaid* and Statius uses it in connection with snakes five times. *Theb.* 2.412, 4.97, 5.506, 8.518, and 11.311. Two of these occurrences describe the snakes in the similes connected to Eteocles' inward mental state discussed here; however, the same verb is also conspicuously used by Statius to reveal Eteocles' sword as he lies on the ground and finally brings it forth from underneath Polynices in the final duel:

> utque superstantem pronumque in pectora sensit,
> erigit occulte ferrum uitaeque labantis
> reliquias tenues odio suppleuit, et ensem
> iam laetus fati fraterno in corde reliquit.
>
> *Theb.* 11.564–7

When Eteocles sensed his brother standing prone over him, he secretly raises his sword, his feeble frame enervated with hate just as his life slips away. Now pleased with fate he leaves his sword in his brother's heart.

Eteocles strikes with "occulte ferrum," which loosely recollects the phrase "tactioque inuadere ferro" (2.487) used to describe the ambush party. The sword raises up in the same manner as the snakes used to describe Eteocles. This action is consistent with expectations attached to the snakes, and we find his inner anger at being offended now physically manifested and directed toward the one person we would expect him to hate the most. Thus Statius elaborates Eteocles' psychological nature through the image of snakes and presents his final act of anger within a trajectory developed in association with that image.[39] An image that defines his character and actions, and that compels readers to anticipate the moment when he may finally strike. Thus, the serpent, by way of the manner in which Eteocles expresses his anger and eventually fulfills his wrath on Polynices, governs characterization of Eteocles, at least the inner psyche until that wrath has an outward expression in the way he kills his brother.[40]

8

Theseus and Concluding the *Thebaid*

The traditional aftermath of the war between Eteocles and Polynices offers a trove of closing scenarios to be exploited.[1] Creon's edict forbidding funeral rites to the opposing forces is critical to the *Thebaid*'s aftermath. Throughout the *Thebaid*, as we have seen, Statius heightens anticipation for the mutual fratricide of Eteocles and Polynices. The previous versions of the myth developed by Statius' tributaries allow for the expectation of Creon's edict, its violation, and often Theseus' intervention. Outside a vague reference to an "alter dux" at *Thebaid* 4.404, however, there is little to prepare us for the arrival of Theseus. Statius puts the narrative's stress on the fratricide. When the fratricide is complete, there is less certainty for what will come next. Readers begin the final movement of the *Thebaid* with only canonical familiarity regarding the burial of the dead; Statius must restructure anticipation for the final events. Statius develops an initial anxiousness for what is to happen next through the simile of Idalian doves, which reflect as much the Thebans' anxiousness after the conflict as the reader's sense for what is to come. Statius then provides the edict of Creon during the funeral for Menoeceus. Creon's irrationality reveals how he perpetuates Thebes' characteristic *nefas* and irrational autocracy. Since the *Thebaid* finds its drive through madness and instability, and as this clearly has not been purged through the deaths of Oedipus' sons, Creon's edict simultaneously opens the narrative possibilities while also creating the need for further resolution. Such sacrilege, as tradition maintains, must not stand. The lone soldier Ornytus provides further direction and anticipation when he announces to the party of Argive women that Creon forbids the burial of their husbands and sons and that two courses are now open to them: they can petition Creon, who will most likely butcher them, or they can go to Athens and ask Theseus for aid. Argia breaks off from the party, speciously to sue Creon for funeral rites, but secretly to perform these for Polynices herself, which threatens Antigone's proud violation of her uncle's imposed law, while the rest of the women leave for Athens. In this way, the temporal arrangement of future events is left in doubt. Though holding out the canonical scenes, Statius creates further uncertainty for how and when these various episodes will come together, and the roles that two prominent post-fratricidal figures, Antigone and Theseus, will play.

The Idalian Doves

Statius presents the "Idaliae Volucres" three times, always as a metaphor for meekness and timidity. The description of the birds in the *Achilleid* informs, to some degree, the nature of the doves in the *Thebaid*. As the birds cheerfully encircle a newcomer to their flock, they demonstrate preference for peace over conflict (*Ach*.1.372–8). The birds are initially timid and suspicious, "cunctae primum mirantur et horrent" (*Ach*. 1.375), before they are willing to fly nearer and welcome the new bird, not unlike the timid emergence they demonstrate in the second simile of *Thebaid* 12.[2] As birds disposed toward peace, their presence in martial epic markedly contrasts with the atmosphere of bloodshed that prevails throughout the epic. The first mention of the Idalian doves in the *Thebaid* comes during Hypsipyle's recounting of the attack at Lemnos (*Theb*. 5.63).

> illa Paphon veterem centumque altaria linquens,
> nec vultu nec crine prior, soluisse iugalem
> ceston et Idalias procul ablegasse volucres
> fertur.
>
> *Theb*. 5.61–4
>
> She departs ancient Paphos and her hundred altars, her appearance and hair are altered; they say she undid her girdle of love and sent her Idalian doves far away.

The birds sacred to Venus are ill-disposed to seeing violence. Before the Lemnian massacre, Venus dispenses with the accoutrements identifying her as a goddess of love and one who subdues martial proclivities.[3] Indeed, Venus assumes the mantle of her half-sisters, the Furies.[4] Before Venus skulks through the city with the Furies she frees her doves in order that they not witness the horrific events. Venus' traditional function brings lovers together. It thus seems fitting that she send the doves away when she is found actively working with the Furies to break lovers apart.[5] We should note, however, that the doves were also proverbial for unexpected misfortune following the relief of a seeming escape. As Diogenianus explains of the Cretan practice of sacrificing doves to Venus: Καὶ γὰρ τῷ Ἀδώνιδι ἐν Κύπρῳ τιμηθέντι ὑπὸ τῆς Ἀφροδίτης μετὰ τὴν τελευτὴν οἱ Κύπριοι ζώσας ἐνίεσαν περιστεράς, αἱ δ' ἀποπτᾶσαι καὶ διαφυγοῦσαι αὖθις ἀδοκήτως εἰς ἄλλην ἐμπεσοῦσαι πυρὰν διεφθάρησαν, "After the worship to Adonis and Aphrodite was finished, the Cyprians would throw live doves into the pyre, which flew off only to fall into yet another pyre and die anyway" (*Diogenian*. 1.49–53). This practice was evidently not unknown to the Romans, nor should we assume that the proverbial freight of Venus' sacred doves in this ritual context was unfamiliar to Statius.[6] The Lemnian episode presents sorrow co-extensive with the Theban horrors, perhaps as an extended simile of the horror that will befall Thebes.

Statius later captures the anxious state of the Thebans, the "metus" and "horror" they experience as they survey the aftermath and seek out their dead, in two similes. In the first, they are compared to men who still feel themselves tossed and buffeted on the sea after they have arrived on land (12.12–13.) But once the Theban conflict comes to an end Statius returns to the image of the doves. This is not surprising. As Statius indicates at 12.18 they are not meant for war. In the final book, they return from their earlier banishment at 5.63 to become a simile for the Theban people who would cautiously come out of their homes, but are still hesitant and frightened. Anxious that they will be charged by enemies:[7]

> sic ubi perspicuae scandentem limina turris
> Idaliae uolucres fuluum aspexere draconem,
> intus agunt natos et feta cubilia uallant
> unguibus imbellesque citant ad proelia pennas;
> mox ruerit licet ille retro, tamen aera nudum
> candida turba timet, tandemque ingressa uolatus
> horret et a mediis etiamnum respicit astris.
>
> *Theb.* 12.15–21

As when Idalian doves have spotted a tawny snake scaling the outside of a prominent tower, they hurry their brood inside and barricade their nests with claws and ready their unwarlike wings for battle. Soon after, the snake hurries backward, but the pale flock fears the open air and though finally taking flight, they still look backward in fear from amid the stars.

This simile offers an anticipatory cue to Statius' closing strategies for the final book. With the deaths of the heroes and the brothers, the core narrative reiterations of the *Thebaid* are satisfied. Statius begins the last book of the *Thebaid* with a focus on the aftermath of the conflict and the burial of the dead. There remains, however, the aftermath that relates to the Argive funeral rites. The antecedent narratives offer Statius a few prominent scenes for closing the epic, but Creon's forbearance of Polynices' burial and Antigone's violation of his edict offer the thrust for the final scenes. Thus, by bringing the doves back into the narrative, despite their cautions, Statius signals an end to the wicked events of his narrative, but with an implied sense that a threat to peace may still loom. Most importantly, the Thebans sense of the unknown possibility, of where things will go from here, mirrors the readers' concern for suitable conclusions. Statius programs the reading of the opening scenes with a simile of Idalian doves that have become suspicious and wary after their home has been attacked by a serpent (12.15–21).This image intends a parallel to the feelings of the Thebans as they emerge from behind the walls to bury and grieve for their dead, or search out the Argive leaders (Tydeus, Amphiaraus, and Capaneus, 12.41–3).

The Edict of Creon

Creon, the only remaining male heir to Thebes, takes power after the death of Eteocles and Polynices and reveals the same disposition toward the violence, cruelty, and unsteadiness as his nephews.[8] After the self-sacrifice of his son, for instance, Creon is overcome with grief and tormented by the persistent memory of Menoeceus' death. Statius creates anticipation for Creon's failure through the suggestion that that he did not learn from the errors of his predecessors. The new king should be wept for ("flebilis," 655) and Statius bodes "numquamne priorum | haerebunt documenta nouis?," "Will the new not keep the example of the old?" (11.656–7). Nevertheless, when Creon assumes power he does focus on the duties of that office. The power of holding Thebes exceeds his mourning for Menoeceus and Creon attempts to separate his private grief and his newly acquired public obligations: "iam flectere patrem | incipit atque datis abolere Menoecea regnis," "Now he begins to turn aside his fatherly love and abolish Menoceus from his received rule" (11.659–60). But even if we suppose Creon does not want his grief to influence his rule, his actions are nevertheless cruel. In his first act as king, Creon exiles Oedipus from Thebes (11.669–72). Oedipus ironically suggests Creon is not taking his new power far enough (11.683–3). Creon grows swollen with power, "tumidus regale" (11.756). The characterization of Creon in this way anticipates corresponding behaviors and actions.

The most critical event to the eruption of further conflict after the mutual fratricide of Eteocles and Polynices is Creon's denial of funeral rites for the Argive dead. The funeral of Menoeceus offers Creon the opportunity to pronounce against his enemies and the cause of his son's death. During the princely immolation of Menoeceus' corpse, no plebeian pyre for his son, Creon reveals his misapprehension of his monarchal position when he speculates that had Menoeceus not died the office might be a happier one ("munus acerbas," 12.75). After expressing his grief over Menoeceus' remains, Creon denies burial to Polynices and the rest of the Argive dead. The funeral of his son kindles his wrath, and he makes his decree with emotion and violence, rather than judicious impartiality.[9] Had Creon the ability he would go so far as to prolong the suffering of the dead ("longos utinam addere sensus | corporibus," 12.96–6). In this way, the personal becomes political, as Creon's private grief poisons his public obligations. Moreover, Creon is aware of his own mind and he knows that he is being cruel when he forbids the burial of the Argive dead (11.662–4).[10] This overwhelming desire to prolong the desecration and violence against one's enemies recollects Achilles' violence toward Hector's corpse. Because Creon's emotional distress fuels his violent attitudes and pairs him with Achilles, this raises the possibility of a diplomatic resolution and a peaceful ending. Traditionally, as I discuss below, Theseus holds the possibility of a bloodless end to the matter. Indeed, as there is no way as yet of anticipating the arrival of Theseus, one might even suppose the possibility or near-possibility of a diplomatic resolution being put forward through Antigone. After all, violence is not a necessary conclusion to martial epic as Achilles' ransoming of Hector to Priam at the end of the *Iliad* proves.

The Choices of Ornytus

Immediately following Creon's injunction the scene shifts to the tearful company of widows, a catalog of heroines in miniature, traveling to Thebes to lay the remains of their beloved men to rest. They are favored by divine agents; Hecate provides torchlight and Juno guides their way (12.129–136). As Juno's aid and messenger Iris is charged with preserving the bodies "ut longius obstent | exspectentque rogum et flammas non ante fatiscant," "so that they hold for a longer time while they await the pyre, and do not rot before they are given to the flames" (12.139–40).[11] This divine order creates a temporal frame within which Statius can develop the narrative. This also makes clear, through a hinting prolepsis, that the bodies will receive their final rites in the end and that these divinities do not side with Creon. This is the most significant reintroduction of divine agency in human affairs since Jupiter called the gods away and departed before the fratricide. And since gods are often motivators in mortal outcomes, their interference and preference for one party over another creates expectation for that outcome. Creon's position, being sacrilegious, finds no support here. Since he has forbidden the burial while Iris prevents the bodies from decomposing, this presents two irreconcilable positions that will require resolution, and which the reader now anticipates.[12] Statius thus establishes a temporal gap to anticipate conflict over the funeral rites, against Creon's wishes the bodies will not be desecrated by wild animals or exposure.

En route, the Argive widows meet Ornytus, a lone-surviving soldier of little importance apart from his usefulness in setting out a number of several divergent narrative possibilities with his recommendations. Foremost, he informs the women of Creon's edict and identifies him with a host of infamously inhospitable characters: Busiris, the Thracian Diomedes, and the Cyclops or Sirens.[13] Ornytus suggests that in all likelihood anyone petitioning him will be slain so it may be best for them to return home and mourn the names of the slain on empty tombs. Or, he continues, they could place the issue before Theseus, newly returned to Athens from his conquest of the Amazons. Ornytus, in fact, implies the character of Theseus, or at least the character needed to improve conditions at Thebes: "bello cogendus et armis | in mores hominemque Creon," "Creon must be compelled with war and arms to humanity and its customs" (12.165–6). Notably, Ornytus indicates that the refusal to bury the dead is not irreligious but inhuman, and against the "mores" of mankind.[14] Theseus will prove consistent with this suggestion. Ornytus' council derails the women's impetus, a paralysis characterized by a simile of heifers suddenly catching the sound of a tigress' distant roar and they are uncertain how to proceed (169–72). Argia resolves the confusion and puts forward a plan. Since she is family, she leads the band of women to believe that she will travel to Thebes and petition Creon. Because of her relationship she is more likely to be heard by the new king without incident. What she intends, however, is to bury Polynices on her own. With this decision, she supplants expectations that Antigone will act as her brother's executor; Argia now appears positioned to seize that role.

ubi incluta fama Antigone?

Whereas Tisiphone controlled the narrative's impetus in the early books and into the final confrontation between the brothers, Argia's impatience hurries along the final book. If the reader expects an end that has as its focus the interventions of Antigone or Theseus, Argia's refusal to wait threatens to overshoot the introduction of either of these characters and their traditional roles. Could Statius be composing an *Argiad* in the final book? As she claims, in a touching sort of prayer to her Polynices:

> anne ait hostiles ego te tabente per agros
> (heu dolor!) expectem quaenam sententia lenti
> Theseos, an bello proceres, an dexter haruspex
> adnuat? interea funus decrescit
>
> *Theb.* 12.209.12

Do I wait (ah, woe!) for slow Theseus' decision while you decay in your enemy's land? Will his council, will his reliable prophet assent to war? Meanwhile your body rots...

Argia reveals that there exists the possibility of further narrative delay in that a decision must be arrived at for Theseus, and perhaps even a scene of augury or haruspicy, like those leading up to the Theban war in which the omens must be divined.[15] Meanwhile, unaware of Iris' preservation, she feels the urgency to attend to Polynices' body. The problem of the decaying corpses is an acute one, and establishes a necessity for the resolution. Notably, in one of the only two surviving fragments from Aeschylus' *Eleusinioi* we find, "ὤργα τὸ πρᾶγμα· διεμύδαιν' ἤδη νέκυς" (fr. 53a), "the matter urged, the corpse decomposing." Argia presses to push past the possibility of delay and to the ending. While ultimately, she pilots readers toward Antigone and Creon, here she oversteps the potential for their endings with one of her own. Indeed, as Argia travels to Thebes, her journey inversely reflects the travels of her husband Polynices in the *Thebaid* 1. Recall that for Polynices the road of return to his homeland is treacherous and filled with anxiety and ominous shadows, all of which bodes ill for the outcome of his desire to rule.[16] Argia, on the other hand, bravely passes dark landscapes, wild beasts, and the dangerous abodes of monsters (12.219–37). The landscape appears even to show her the way as she "magno Megareia praeceps | arua rapit passu, demonstrat proxima quisque | obuius," "consumes the Megarian fields in hurried haste; each one she encounters points her to the next" (12.219–21).

Once near Thebes, Argia prays to Thebes, in a way that attempts to signal peace and requests help in guiding Argia's way. Argia asks the city, very humbly and simply: "rogos hospes planctumque et funera posco," "though a stranger I ask a pyre, a lament, a corpse" (12.261). As Argia searches the battlefields, in the dark and in vain, Juno pities her and enlists Cynthia to cast moonlight down on her toil. Just as Argia seeks a truce between herself and the city where Polynices died,[17] so too Juno uncharacteristically desires to set enmity aside when she tells Cynthia "veteres sed mitto querelas," "but I set aside the old arguments" (12.301). These accords contrast with Creon's decree, which sustains hostilities. Statius establishes mortal and divine climates in which parties are actively looking for peace, rather than, as before, violence. Given that the battlefield took three days for the Thebans to survey (12.50), the divine interventions of Juno and Cynthia quicken the pace and expedite her search.

With divine assistance, Argia finds her husband quickly. As she addresses his corpse it becomes clear, as much to her own wonderment as the reader's, why she is the only mourner there. She asks: "nullasne tuorum | mouisti lacrimas? ubi mater, ubi incluta fama | Antigone? mihi nempe iaces, mihi uictus es uni!" (12.331–3), "Was no one from your family moved to weep over you? Where is your mother? Where is Antigone glorious in fame? For me only you seems to lie dead, for me only you were defeated." Antigone, and other characters appear to have been edged out of the narrative as Argia reveals that only she appears to be the one to carry the funeral of Polynices to its end. But then suddenly, and probably unexpectedly, when Argia finishes her obsequies, Antigone arrives.[18] The sense of surprise the reader should feel is provided in the transitional exclamation: "Ecce" (12.349). Statius then provides a hurried analepsis of why she was tardy at the scene, "ergo deis fratrisque moras excusat," "She offers excuses to the gods and to her brother for her tardiness" (12.354). But, of course, for readers there is no sense of delay at all. Her experiences are compressed and treated elliptically so that she is quickly brought up and into the narrative. And once Antigone takes the field, she contests with the usurper of her night, "'cuius' ait 'manes, aut quae temeraria quaeris | nocte mea?'" (366–7) "'Whose body do you look for?,' she asks, 'And who are you that dare do this when it is my night?'" This night we infer as the scene in which she buries Polynices, upon which literary tradition Argia has now encroached.[19] To some degree the meeting of Argia and Antigone reflects the first meeting of Polynices and Tydeus. The sisters, however, quickly realize their common aims and proceed to take care of the body of Polynices. In this way, and in a way that proves consistent with Statius' epic program, the most expected narrative direction becomes suppressed in order to deliver it in a more sudden and surprising manner. Argia appears well positioned to dominate the funeral scene, and she herself wonders where Antigone could have got to. Antigone suddenly arrives, and with apologies in order to participate, as if to say "no, wait, here I am."

The Twin Flames

As Argia and Antigone (and Menoetes) search out a suitable pyre for Polynices the one they find happens to be that of Eteocles, still smoldering. When Polynices' corpse is brought into contact with his brother twin flames erupt combating one another and shoot into the sky:

> ecce iterum fratres: primos ut contigit artus
> ignis edax, tremuere rogi et nouus aduena busto
> pellitur; exundant diuiso uertice flammae
> alternosque apices abrupta luce coruscant.
> Pallidus Eumenidum veluti commiserit ignes
> Orcus, uterque minax globus et conatur uterque
> longius
>
> *Theb.* 12.429–35

Behold the brothers again! Once the devouring flames touched their limbs, the pyre trembled and the intruder is driven away. The flames rush upward, cleft at the crown with two points of flashing light. As though pale Orcus had brought the Erynian torches into conflict, each shape of flame vies to outdo the other.

Statius' description of the flames recollects Oedipus and his own curse delivered by Manto in Seneca's *Oedipus*: "sed ecce pugnax ignis in partes duas | discedit et se scindit unius sacri | discors fauilla," "But oh! The contentious flame separates into two, the spark of a single rite divides into conflict" (321–3). This move strikes a tragic note by reminding the reader that the losses incurred throughout the epic are genetically linked to Oedipus, who was himself cursed by the actions of his father. The brothers were doomed because Oedipus was doomed. Yet, where the omen that Manto describes prefigures the catastrophe that Oedipus is about to face in Seneca's treatment, Statius means to conclude their conflict by pointing backward through the allusion of twin flame to Seneca as "father."[20] These flames indicate that even after their mutual fratricide, as corpses, their enmity persists and fully presents the depth of their hatred. Statius' scene reveals Statius' awareness of continuity within the story. When the flames burst forth, the curse, which marks the beginning of the text,[21] concludes. No further action remains to develop between Eteocles and Polynices; however, he does insist that their hatred endures even after their deaths. Notably, one particular condition of the enmity between the sons is preserved by Athenaeus. After indicating Oedipus cursed his sons—in front of them rather than in subterranean exile as Statius has it—Athenaeus records: ἀμφοτέροισι δ' αἰεὶ πόλεμοί τε μάχαι τε ... (*Ath.* xi.465 E).

The assertion that a cursed party will "always" suffer is a standard clause in utterances.²² No reconciliation between them is possible. This is fully delivered in the *Thebaid* when Argia and Antigone place the corpse of Polynices on his brother's pyre.²³

Choosing Theseus

Statius' epic does not build around Theseus, nor does it anticipate his arrival. Until the final book, Statius never looks toward the arrival of Theseus beyond the presentation of a world that utterly lacks, and desperately needs, a stable figure.²⁴ But as a stabilizing figure, a leader who can bring peace to Thebes, Theseus is deeply ambiguous.²⁵ Theseus has a pronounced capacity for war, and, as his conquest over the Amazons indicates, subjugation. Certainly Statius intends to create associations between Theseus' triumph over the Amazons and his imminent conflict with Thebes. Aside from the need for political stability at Thebes and the structural requisites of a narrative terminus, little prepares readers for the arrival of Theseus to conclude the *Thebaid*. To be sure, Theseus' intervention in Theban affairs is a canonical mainstay, whether securing funeral rites for the dead is the result of diplomacy or armed conflict.²⁶ With the exception of Pindar, who makes no mention of the funeral rites,²⁷ Thebes typically yields to either diplomacy and reason, or the force of a superior military force. Aeschylus, as Plutarch reports, finds a peaceful resolution in "πείσας καὶ σπεισάμενος." Isocrates²⁸ similarly presents a tradition in which good sense, as presented through heralds, wins over the leaders in charge of Thebes.²⁹ On the other hand, Euripides' Theseus, while attempting a diplomatic resolution is compelled to war in the *Suppliants*.

The central action of Euripides' *Suppliants* is gaining burial for the dead heroes. A significant moment in the play occurs when Theseus asks Adrastos to relate how these fallen men came to be so distinguished among mortal heroes and eulogize their deeds.³⁰ The virtues related by Adrastos reveal their importance to the betterment and health of the *polis*, a consistent theme throughout the play.³¹ The presentation of their virtues reveals, from Adrastus' perspective, that the heroes warrant a burial, that they are worth the war Theseus prepares to bring should Creon persist in refusing to bury them. Euripides makes a strategic shift from Aeschylus' presentation of the heroes in the *Septem*. Granted, the use of a particular myth does not necessarily constitute fidelity to one particular tradition. Often, in fact, traditions are tailored to meet narrative demands or compete with previous expositions. A case in point is easily found in the various castings of Tydeus. Homer uses the historical image of Tydeus as a comparative ideal. At *Iliad* 4.370–400, Agamemnon rouses Diomedes through an ignominious imputation that he does not attain in battle the same glory as his father. He recounts Tydeus' embassy to Eteocles and his victory over the ambush sent by Eteocles. Agamemnon rebukes Diomedes with the final judgment: ἀλλὰ τὸν υἱὸν | γείνατο εἷο χέρεια μάχῃ, ἀγορῇ δέ τ' ἀμείνω, "but his son proves to be worse in battle, but better in talk" (*Il.* 4.399–400). Aeschylus' view of Tydeus, on the other hand, is less approving. Tydeus is filled with battle-lust (*Sept.* 380). Amphiaraus, the only one Aeschylus casts favorably among the invading contingent, denounces Tydeus as a murderer (ἀνδροφόντην,), a public nuisance (τὸν πόλεως ταράκτορα), and a great teacher of evil (μέγιστον. . .τῶν κακῶν διδάσκαλον) (*Sept.* 572-3). In order to support Theseus' purpose, Euripides hinders the seepage of taint through Adrastus' funeral oration, a eulogy that stabilizes their character and natures as worthy heroes against competing traditions. The dead are rhetorically positioned as worthy recipients of Theseus' intervention. In Statius' *Thebaid*, Capaneus' wife offers justification for their recovery and burial that is not particularly persuasive. Her argument is essentially that they are men, not monsters, and deserve burial: "nec querimur caesos: haec bellica iura uicesque | armorum; sed non Siculis exorta sub antris | monstra nec Ossaei bello cecidere bimembres" (*Theb.* 12.552-4).

In Statius' *Thebaid*, Adrastus comes closest to a moral hero. Granted, the events of the war are beyond his control and he is not without flaw. In contrast to the other leaders, Adrastus appears the least disposed toward tyranny, irrespective of his shortcomings. Statius provides him with a certain dignity by letting the best leader of the invading contingent simply recede into the background. At 11.424 Adrastus hears that Polynices and Eteocles are rushing to duel one another. He hurries to set himself physically between them. Adrastus pleads with them and goes so far as to offer his own kingdom, but to no purpose. Adrastus realizes the situation is lost and he departs.[32] This is the last we see of Adrastus. As Vessey notes: "Statius says nothing more of him, for there is nothing more to tell. The gentlest of kings, through the harshness of destiny, has been utterly defeated."[33] Statius, however, never explicitly informs us on Adrastus' whereabouts after he departs, and we can only assume that he returned to his kingdom along with the routed parties (11.757–61). In Euripides' *Suppliants*, however, Adrastus leads the party to Athens that requests Theseus' intervention. His absence from the petition scene of *Thebaid* 12 has an interesting effect. If he were involved in the plea at Athens, he would invariably be characterized as a much weaker character next to Theseus, which is certainly the case in Euripides' *Suppliants*. In lieu of Adrastus' supplication, Statius offers the more histrionic and grief-stricken lament provided by the wives of the fallen heroes, which offers more raw emotional appeal than Adrastus, as he is characterized by Statius, could. The presentation of the Argive cause in *Suppliants* is made by Adrastos, contrary concerns being made by Theseus' mother, Aethra. In the *Thebaid*, however, Theseus is moved entirely by feminine lament.[34]

The absence of Adrastus during the embassy clears the way for Theseus. When Creon takes his position as ruler of Thebes, he is not a particularly stable (or stabilizing) leader. This is evident in his mental state and self-interest. Nevertheless, because he is a cruel tyrant, there is a demand for an oppositional figure, which makes Theseus a savior of Thebes.[35] Despite being the last and strongest man standing at the end, and no matter how much Theseus might control his anger,[36] we should be reluctant to make Theseus more than he is.[37] Statius' troubling characterization of Theseus invites comparison with his Euripidean predecessor. Theseus' behavior does not fall on the side of virtue, or even alliance, which is strongly emphasized in the dramatic treatment. He claims his purposefulness as ἀεὶ κολαστὴς τῶν κακῶν, "always the punisher of evils" (*Supp.* 341).

fidissime Phegeus

Messengers in Statius' *Thebaid* generally receive little attention. There are three named messengers: Mercury, who faithfully discharges the orders of Jupiter; Iris, who visits Somnus on behalf of Juno; and Theseus' "fidissime Phegeus." There is also an unnamed character that Eteocles hates for delivering bad news ("odit | narrantem," *Theb.*7.232–3). Tydeus' embassy to Thebes on behalf of Polynices also associates him with messengers (though he obviously plays a much greater role) and draws some interesting contrasts between the divine and mortal office of "nuntius." Generally, messages are faithfully delivered without omission or embellishment among divine characters. Hermes, for instance, has two major scenes: leading Laius out of Hell and chiding Mars on Jupiter's behalf. At *Thebaid* 1.292–302 Jupiter orders Mercury to bring Laius to his son Eteocles so that he may carry Jove's order of war to his "diro nepoti" (1.298). Mercury and Laius accomplish this through a dream to Eteocles (2.1–124).[38] The second major scene involving Mercury comes when Jupiter is irate over Mars' dallying. Eager to get the war under way, Zeus storms a message to Mercury (7.6–33) and "ille refert consulta patris" (7.81). In both instances divine messengers do as directed. Iris is just as faithful. In order to provide the Argives with a successful night-raid against the Theban camps, Juno sends Iris to the house of Sleep to request that the god provide a dire somnolence among the opposing troops. Iris delivers the request of her mistress to the ever-drowsy god (10.126–31); however, she is not certain that she has been heard and so demonstrates further evidence of being faithful to her duties: "dixit, et increpitans languentia pectora dextra, | ne pereant uoces, iterumque iterumque monebat," "She spoke, and striking his drowsy chest with her hand commanded him again and again, so that her words would not be lost," over and over advising (*Theb*. 10.132–3). Sleep slowly nods, and her task is complete.

The messages and the messengers on the mortal plane, however, do not always reflect the same fidelity as divine messengers. Tydeus is a poor selection to represent Polynices.[39] Statius describes him: "utque rudis fandi pronusque calori | semper erat, iustis miscens tamen aspera coepit," "thus always raw in speech and prone to rage he began mixing true but nevertheless harsh words" (*Theb* 2.391–2). While it is unlikely that Eteocles would relinquish control of the throne to his brother no matter who the messenger was, Tydeus' rash disposition and inability to conform to the model behavior of "nuntius" provides Eteocles with further grounds for holding the throne (2.420–6). Tydeus provokes Eteocles and provides, to his mind at least, sufficient cause for an aggressive response. Indeed, when Eteocles notes that Tydeus shares Polynices' mind (2.417–18), he draws attention to the fact that messengers represent the persons for whom they deliver messages.

Like Tydeus, Theseus' messenger Phegeus cannot control his temper or restrain exaggerations when delivering a message to Creon.[40] As Antigone and Argia are hauled before Creon (dragging their captors in their haste to be punished), Phegeus arrives from Athens bearing the message to the Theban court from Theseus:

> ille quidem ramis insontis oliuae
> pacificus, sed bella ciet bellumque minatur,
> grande fremens, nimiumque memor mandantis, et ipsum
> iam prope, iam medios operire cohortibus agros
> ingeminans.
>
> *Theb*. 12.682–6

He comes peaceful enough with guiltless olive branches, but he rouses war, he threatens war. Boisterous and too mindful of the one who gave him his mandate, he adds that Theseus himself is near, already with his troops overrunning the territories between.

When Theseus calls on Phegeus, "fidissime Phegeu" (12.596), to deliver his message to Creon he relates the ultimatum to his trusted messenger that he is to deliver: "aut Danais edice rogos aut proelia Thebis," "give either pyres to the Danai or war to Thebes" (12.598). Theseus' ultimatum, while not demonstrating more than a modicum of diplomacy, at least offers Creon a choice. Instead of relating the ultimatum, Phegeus zealously declares war. This is quite a subtle detail, but we cannot help but suppose that had Phegeus been truly, rather than ironically, "fidissime Phegeus" things might have gone differently. While Statius undoubtedly develops events at Thebes around large powerful forces, he is acutely aware of how even small details can have larger ramifications. Phegeus' attitude perpetuates the martial spirit that has ravaged Thebes and threatens Creon's newfound position and his war weary people. Phegeus vociferously advocates war, focusing on only half of the offer that Theseus intended for Creon.[41] Phegeus' personal demonstration and exaggeration, his "nimium memor," indicates a further instance of the inability of persons in power to have full confidence in their subjects. Theseus' announcement that Phegeus is "fidissime" smacks of irony. With his zealous embellishment, and the threat of impending war, Phegeus extends Creon no other choice but to prepare the Thebans for a second fight. Before Creon summons his matching response, however, Statius focuses attention on his psychological disposition. The new ruler wavers: "stetit ambiguo Thebanus in aestu | curarum, nutantque minae et prior ira tepescit," "The Theban stood indecisive, worry rises within him; his menace falters and his previous anger cools" (12.686–7). Based on this description of Creon's state and the hallucination that follows, in which he sees the Furies in the palace, Menoeceus weeping, and the Pelsagi on pyres (12.695–97), Creon is undoubtedly overwhelmed.

The image of the overstepping messenger, elaborately adapted to the *Thebaid*, has roots in Euripides' *Suppliants*. After discussing the intervention of Athens against Creon's decree with Adrastus and Aithra, Theseus reaches his decision to intervene. He presents the order his plan is to take, and declares: δράσω τάδ᾽· εἶμι καὶ νεκροὺς ἐκλύσομαι | λόγοισι πείθων· εἰ δὲ μή, βίαι δορὸς | ἤδη τότ᾽ ἔσται κοὐχὶ σὺν φθόνωι θεῶν, "I will do these things: I go to liberate the dead, persuading with words, and if not with the force of spears, the gods will not disagree" (*Supp.* 346–8). Theseus relates how he intends to persuade the Athenian people in this cause and the importance of involving them in the decision.

Faithful to his declaration, Theseus informs the Athenian herald of the message to be taken to Creon (382ff.). The messenger is to relate that the bodies are to be returned to Theseus as χάριν, "goodwill" (385), and that Creon should establish favorable relations with Athens. If not, Creon can prepare for war. This is not wholly dissimilar from the ultimatum delivered by Statius' Theseus.

As Theseus relates the message the herald is to deliver, a messenger from Thebes enters. Theseus plays along with the Theban herald, who adds more than he should to the message he delivers: κομψός γ' ὁ κῆρυξ καὶ παρεργάτης λόγων (*Supp.* 426). Theseus enters into a political *agon* with the herald over the better form of government between tyranny and democracy. Notably, the freedom enjoyed by the herald to speak as he does casts a lackluster light on tyranny, which allows the messenger to put forward a discourse on politics before his task. At the end of their exchange, Theseus gives the herald a stronger rebuff than he had earlier in his critical accusation: περισσὰ φωνῶν (459).[42] Theseus also defines the appropriate discharge of the heraldic office (*Supp.* 459–61). This scene (399–510) provides standing political debate between the two forms of government in Thebes and Athens. It is politically charged, and does nothing to advance the plot or heighten dramatic tension. The messenger scenes between mortals in Statius' *Thebaid* are a skilful adaptation of this exchange. Instead of using the antagonism of messengers toward kings to formulate political positions, Statius uses them to advance war against the Theban people. Statius thus seems to have found exceptional use for a messenger who oversteps what he is charged to say and speaks for himself instead of for his leader to advance the narrative. In two instances, perhaps, things might have been different if reliable messengers were sent. In the *Thebaid*, it almost appears that disaster could have once more been averted if someone had more effectively discharged their duties. Whereas Tydeus' embassy reveals aspects of Eteocles' character (and Tydeus' as well), Phegeus' speech heightens, even exaggerates, the furiousness of Theseus and indicates Creon's inability to govern, which is consistent with the instability present throughout the epic.

Perhaps under the strain of losing his son, enduring one war, and entering another with Theseus, Creon reveals himself unfit for rule; we have now, to some degree, Theseus as a model, though not ideal, ruler.[43] Creon leads Thebes into a fresh conflict; the first under its new king. We may be tempted to examine Creon as yet another tyrant in what is clearly an unfortunate succession of cruel and unjust rulers; however, this misses something of the point Statius seems to stress. Eteocles and Creon are not only heavy-handed and uneven (and even Polynices promises to be equally bad) they are not models of stability. Until the arrival of

Theseus, Statius offers only examples of unstable leaders and the effect they have on those they lead. As Vessey remarks: "To have concluded the tale with the death of the sons of Oedipus and the accession of Creon would have been to make the *Thebaid* a statement of despairing nihilism."[44] I do not agree completely with Vessey's statement, only that Theseus' image, especially as a leader, provides a counter-point to the image of leaders already endured. In the latter half of the final book Statius casts Theseus as a ruler capable of bringing stability to Thebes—whether anyone likes it or not. And this promise of stability anticipates at least a temporary closure to the narrative.

Particularly noteworthy is the powerful effect that Theseus has on the people that he leads. Not only is he unmindful of his own exhaustion from the march home, but he inspires his men with new vigor when they are to set out for Thebes (12.599–600). His weary troops, and even the untrained people of the countryside, are inspired to follow him against Creon (12.611–13).[45] More remarkable still is the way in which Hippolyta and her vanquished people have been assimilated to Theseus' army. She herself wants to lead the Arctoas against Thebes but, being pregnant, Theseus insists that she remain behind. These preparatory moments as Theseus rallies for battle invite comparison with the departure of the Argives for Thebes in *Thebaid* 4: "illi, quis ferrum modo, quis mors ipsa placebat, | dant gemitus fractaeque labant singultibus irae," "Those who had clamored for the sword, for even death itself, now offer groans; broken, their anger gives way to weeping" (4.22–3). Similarly, in contradistinction to Theseus' eager army, Creon's Theban forces are in no fit condition for another war.[46] When the moment of engagement arrives, much of the Theban army is routed in fear (12.736). Creon makes an effort to command his army. When Theseus sees him on the battlefield he notes:

> ... hortantem dictis frustraque extrema minantem
> conspicit; abscedunt comites: sed Thesea iussi
> linquebant fretique deis atque ipsius armis,
> ille tenet reuocatque suos; utque aequa notauit
> hinc atque hinc odia, extrema se colligit ira
>
> *Theb.* 12.755–9

He sees him rousing his men with words, threatening them with hollow ends; his allies withdraw: but Theseus' so ordered depart him, confident in the gods and Theseus' arms. Creon holds and recalls his men, and where he finds his hatred matched, he draws on the extent of his wrath.

Thus, Statius provides one of the most important and decisive contrasts between a stabilizing and effective leader and failure. Creon has the superior position, but cannot comparably command his forces. Similarly, Adrastus, Polynices, and Eteocles fail to exercise the same degree of power over their military forces as Theseus. Theseus stabilizes Thebes. His army was weary, but he inspired them. The Amazons were so well and effectively conquered that they, as well as the people from the countryside, would follow him into battle. Moreover, the substance of their conviction is retained in the chaos of war. His men still follow his command.

After the death of Creon,[47] the people of Thebes give themselves to the victor. While there seems to be little choice for them, their response is consistent with the fealty that Theseus inspires (*Theb.* 12.782-7). While opinion of Theseus and his sincerity remains divided, we cannot overlook that he brings peace to a city lacking stability.[48] That appears to be the explicit message put forward at the end of the epic. Pollmann suggests that Theseus' willingness to enter the houses reveals his wish not to destroy Thebes, which invites a comparison to Euripides' *Suppliants* 723-30 where Theseus refuses to occupy the city.[49] This visitation does not necessarily mean that he would be quick to release what he has captured. Tacitus' most cutting criticism against Domitian is that Rome too quickly lost what it had acquired.[50] It seems unlikely that, with a prevailing "forma mentis" of imperial expansion in Flavian Rome, once Theseus conquers Creon he should pass up any claim to Thebes. Instead, the implication here is that force and might prevail. What Theseus brings to the Theban situation, what political order remains, is left undisclosed by Statius.[51] It is a disappointment that Statius introduces Theseus (a third ending to the poem) only to leave this aspect of the finale so wide open and inconclusive. Yet, in the end, an order that the Thebans welcome is brought to their city; this is what Theseus offers the Theban tragedy.

Notes

Introduction: notum iter ad Thebas

1. Translations are my own throughout.
2. Cf. Heuvel (1932) 101 and Bernstein (2008) 75.
3. For other instances of distance to be traveled as a metaphor for narrative in the *Thebaid* see "unde iubetis | ire deae," "From what point would you have me begin, gods?" (*Theb*. 1.3–4) and "quo tenditis iras," "where does the wrath tend?" (*Theb*. 1.155).
4. See Watson and Watson (2003) 96 who consider the possibility Martial attacks Statius in this passage. See also McNelis (2007) 178ff.
5. For further discussion of Statius' *saphragis* see Dominik (2003) 91–109.
6. See Schachter (1967) 1–10.
7. On Statius' familiarity with Antimachus' *Thebais* see Fillipis (1901) 125–8; however, Vessey (1973) 69 is doubtful.
8. See Matthews (1996) 21–2.
9. Notably, Hadrian preferred Antimachus to Homer, which suggests that Antimachus was still being circulated and enjoyed after Statius. See *Vita Hadriana* 16.2 and Dio 69.4.6. See also Propertius 2.34.45 and Quintilian 10.1.53.
10. Pollmann (2004) 28.
11. Propertius 1.7.1–2. Propertius also touches on some the story's highlights (2.34.32–42).
12. McNelis (2007) 21–22.
13. Burnett (1988) 107ff. provides a concise review of this debate.
14. Hardie (1983) 10. Cf. Holford-Strevens (2000) 47–8.
15. Burnett (1988) 113–4, 119.
16. Tarrant (1978) 230 argues that the drama is complete and represents an attempt at a new experimental form of tragedy. If Seneca's play is complete, it is a poor adaptation of the traditional episodes and perhaps deserves to be called "experimental."
17. Cf. Braun (1867) 245–75, Vessey (1973) 271 and Davis (1993). Mendell (1967) 120 suggests that Statius is to the rhetorical epic what Seneca is to the rhetorical tragedy. Likewise, Barchiesi (2001) 326 declares "the *Thebaid* is a tragic spectacle, a post-Senecan epic." Both authors are concerned with tyranny, excessive power, *nefas*, and strife between brothers. See in particular Frings (1992) 15–36, as well as Herington (1966) 438, Poe (1983) 141, Henry and Henry (1985) 157–76, Boyle (1988) 95, Schiessaro (1994) 196–210, Tarrant (1995) 228–9, Fantham (1997) 190–9, Delarue (2000) 141–76, Aricò (2002) 169–84, and Davis (2003) 84.

18 For catalogs and discussions of the several intertexts between Euripides' *Phoenissae* and Statius' *Thebaid* see Legras (1905) 125ff., Fiehn (1917) 76ff., Reussner (1921), Vessey (1973) 69–78, and Fernandelli (2000) 89–98. Heslin (2008) brings in a broader reading of tragedy and Statius generally. See also Henderson (1993) 182 and Fantham (1997) 190.
19 Aélion (1983) 197–227, Natanblut (2005) 17–20, and Lamari (2010) 16–20.
20 Cribiore (2001) 241–59. See also Bremer (1985) 281–8.
21 Bremer (1985) 287–8 offers a convenient review of these.
22 Cf. Pollmann (2004) 287. The theme certainly marries well with the priorities of Roman education, see Keith (2000) 8–35.
23 Cf. Williams (1986) 212–14.
24 Dominik (2005) 525–6.
25 Segal (1983) 176.
26 Fuchs (2000) 89–202. See also Cave (2009).
27 Ortony, Clore, and Collins (1988) 131.
28 Gerrig (1993). Fuchs (2000) applies a similar method to his study of *Electra*, and affords this advantage to the performance of drama. Additionally, Duckworth (1931) and (1933) warrant consideration.
29 Beecher (2007) 255.
30 Pratt (1939) 1, following Flint (1922) 84–7, suggests that there are two types of dramatic suspense: "uncertainty" and "anticipation," as well as other variations and combinations.
31 Ogilvie (1980) 233.
32 Cf. Heath (1989) 69. Moore (1921) 167 suggests that "the fratricide had long been fixed by literary tradition as the crisis of the Theban story."
33 See Moore (1921) 167. Hutchinson (1993) 175 remarks that "we are often pointed explicitly forward, and the resemblance and especially the contrast with the coming war are repeatedly dwelt on." Nugent (1996) 274 maintains that lament is central to the poem's forward narrative. Dominik (1994b) 23 and Markus (2004) 114 note the use of speech acts to advance the narrative, which may also take cues from drama.
34 The most reasonable division is in halves: a "praeparare bellum gerareque." So Reussner (1921) 2, Kytzler (1996) 25ff., and Frank (1965) 309–18 who argue for a bi-partite structure based on the *Aeneid*: books 1–6 relate the preparations for war, books 7–12 relate the events of the war with a sophisticated system of parallelisms between the two halves. Frank argues the *Thebaid* further subdivides into four less emphatic triads. Vessey (1973) 317–28 and Schetter (1960) 89–90 and 96–121 divide the book into four fairly distinct triads. Dominik (1996) 55 divides the *Thebaid* into three "broad" sections: the initial "impetus of the narrative toward war," the delay at Nemea, and "the reactuation of the narrative toward war." Vessey (1973) 320 further reads the *Thebaid* as a *carmen perpetuum*; although, this forces an unsuccessful analog to Ovid's *Metamorphoses*.

35 See Duff (1960) 377, Gossage (1972) 233, and Dewar (1991) xvii.
36 Vessey (1973) 55–8. See also Markus (2002) 431–67.
37 Feeney (1991) 339.
38 Cf. Brooks (1992) 12.
39 Cf. Tversky (1974) 1124–31.
40 As Else (1986) 163 points out, Aristotle offers only comparison. Aristotle's *Poetics* honors the *Iliad*; however, it does not offer a definition of epic equal to its definition of tragedy.
41 For further discussion of Aristotle's views on epic in the *Poetics* see Hogan (1973) 95–108.
42 Hogan (1973) 95. For a discussion of the narrative affinities between epic and dramatic tragedy see Goward (1999) 2–20.
43 Vessey (1970c) 48 notes the compression expected in tragic drama in relation to the Hypsipyle narrative and the "broader canvas" of expansion allowed by epic. Similarly, Mendell (1967) 118 suggests that Statius "introduced a vast amount of additional material in order to extend the tale to a total of twelve books, which he took as the orthodox number set by Virgil."
44 Vessey (1973) 55 uses the inherent expansiveness of epic to defend the *Thebaid* for being episodic, though the *Thebaid* is too well oriented toward its climax to be dismissed as episodic.
45 O'Neill (1996) 33.
46 Bal (1985) 175–216. Bal regards these as the elements of "fabula." It is an unfortunate matter, but one that cannot be overlooked, that terms often undergo some slippage or tuning from one narratologist to the next, some of which I address in the next chapter. Here, by narrative I mean, broadly, what O'Neill calls "story" and Bal calls "fabula." For a helpful crib to this terminology see O'Neill (1996).

Chapter 1

1 Genette (1980) 36 and Bal (1985) 53. As DeJong (2004) 90 notes, the use of anachrony can "create a dramatic irony and suspense, incite pathos, elicit pity, signal the importance of symbolical value of objects, recall important information and provide background information." For a helpful summary of uses among canonical Greek authors see DeJong and Nünlist (2007) 508–15.
2 Genette (1980) 40. See also Bal (1985) 53 who defines anachrony as "chronological deviations."
3 Genette (1980) 40.
4 Genette (1983) 48.
5 Nünlist (2009) 45. Bal (1985) 54 eschews "flashback" as well as "flashforward" in the case of prolepsis due to their "vagueness and psychological connotations."

6 Bridgeman (2005) 130.
7 Cf. Bal (1985) 60 who defines analepses as "external retroversions" that "often provide indications about the antecedents, the past of the actors concerned, in so far as that past can be made of importance for the interpretation of events."
8 Brooks (1992) 93-4. Cf. τὸ δὲ τέλος μέγιστον ἁπάντων (*Poet.* 1450a23).
9 Indeed, Meir Sternberg (1978) 50 suggests a narrative is just a "dynamic system of gaps."
10 Cf. Craik (1988) 167.
11 Pratt (1939) 1-14.
12 Pratt (1939) 5. Pratt further cites Aristotle *Poetics* 1451b and Athenaeus 6.222-3a.
13 See Aélion (1983) 199, Luschnig (1995) 171, Falkner (1995) 193, Mastronarde (1994) 25, and Craik (1988) 41.
14 On the formulaic qualities of this Euripidean prologue see Rutherford (2012) 179-181.
15 Because Jocasta acts as a narrator, despite her position as a subject within the drama, the application of narrative theory becomes that much more compelling. On the application of narrative theory to drama see Lamari (2010) 5-16 and Goward (1999) 9-13. Historically, we should bear in mind, the drama has been read much more often than it has been seen. Cf. Brian (1997) 195.
16 See Rutherford (2012) 181.
17 On the theatrical space in the prologue see Papadopoulou (2008) 92-3 and Luschnig (1995) 182-3.
18 Hall (2010) 282. On Thebes as a counter-Athens see Zeitlin (1986) 101-41.
19 For narratological analysis of Jocasta's relationship with the past and its misfortunes see Lamari (2010) 23-33.
20 See Mikalson (1989) 97-8 on Helios as an impassive god.
21 For general review see Arthur (1977) n. 2.
22 Zeitlin (1986) 102.
23 Cf. Arthur (1977) 163: "Thus, the present disasters of the city are linked with its origins; the act of Cadmus has culminated somehow in fraternal hostilities."
24 Cf. Sternberg (1978) 35-41. Yet as Bal (1985) 52-3 notes: "Playing with the sequential ordering is not just a literary convention; it is also a means of drawing attention to certain things, to emphasize, to bring about aesthetic or psychological effects, to show various interpretations of events, to indicate subtle differences between expectation and realizations, and much else besides."
25 As Lloyd (2007) 295 notes Euripides' use of a prologue speech to lay out the prehistory "leads to problems identifying the point in the story at which the plot begins."
26 In principle, as Genette (1980) 36 notes, beginning a narrative *in medias res* requires a later "expository return to an earlier period of time."

27 Treating the speech act of a character remains somewhat challenging. As a mimetic presentation, some would argue against using Jocasta's opening speech as an example of analepsis. As Bal (1985) 57 notes, when what has or will have happened is presented as direct discourse "the moment of speech is simply part of the (chronological) story; only in the contents are the past or future mentioned." For Lloyd (2007) 296 and de Jong and Nünlist (2007) 511 dramatic prologues serve as a "retrospective narrative" with a function similar to analepsis. Jocasta's "retrospective narrative" presents a fundamentally analeptic content, through which hearers are refocused in the past, thus the more developed aspects of non-chronological narration found in analepsis appear germane.
28 Cf. Toolan (1988) 54.
29 On scripts and their relation to temporal and causal expectations in narrative see Herman (1997) 1046–59.
30 Mastronarde (1994) 139.
31 Craik (1988) 41.
32 As Flint (1921) 47 discusses, there were two narrative traditions in play. In one, popular among dramatists, Jocasta commits suicide after the anagnoresis, as in Homer, Sophocles, and possibly Aeschylus since she is not present in the *Septem*. Citing Pausanias 9.4.2 and 9.5.11, Flint maintains that another tradition, likely present in the Cyclic *Thebais* preserved Jocasta until the fratricidal conflict. This, of course, depends on Jocasta and Euryganeia being the same person.
33 Cf. Lamari (2010) 23–4.
34 On Jocasta's emphasis on family background as she "makes the various ties of kinship clear ... and with this the ways in which the family relationships have become confused and poisoned" see Rawson (1970) 114. See also Sewell-Rutter (2007) 36–7.
35 Lamari (2010) 25.
36 So also *Antigone* 53 where the successive force of ἔπειτα puts her suicide just after the revelation of Oedipus' identity, not after the death of her sons.
37 So Aélion (1983) 199, Luschnig (1995) 171, Mastronarde (1994) 25, and Craik (1988) 41. See also Segal (1992) 91–2.
38 Lowe (2004) 71.
39 So Aélion (1983) 199, for instance, remarks: « Si la présence d'Oedipe est une innovation frappante, plus frappante encore est la présence de Jocaste. Mais Euripide n'a peut-être pas inventé le personnage de la mère, déchirée par la lutte sans merci que se livrent ses fils. »
40 See Aélion (1983) 197–227 and Lamari (2010) 16–20.
41 Cf. Craik (1988) 164 and Papadopoulou (2008) 49.
42 This kind of anachrony can get messy. As Herman (2002) 211–26 alerts us, what constitutes temporality within the classical discussions led by Genette is rarely

distinct, and is often quite "fuzzy." Cf. Genette (1980) 83. The power of the prophecy here is precisely in its being both present and absent, both affecting the narrative outcome, while being removed from those events.

43 Falkner (1995) 197 reads this as their "rite of passage *manqué*."
44 Craik (1988) 41.
45 The two longest surviving fragments of the cyclic *Thebais* cite Oedipus' poor treatment by his sons and the curse he invokes against them. See Davies (1989) 23–25.
46 Euripides' use of supernatural devices like prophecies and curses to anticipate future events is uncommon, but serves a vital, though conventional, purpose here. See Rawson (1970) 124, Goward (1999) 122, and Lloyd (2007) 299.
47 See LSJ *sub*. συμβαίνω.
48 See *Phoen*. 1359–76. See Mikalson (1989) 81–2 for discussion.
49 Cf. Brooks (1984) 109: "It is characteristic of textual energy in narrative that it should always be on the verge of premature discharge, of short-circuit. The reader experiences the fear—and excitation—of the improper end, which is symmetrical to—but far more immediate and present than—the fear of endlessness."
50 Lamari (2010) 28. Cf. Lowe (2004) 39: "…if the anticipation of an ending is to feed into our narrative model, we need to know in advance when the clock is going to be stopped—to have, as it were, an alarm set."
51 Lamari (2010) 30–1.
52 Falkner (1995) 198 reads this as an effeminization and domestication of Oedipus.
53 See Mandler and Johnson (1977) 111–51.
54 As Ricoeur (2002) 40 notes: "Following a story, correlatively, is understanding the successive actions, thoughts, and feelings in question *insofar as they present a certain directedness*. By this I mean that we are pushed ahead by this development and that we reply to its impetus with expectations concerning the outcome and the completion of the entire process" [my italics].
55 Cf. Braund (2006) 262.
56 So Moore (1921) 167 suggests that "the fratricide had long been fixed by literary tradition as the crisis of the Theban story."
57 See Hall (2008) 395 v. III. See also related discussion on Barthius' manuscripts generally 64-8.
58 Vessey (1986) 2969–70.
59 Dominik (1994b) 71 on Eteocles' initial innocence and the disparity between Jupiter's actions and his claim at 1.300.
60 See also Ganiban (2007) 45.
61 Cf. Vessey (1986) 2971.
62 Morson (1994) 234–5.
63 See Vessey (1986) 2969. See also Caviglia (1973) 87 and Braund (2006) 262.
64 See Mandler and Johnson (1977) 111–51.
65 Vessey (1986) 2968.

66 On the use of ellipsis as narrative device see Toolan (1988) 56-7.
67 As Genette (1983) 83 remarks: "when later is earlier, and earlier later, defining the direction of movement becomes a delicate task." For discussion of the "present" and perspective in the *Aeneid* see Kennedy (2013) 67-9. Markantonatos (2002) 30 sagely notes: "unqualified command of the past allows the narrator to stake a mighty claim on the future."
68 See also Hyginus *Fabulae* 6.76. Antimachus fr. 3 references the rape of Europa and her being hidden in the Teumissian cave by Zeus, though Vessey (1970a) 121 conjectures Antimachus' development of preliminary material was limited, based on Tydeus' presence in *Thebais* 1. See also Matthews (1996) 84-91.
69 Notably excess is a charge brought against Euripides *Phoinissae*. See Dunn (1996) 190-7. Kitto (1939) 356 summarizes several views in his claim that "[o]ut of the Theban legend he is creating what we may call a dramatic pageant, presenting scene after scene for the sake of their immediate and cumulative effect, but not for the sake of an inner drama; therefore he needs a lot of material but need not be particular about its cohesion."
70 *Metamorphoses* 1.2-4. Cf. Fantham (2004) 5.
71 Rosati (2002) 231 notes "longa retro series" admits the tensions of defining the *Thebaid*'s place within a long literary and mythic tradition.
72 Heath (1989) 69 suggests: "Statius has chosen, not simply a 'single action,' but that kind of unified action of which Aristotle approved most highly; to reject the whole story of Thebes or the Labdacid house is precisely to reject a unified plot of many parts."
73 The *Thebaid*'s proem has enjoyed pronounced discussion. See notably Carrara (1986) 146-58, Criado (1998) 122-35, and Rosati (2002). The Domitianic interlude has been a particular sticking point, so Kytzler (1960) 331-54, Schetter (1962) 204-17, and Criado (1996) 53-76.
74 On the order of presentation in the proem and the *aristeia* of the heroes see Vessey (1973) 65.
75 For discussion of Clio within Statius' *oeuvre* and in lyric intertext with Horace see Georgacopoulou (1996) 171-5. Notably, Clio was also Valerius Flaccus' choice (*Argonautica* 3.15).
76 Cf. Vessey (1973) 65.
77 Cf. Bruner (1991) 11-13. See also Lowe (2004) 28-9, 52.

Chapter 2

1 Taisne (1994) 179. See Goward (1999) 35 on the use of the supernatural to "create a structure of expectation, mingled hopes and fears, toward a particular outcome ... built up by the use of prophecy and dream." Cf. Moore (1921) 166-72.

2   So de Jong and Nünlist (2007) 514: "Actorial internal prolepsis regularly takes the form of either apprehensive or optimistic emotions. A special type are prophecies, dreams, and omens which can be found in several texts."
3   Cf. Carroll (2001) 265 who insists that suspense requires an affective disposition toward characters, mainly moral and positive. Cf. Tan (1985) 102. See also Nünlist (2009) 38 who supposes narratorial prolepsis increases sympathetic feeling.
4   The operation within epic is not so dissimilar from that of tragic drama. As Goward (1999) 25 describes: "The stage action manifests itself as a series of events seen with the heightened perception of foreknowledge as working towards an inevitable end. This perspective contrasts ironically with the stage figures' inability to understand what will happen (despite receiving the same advance notification) until too late."
5   Cf. Euripides *Phoen.* 343.
6   The Klotz-Klinnert, Hill, and Hall editions prefer "adiuncta" at 244. I prefer, however, the reading offered by Garrod, following Lachmann, who places an interjective "a" before "iuncta," which dramatizes the decree.
7   See Legras (1905) 36, Reussner (1921) 6, and Vessey (1973) 134–9.
8   See Hulls (2014) 199–201. As Statius indicates the motivation for conflict has little to do with the value of Thebes, but much to do with a perverse desire for power: "sed nuda potestas | armauit fratres, pugna est de paupere regno" 1.151. In Euripides' *Phoenissae* (552–67) Jocasta argues that a war against Argos will be costly and cut into the wealth that Eteocles covets, and by implication that which Polynices would retain if he were successful.
9   As Franchet d'Espèrey (1999) 235 observes Adrastus is the first non-violent character Statius introduces in the epic.
10 The narrator, however, had contradicted this at *Theb.* 1.425.
11 Reussner (1921) 11–15 discusses the cloaks in relation to Euripides' *Phoenissae*. See also Holland (1976) 32 who maintains that the garb of the heroes prefigures "the brutal potential of the principal warriors and their fate."
12 The sentiment recalls Aeneas' hopeful speculation: "Forsan et haec olim meminisse iuvabit," "Perhaps even these things will be a delight to recall" (1.203). Note, however, that a positive telos has been established for Aeneas, despite his obstacles and sufferings.
13 Bernstein (2008) 72–7 argues that this claim reveals how very limited Adrastus' awareness of the situation truly is. See also Bernstein (2003) 364–9.
14 Ten Kate (1955) 105 suggests that Statius is careful to supress Adrastus' genealogical closeness to Capaneus and thus spare him violent actions. Similarly, as Braswell (1998) 80 speculates, Pindar's *Nemea* 9 selectively handles Adrastus' lineage, suggesting "the poet has told only half the story, and the less incriminating part at that, presumably to spare the reputation of Adrastos."
15 For discussion of Adrastus' reluctance to proceed with the war see Franchet d'Espèrey (1999) 99–102.

16 Adrastus is also sleepless and indecisive about the war (3.440-51) and at 8.260 he listens to the merry making Thebans and anticipates a bad future.
17 Statius appears to borrow from Evander's speech in which he offers military aid to Aeneas for Adrastus. See McNelis (2007) 27-9 and Gervais (2017a) 120.
18 Polynices will claim, in his last conversation with his father-in-law that he is "an accursed guest, better to have arrived in some other city," "infelix utinamque aliis datus urbibus hospes" (11.166).
19 If Lucretius 4.1274-7 is a reliable authority, Tydeus and Polynices can expect a subdued and uneventful honeymoon with their brides. Vessey (1973) 100 suggests Statius may have had his own stepdaughter in mind.
20 See Gervais (2017a) 152-3.
21 So Jupiter had anticipated: "superis ah, iuncta sinistris," 1.244.
22 As Gervais (2017a) 158 points out the presence of Lachesis, one of the three canonical Fates, demonstrates that there are multiple agencies engaged in bringing about suffering and misfortune.
23 Mulder (1954) 185 recognizes the creation of a shift in expectation created by "ecce meto subito...," which creates a sudden shared experience in fright.
24 Cf. Duff (1960) 473.
25 Gervais (2017a) 162 suggests the event undermines the people's confidence in their leader.
26 The necklace has strong referential similarities with Virgil's description of Allecto's infection of Amata at *Aeneid* 7.346-53. See McNelis (2007) 55. So Davis (1994) 468 claims the necklace is "virtually coeval with Thebes itself." Similarly, Feeney (1991) 364 maintains, the necklace is an "internally bound miniature of pettiness and vice."
27 Gervais (2017a) 177 suggests that Statius' "appeal to tradition actually signals that St[atius] has invented the involvement of Harmonia's necklace in the history of Thebes."
28 Apollodorus (*Bibl.* 3.6.1) and Diodorus Siculus (4.65.5) both attest that Polynices took with him into exile the necklace and robe of Cadmus' wife Harmonia, daughter of Venus and Mars.
29 On the emphasis Statius places on the necklace as a gift see Coffee (2009) 192.
30 Cf. Coffee (2009) 192-3.
31 Argia's apprehensiveness constitutes an actorial internal prolepsis. See de Jong and Nünlist (2007) 514.
32 Dominik (2005) 521.
33 Hershkowitz (1997) 37-42 maintains a Virgilian connection between this scene and Venus' plaint to Jupiter and his comforting response (*Aen.* 1.223ff.), and correspondence with Lucan's Cornelia and Pompey (*BC* 5.734ff.). See also Gervais (2017a) 192.
34 Bessone (2002) 199 demonstrates Argia's relationship to the *relicta* theme emphasizing the generic confluence of elegy in Statius' epic.

35 The presence of Melampus is, as scholars have noted, peculiar. Vessey (1973) 183 and Fantham (2006) 150 each note the dramatic features provided by the use of the second priest.
36 Cf. Fantham (2006) 147.
37 Fantham (2006) 153 suggests this is modeled on *Bellum Civile* 1.685–6, the vision of Pompey's death.
38 Other characters similarly have foreboding knowledge of the future, though without the intensity and pathos of Amphiaraus. Maeon also has a minor vocation in augury and foresaw all that would happen, but Cassandra-like was denied by Fate the ability to convince anyone (2.690–5). Lycurgus (3.650ff.) knows before he returns to his kingdom that something horrible has befallen his family.
39 Snijder (1968) 251.
40 See Vessey (1973) 157–9.
41 Cf. Sheppard (1913) 81–2.
42 Fantham (2006) 160 reads "ibimus" as an intertextual echo of the declaration of Aeschylus' Amphiaraus on the banks of Ismenus: "μαχώμεθ," "We fight" (Sept. 589).
43 Cf. Ahl (1986) 2899.
44 *Bellum Civile* 1.673–95.
45 As Parkes (2012) 212 notes this is a rare occurrence, which "reflects the brothers' reciprocal destruction."
46 Parkes (2012) 213.
47 For intertext see *Odyssey* 11.13–640 and *Bellum Civile* 6.642–51 (note the courteous nod to Lucan's Thessalian witch at 4.504–5). Parkes (2012) 214–15, 217 cites parallels with Seneca's *Oedipus*.
48 Cf. Laius' prophecy offered as a dream, which also reassured Eteocles.
49 For the Stoic context to this passage see Vessey (1973) 156. Tacitus also condemns telling the future, where Otho's trust in the predictability of the future allows a round attack of his character (*Hist.* 1.22).
50 See Goward (1999) 42, Bal (1985) 19–23, and Rimmon-Kenan (1983) 22–7.

Chapter 3

1 On Statius' use of "morae" see Parkes (2012) xvii–xx and 284; McNelis (2007) 93 and Feeney (1991) 339 find in Archemorus' name the "Originator of Delay" (ἀρχή and *mora*) *contra* Mozley (1928) 560 who explains the name's etymology (ἀρχή and Μόρος). See also Vessey (1973) 165–7 and (1986) 2988–93.
2 For instance, in *Aen.* 1.124 "interea" marks the shift between the storms that have overtaken Aeneas' fleet and Neptune's realization of the unsanctioned inclement weather.

3   Parkes (2012) 282 suggests that "interea" draws attention the narrative's digressive nature.
4   Parkes (2012) 283.
5   Statius calls on Apollo to impart, "doce," historical or factual, rather than poetic, inspiration. Compare his role in revealing protoempirical knowledge of phenomena at *Theb.* 6.360–64. Cf. Brown (1994) 41–3 and Myers (2015) 43.
6   Hartung (1843) suggests Euripides' *Hypsipyle, Antiope*, and *Phoenissae* belong to the same sequence, based on the Scholia for Aristophanes' *Ranae* 53.
7   Aricò (1961) nominates the Hypsipyle as a possible source for Statius. Vessey (1970) 48–51 is more skeptical, as is Brown (1994) 99. More often, Statius' *Thebaid* is used, rightly or wrongly, to understand aspects of Euripides' play. Cf. Görschen (1966).
8   Cicero's *Tusculan Disputations* 24 describes how Carneades condemns Amphiaraus' platitudinous speech in the *Hypsipyle*.
9   Notably, *Hypothesis* 2 and 4 of Pindar's *Nemean Odes* offer thirst (διψήσαντες), rather than a religious rite, as the motivation for the Argives' search for water. See Bond (1963) 148.
10 As Henderson (1993) 183 notes "it is as if Virgil's Andromache were to step out of her narrated inclusion within Aeneas' perspective and takes over the telling of *Aeneid* 2 and 3 for a *Troades*-style narrative."
11 See Legras (1905) 152. Butler (1909) 165 suggests her narrative is a "digression within a digression," though Nugent (1996) 69 maintains the episode is more than mere digression. See also Ogilvie (1980) 233.
12 Götting (1969) reads Hypsipyle's narrative against Odysseus' narrative in the palace of Alcinous and Aeneas' narrative in Dido's court. See also Gruzelier (1994) 154, Brown (1994) 99–102, Nugent (1996) 49, and Casali (2003) 60–8. Moerner (1890) 23–35 identifies similarities between Statius' Lemnian treatment and that of Apollonius and Valerius Flaccus, noting also the loss of possible sources from Sophocles and Aeschylus. For Statius' complex positioning of Hypsipyle within the allusive framework of his own epic program see Gibson (2004). Aricò (1961) draws a number of parallels between the Statian and Euripidean texts.
13 Götting (1969) 84–6, Vessey (1970) 45–7, and Vessey (1973) 170. Augoustakis (2011) 32 Hypsipyle's narrative as presage to the Theban war.
14 Dominik (1994) 54–63.
15 Vessey (1973) 177 suggests Hypsipyle has an affinity with Jocasta in that both are "majestic and sad."
16 As Dominik (1994) 56 notes, it is a "mini-epic…an epic within an epic."
17 Vessey (1970c) 44–8.
18 Vessey (1986) 2993 finds in Adrastus' exhortation "an invitation to compose a poem."
19 This recalls Aeneas' "Infandum, regina, iubes renouare dolorem," "Awful woes you have asked me to revisit, Queen" (*Aen.* 2.3).

20 Note the epic flavor of "debellatos manes," where the sense is to be completely conquered at the end of a war.
21 Her *ersatz*-vatic prelude invites comparison with Statius' introduction to the *Thebaid* in which he is overcome by the scope of the Theban mythos. The horror of the story overwhelms her and a Fury, "Eumenis," rather than Pierian fire, "inspires" her. Cf. Hypsipyle's response to Euneos, her son, in Euripides' *Hypsisyple*. When he asks about the Lemnian massacres, she replies: φόβος ἔχει με τῶν τότε κακῶν, "Fear seizes me—these evils!," 757, 1597).
22 Note in this sequence the emphasis of pronouns: "illa ego," "illa," "quae," and capped with "sola."
23 Cf. Brooks (1984) 109 who maintains that "it is characteristic of textual energy in narrative that it should always be on the verge of premature discharge, of short-circuit. The reader experiences the fear—and excitation—of the improper end, which is symmetrical to—but far more immediate and present than—the fear of endlessness."
24 Hypsipyle baits the Argives with poetry, so Persius 1.23 and Petronius 3.4. For discussion see Bramble (1974) 143-6.
25 Notably, Augoustakis (2011) 32 suggests that Hypsipyle "lulls the Argives into a metaphorical sleep."
26 Statius' description is brief. Valerius Flaccus, whose Venus enters Lemnos like a Fury rather than with the Furies as in the *Thebaid*, outdoes Hypsipyle's description in terrible aspect at *Arg*. 2.104-6.
27 The play of knowledge between audience and character to create suspense is ubiquitous throughout literature, Lowe (2004) 12.
28 Cf. Apollonius Rhodius *Arg*. 1.668, Hyginus *Fab*. 15, Valerius Flaccus *Arg*. 2.315ff. As a culprit in liege with Furies, Pausanias 3.19.9-10 recounts an interesting story in which one mytho-historic Polyxo married Tlepolemus, leader of the Rhodian forces at Troy, who was murdered by Helen. To avenge her husband Polyxo sent servants dressed as Erinyes to murder Helen in turn.
29 See Euripides' *Medea* 1236-50.
30 Vessey (1970c) explores several parallels between the Lemnian episode and the Theban narrative.
31 Nugent (1996) 63 finds a seed of anticipation in this murder scene, where "at this moment of fatal encounter between husband and wife, the text seems poised precariously between murder and rape."
32 Cf. *Hyps*. 752g 1-15.
33 Nugent (1996) 51 points out "Hypsipyle's response to Adrastus' request that she narrate her painful past uncannily prefigures 'the talking cure' that is the discourse of psychoanalysis."
34 Cf. Lesueur (1992) 238, Nugent (1996) 54-5, and Gibson (2004) 161.
35 Cf. Scodel (1997) 93.

36 *Hyps.* fr. 754 similarly describes Opheltes in the meadow collecting flowers: ἕτερον ἐφ' ἑτέρῳ †αἰρόμενος† | ἄγρευμ' ἀνθέων ἡδομένᾳ ψυχᾷ | τὸ νήπιον ἄπληστον ἔχων. The use of ἄγρευμα ascribes qualities to the infant that are not characteristic of a child. The flowers are his prey, the spoils of his conquest. The image is strong in its juxtaposition of violent capture and the picking of flowers. Statius, however, elevates the association of Opheltes not to that of adult hunter but divinity (i.e. Mars and Apollo 5.801-3).

37 Cf. Hor. *Epod.* 1.19-22.

38 Her anxiety for punishment was similarly critical to the dramatic effect in Euripides' *Hypsipyle.* At 753d.16 she cries to the chorus: ὠλόμαν, "I am lost" and at 754b.7 she fears what will happen to her (δέδο[ι]κα θ[αν]άτῳ παιδὸς οἷα πείσομ[αι, "With the child's death I fear what I will suffer"). She also conceives a plot to escape, no doubt to avoid a likely death sentence against her. Cf. Bond (1963) 96-7. Hypsipyle discusses her plans with the chorus. The reality that she is powerless to make an escape on her own is made clear as she asks: τί δ' εἴ τιν' εὕρ[ο]ιμ' [ὅστ]ις ἐξάξε[ι] με γῆς; "Yet who will free me from this land?" (754b.15). The remaining lines are badly damaged but Grenfell and Hunt (1908) 95 speculate that the chorus responds that no one is willing to help a slave.

39 Bond (1963) 65.

40 Wilamowitz-Möllendorff suggests that Hypsipyle is petitioning the strangers at Lycurgus' palace (who will turn out to be her sons) for rescue from her slavery. As recorded in Grenfell and Hunt (1908) 102 who consulted Wilamowitz-Möllendorff and other scholars on the fragments. Bond (1963) speculates that at this point Hypsipyle would have mentioned her hopes of acquiring freedom through Opheltes. The fragment, however, is too incomplete and resists definite conclusions.

41 See Bond (1963) 92 and Grenfell and Hunt (1908) 97.

42 Cf. Euripides *Hyps.* 757.847-8 where Hypsipyle appears to plead for her life to the family: ὦ μάʳντι πατρὸς Οἰκλέους, θανʹούμεθα. ἄρηξʳο[ν, ἐ]λθέ, μή μ' ἴδῃς ὑπ' αἰτίας / αἰσχρʳᾶς θανοῦσαν, διὰ σὲ γὰρ διʹόλλυμαι, "O seer, Oicles' son, I am about to die. Come and defend me! Don't see me die so shamefully. Because of you I perish!"

43 Compare "sed uidet haec, videt ille deum regnator, et ausis, | sera quidem, manet ira tamen" (*Theb.* 5.688-9) and "Vindices aderunt dei; his puniendum uota te tradunt mea" (*Thy.* 1110-1).

44 Euripides' *Hypsipyle* also makes reference to Opheltes' toys. The place of this fragment in the play is uncertain. Bond (on *fr.* 1.i in his edition) conjectures the fragment should be placed early on as it suggests the infant is still alive.

45 Fortgens (1934) 68.

46 Garrod and Klotz punctuate *spes avidae* in their editions with an exclamation. Hill indicates in his that he was once tempted to do the same but rejected this reading in favor of *spes avidi*.

47 Fantham (1999) 228 condemns Eurydice's demand to bar Hypsipyle from the funeral as "unwomanly."
48 As Chong-Gossard (2009) 18–19 and (2013) 58 demonstrates, Amphiaraus' consolation in Euripides' *Hypsiplye* enjoyed a sustained shelf-life in antiquity. The speech of Amphiaraus was translated in Cicero's *Tusculan Disputations* 25, thoughtfully cited and considered in Plutarch *Consolatio ad Apollonium*. Given the popularity of the speech it would seem unlikely that Statius was unfamiliar with it, and may, in his way, indicate here that the platitudes that comfort some are not always sufficient.
49 Bond (1988) 16–19.
50 Ortony, Clare, and Collins (1988) 131. See also Goward (1999) 39 who regards the structure of drama to elicit suspense as agonistic, marked by a kind of "dolos" wherein the competing endings offset one likely outcome with another less likely outcome.
51 Ganiban (2013) 263 "By taking control of the rites, the Argives undermine Lycurgus' and Eurydice's status as both rulers and parents, while they promote their view of Hypsipyle as the Argive's saviour, who must therefore be protected."
52 Cf. Parkes (2012) 284.

Chapter 4

1 So also Soph. *Ant.* 53, the successive force of ἔπειτα puts her suicide just after the revelation of Oedipus' identity, not after the death of her sons.
2 For broader discussion of the limitations imposed on reading the *Septem* without the preceding plays see Winnington-Ingram (1983) 40–3.
3 Cf. Mastronarde (1994) 25 and Craik (1988) 36. Smolenaars (2008) 222–3 raises the possibility that Euripides explored both traditions, treating the intercession in the *Phoenissae* and the early death of Jocasta in his lost *Oedipus*. Thalmann (1982) draws sufficient corollaries between Aeschylus' *Septem* and the Lille fragments concerning the drawing of lots to suggest Aeschylus was familiar with both traditions as well.
4 There are strong similarities between Jocasta in the *Phoenissae* of Euripides and the female speaker in the fragments. Gostoli (1978) 24 suggests the identity of the female speaker could be Euryganeia, who in less developed traditions was the second wife of Oedipus and the mother of Eteocles and Polynices; however, Bremer (1987) 165, agreeing with Robert (1915) 110, reasonably but without much certainty suggests that if Oedipus were too distraught over the horror of his first marriage to take a second wife then Euryganeia may simply be another name for the mother of Oedipus. See also Tsitsibakou-Vasalos (1989) 60–88.
5 See La Penna (1994) 123–34.
6 See also Prop. 2.9.50.
7 On discussions of Jocasta, her role in the *Thebaid*, and her interrelation to dramatic tragedy see Vessey (1973) 270–82. Soubiran (1969) 699 makes the compelling

argument that Statius models his Jocasta on the Veturia of Livy. See also Legras (1905) 95–7 and Reussner (1921) 16–18. Despite the tradition of Jocasta, Mendell (1967) 118 suggests she intends to rival Virgil's Amata. Markus (2004) 118 points to the "intertextual dialog" with Euripides and Seneca's productions. As does Lovatt (2010) 81–2 who argues for an enfolding of tragic and historic character modeling.

8   See Bal (1985).
9   A characteristic feature of the Fury who does not like to work alone. See *Aen.* 6.572.
10 Compare Tisiphone's arrival at Thebes (1.100).
11 Cf. Dominik (1994) 37.
12 See McNelis (2007) *passim* and Ganiban (2007) 159–65.
13 Readers will also recall Antigone's persuasive force in Seneca's *Phoenissae* (417–18), where Frank (1995) 190 argues she has pleaded with her brothers once before.
14 Cf. Korneeva (2011) 205.
15 Prince (1988) 6. Cf. Augoustakis (2010) 71: "contrafactual scenarios."
16 Ortony, Clore, and Collins (1988) 131.
17 See Keith (2000) 96 on Jocasta recognizing that she is aligned with the Furies. See also Korneeva (2011) 208–9.
18 Smolenaars (1994) 223.
19 See Sen. *Phoen.* 420–6. So notes the messenger describing Jocasta's entrance between the battle-lines: "vadit furenti similis aut etiam furit" (427).
20 Cf. Ganiban (2007) 111 who suggests that association with Furies "doom her from the start."
21 Dominik (1994b) 266 is sensitive to the harsh sounds and alliterations Statius uses to express anger in her speech.
22 We should not underestimate the likely views Roman audiences would project unto this scene. No doubt the separation from Jocasta would be expected to grieve for a man who was unable to visit his mother regularly. On the close bonds between Roman mothers and sons see Dixon (1988) 168–202.
23 See Conacher (1967) 238.
24 Seneca's Jocasta declares for the weaker party: "infirmo favens" (*Phoen.* 385).
25 Augoustakis (2010) 66.
26 See Smolenaars (1994) 235 for allusions to Seneca's *Phoenissae*.
27 See also Hershkowitz (1998) 280–2, note especially the sexual undertones of Polynices' reunion and Eteocles' persistence.
28 On the importance of repetition in narrative see Brooks (1992) 316.
29 See Ganiban (2007) 161–3 on the Senecan prototypes to this scene with especial regard to *pietas*.
30 Compare Polynices' yielding to Jocasta in Seneca's *Phoen.* 498–9.
31 Cf. Duchemin (1968) 80.

32 The most overt differences are cultural and aptly summarized by Bremer (1987) 171: "the scope of the conflict and of the attempted solution—which we considered to be still rural-aristocratic in Stesichorus, and urban-democratic in Euripides—widens into the vast dimensions of an empire. No more talk of movable/unmovable property (Stes.), of citizens in a polis (Eur.), but: regnum, imperium."

33 *Contra* Tarrant (1978) 230.

34 See Maignon (1989) 53. Cf. Smolenaars (1994) 215 on chronology and placement.

35 Cf. Thalmann (1982) 389 suggests that despite Stesichorus' innovative treatment of mythic subject matter he was not likely to change the outcome of the final conflict. See also Burnett (1988) 111, Maignon (1989) 56, and Martin (2007) 11-12.

36 Lovatt (2010) 81-2 suggests placing the scene further from the critical moment (as in Seneca), but this diminishes the dramatic impact of the scene. This is however, part of the misleading, noting the expectations in place from familiarity with previous versions, putting in place further delay (83).

37 See Craik (1988) 230.

38 Conacher (1967) 247 claims, this "is little more than a lamentation for the coming fratricidal slaughter."

39 Gerrig (1989a) 277-80 and (1989b) 633-48.

40 Bal (1985).

41 Bremer (1987) 172.

42 Vessey (1973) 271.

43 E.g. Euripides' *Phoenissae* 454-64 which implies that they are not looking at each other. See also Lamari (2010) 106 and Craik (1988) 195. Cf. Venini (1970) 95-6 and Smolenaars (1994) 233.

44 Goward (1999) 39 regards the structure of drama to elicit suspense as agonistic, marked by a kind of "dolos."

Chapter 5

1 Franchet d'Espèrey (1999) 52-7 reviews the tragic predecessors who shape the malediction of Statius' Oedipus.

2 On Oedipus' limited presence in the *Thebaid* see Ganiban (2007) 33.

3 So Lovatt (2013) 59 suggests "Oedipus' curses will win the ultimate victory" and Ganiban (2007) 39 holds that "the progress and fulfillment of his prayer essentially become the *Thebaid*." See also Franchet d'Espèrey (2001) for discussion of causality and Hershkowitz (1998) 248 on the curse. See also Marinis (2015) 359.

4 Statius heightens the violence of Oedipus' self-blinding by having him tear out his own eyes rather than pierce them with the gold brooch pins. Cf. Sophocles *OT* 1269-70, Eur. *Phoen.* 59-62, and Seneca *Oed.* 962-4. Keith (2002) 385 argues

that Oedipus' "self-blinding is itself the literary descendant of the blinding of the Ovidian Tiresias." In this instance, however, Statius' Oedipus is much closer to his antecedents in Euripides and Seneca. There is greater dramatic effect in Oedipus' attack on himself than Juno's attack on Tiresias. Aricò (2002) 169-72 argues that Statius' Oedipus is much closer to Seneca's but is not unmindful of the Euripidean model. See also Delarue (2000) 144-52.

5   On beginning *in medias res*, see Horace *Ars P.* 146-50. See also Sternberg (1978) 35-41 and Genette (1980) 36.
6   Cf. Seneca's *Phoen.* 40-44 in which Oedipus sees in his mind's eye the *eidolon* of Laius beckoning to him.
7   Podlecki (1962) 356 suggests that when Euripides' Oedipus emerges he is "the self-blinded Oedipus, the glory and the shame of the house of Laius, a mere dream-image of his former self, living in the empty memories of his vanished greatness."
8   Moreland (1975) 20.
9   *Theb.* 1.236-37. Cf. Dee (2013) 183-4.
10 So Virgil *Aen.* 2.687-78: "at pater Anchises oculos ad sidera laetus extulit et caelo palmas cum uoce tetendit" and 10.667: "et duplicis cum uoce manus ad sidera tendit;" Ovid *Met.* 6.367-78: "supplicat indignis nec dicere sustinet ultra | verba minora dea tollensque ad sidera palmas;" and Petronius *Sat.* 154.5: "ambas | intentans cum uoce manus ad sidera dixit."
11 While Jupiter ratifies Oedipus' prayer at 1.239-40, this moment offers a convenient pretext to end the Cadmaean line. Oedipus receives no direct satisfaction from Jupiter. Indeed, given the grief that the outcome presents for Oedipus, Jupiter's ratification, is telling in its cruelty. It is a perversion to grant Oedipus his wish. Cf. Hubert (2013) 111-16 on the selfish nature of Oedipus' prayer and its ultimate betrayal of his interests.
12 Cf. Dominik (1994) 103 who suggests the broad invocation gestures to as many gods as possible.
13 Cf. Dominik (1994) 103.
14 Cf. Gossage (1972) 196.
15 Tisiphone routinely undercuts Jupiter. She is first to stir conflict at Thebes (1.123-30), which makes Jupiter's pronouncements during the *concilium deorum* appear tardy. As Ganiban (2007) 52 points out: "That questions of *nefas* and fraternal strife do not enter into Jupiter's plans or elsewhere shows his ignorance of his world and the weakness of his moral authority." Moreland (1975) 28 suggests that "Jupiter is a symbol of order among the gods, as is Adrastus on the human level." In fact, however, Adrastus is as woefully inept as Jupiter. Cf. Delarue (2000) 304-6 and 374-5. See also Hill (1996) 35 who declares him "a bumbling and ineffective Jupiter who retained the outward paraphernalia of power but none of its substance," though he makes too

great a leap in claiming that "Jupiter is now seen as an ineffective figure still groundlessly confident that he is in control. The evil forces in the universe are too strong for him; what is needed is a greater force, a new Jupiter, a Domitian" (52–3).

16 Cf. Vessey (1971) 377.
17 As Davies (1989) 24 notes, scholars have long been disappointed over the presentation of the curse here, which fails to achieve the caliber and drama of that presented by Oedipus against his sons in Sophocles' *Oedipus at Colonus*.
18 Cf. Herman (1997) 1046–59 and for general survey see Herman (2002) 85–114.
19 See Mastronarde (1994) 162.
20 See Mastronarde (1994) 248–9.
21 Cf. Sewell-Rutter (2007) 65.
22 Cf. Reussner (1921) 5: "Conclusio autem orationis Oedipi, quam in exemplo prologi tragici res gestas exponere diximus, ad ipsum carminis argumentum traducit." See also Pratt (1939) 53; Caviglia (1973) 13; Mendell (1967) 120; Mikalson (1989) 95; and Duff (1960) 472.
23 See Frings (1992) 18 and Ahl (1986) 2822–30. An earlier type for this opening gambit is likely to be found in Seneca's *Agamemnon*; see Calder (1976) 29–30. Note too that Jocasta is compared to a Fury at *Thebaid* 7 when she approaches Polynices. Vessey (1973) 72 comments that "the Oedipus of the *Thebaid* is the Senecan Oedipus; it is as though Statius was continuing the story from the point at which the tragedian had left it." See also his discussion of Statius and the *Thyestes* (pp. 77–8). Of course, Statius shares much with the substratum of Senecan tragedy generally. Cf. Braun (1867) 245–75 and Vessey (1973) 271. Mendell (1967) 120 suggests that Statius is to rhetorical epic what Seneca is to rhetorical tragedy. Likewise, Barchiesi (2001) 326 declares that "the *Thebaid* is a tragic spectacle, a post-Senecan epic." Both authors are concerned with tyranny, excessive power, *nefas*, and strife between brothers. See, in particular, Frings (1992) 15–36, as well as Herington (1966) 438; Poe (1983) 141; Henry and Henry (1985) 157–76; Boyle (1988) 95; Schiesaro (1994) 196–210; Tarrant (1995) 228–9; Fantham (1997) 190–9; Delarue (2000) 141–76; Aricò (2002) 169–84; Davis (2003) 84.
24 Tarrant (1985) 91. Cf. Mendell (1967) 120. See also Pratt (1939) 53 who comments: "the prologue creates full anticipation of subsequent events; throughout the remainder of the drama, this foreknowledge, resulting from the play of foreshadowing upon preknowledge, is reinforced and utilized in diverse ways for the maintenance and intensification of anticipative suspense."
25 For further discussion of Seneca and Statius, see Vessey (1971b) 378–9, Frings (1992) 15–36; Delarue (2000) 141–76; Aricò (2002). Oedipus will eventually become a reflexive model for Polyxo, so Schetter (1960) 5–8.
26 Cf. Dion. Hal. *Ant. Rom.* 2.26–27 who approves Romulus' bestowal of the law to fathers which made even the greatest of Roman citizens subject to their fathers.

27 The *Nuntius* of Seneca's *Phoenissae* suggests Oedipus holds a bare sliver of authority when he asks for his help in preventing the fratricide (320-6). Oedipus in his wrath and bitterness chooses not to intervene, which is a way of exercising power over his sons.
28 Statius is sensitive to the topic of castration. See *Silvae* 3.4 on Flavius Earinus, and related discussion in Newlands (2012) 112. More to this point, see Gunderson (2003) 59-89 who explores paternal authority and castration in the declamatory tradition on which Statius cut his teeth.
29 On the longing for release from their father's authority among Roman males see, Veyne (1987) 27-30 and Cantarella (2003) 287, 293-8. See also Sussman (1995) 179-92 on declamation an arena in which to work out such latent anxieties concerning parricide among Roman youth.
30 On Thebes as an "other" Rome. See Braund (2006) 259-73 and Hardie (1990) 224-35. As Vessey (1971) 382 suggests, the *Thebaid* "must have been thought by its author to be not without relevance to his own time." See also Zeitlin (1986) 101-41 on Thebes as a reflection of Athens. For discussion of the parent-child theme in the *Thebaid* see Gervais (2015) 221-39.
31 As Augoustakis (2016) 171 notes, "Oedipus' representation as a sadist, who now for the first time enjoys a meal and on whose face joy can be discerned, casts the king as a miserable, deformed, and malicious being."
32 Cf. *Thebaid* 1.53-4.
33 See Poe (1983) 150.
34 Vessey (1971b) 375 points out of the strong interest in exploiting pathos and creating emotional interest in the *Thebaid* that grew out of Statius' rhetorical training.
35 Oedipus refers to himself as the "infaustum patrum" of Antigone (Sen. *Phoen.* 3); he bemoans his fate (*Phoen.* 383); expresses a slowness in understanding his fate, "haerebo fati tardus interpres mei" (*Phoen.* 139); Jocasta in her pleas to Polynices and Eteocles claims that the error belongs to Fortune (*Phoen.* 452-3); and cautions: "ne quid e fatis tibi | desset paternis" (*Phoen.* 513-14).
36 Sen. *Phoen.* 295-302, and 331-5. Compare Oedipus' declaration: "facietis, scio: | sic estis orti" (*Phoen.* 337-38) to his prayer to Tisiphone at *Thebaid* 1.86-7: "nec tarda sequitur | mens iuuenum."
37 Cf. Fantham (1983) 64-5.
38 Cf. *Phoen.* 287-94 and 553-5.
39 Cf. Vessey (1971b) 377.
40 Cf. Mastronarde (1994) 584.
41 Cf. Marinis (2015) 360 who claims a Euripidean model for the scene but which "conveys a heightened pathos."
42 Some scholars read "nil ego" as Oedipus' efforts to distance himself from responsibility. Shackleton Bailey, for instance, translates the words as "I had no part."

Venini (1970) reads the declaration in reference to *Iliad* 19.86. While there may be some intertextual referencing, Oedipus nevertheless implicated himself when he referred to his falling eyes, and when he asked which god stood by him and told his prayers to fate. While complete culpability is impossible, Oedipus cannot make a reasonable claim to have had no part in the events, since he had already acknowledged that he did. Even if we suppose he had no direct influence, then neither did Laius. Blame directed at Jocasta is also problematic (perhaps because she bore him? Or because she failed to dissuade Eteocles and Polynices?). The precise sense of "nil ego" presents an interpretative crux, and my own preference is to read the lines as a tragic acknowledgment of the collapse of his house and family line. Cf. Vessey (1973) 280 and Dominik (1994) 46-7 who suggest the moment indicates Oedipus' realization of ancestral pollution. Cf. Eur. *Phoen.* 1610. See too Ganiban (2007) 196-7.
43 Ganiban (2007) 196 suggests that Oedipus "lacks a full understanding of his role in his sons' death." See also Ryzman (1989) 21 who, in her discussion of Aeschylus' *Septem*, maintains "the curse results in the annihilation of the family, while the individual lacks independent responsibility."
44 For discussion of the humanization of Oedipus through his scene of lament see Franchet d'Espèrey (1999) 297-301.
45 See Venini (1970) 157.
46 The suicidal nature of Oedipus is narrated early in Euripides' *Phoen.* 326-36 by Jocasta and plays little role in heightening the drama after the sons are dead. Calder (1976) 10 suggests: "Oedipus in the *Phoenissae* made the mistake of refusing suicide because he heeded Antigone's ignorant request to survive because of his *pietas*."
47 Vessey (1971b) 376.

Chapter 6

1 See Vessey (1970b) 426-41, Vessey (1973) 209-29, and Lovatt (2005) 258-61.
2 So Fortgens (1934) 35.
3 See Legras (1905) 82-3, Vessey (1973) 209, and Lovatt (2005) 12-19. The seeds of Statius' use of games to prefigure future outcomes are perhaps found in Virgil. During the foot race, Nisus slips in blood: "levi cum sanguine Nisus | labitur infelix" (*Aen.* 5.328-9) and Nisus falls "immundoque fimo sacroque cruore" (5.333). The significance of this moment has not been lost on scholars reading the prefiguration of a tragic moment in this episode. Virgil identifies Nisus with the same epithet that marks Dido as a figure soon to approach an unfortunate end, and ubiquitous throughout the *Thebaid* as a marker of someone on whom misfortune will fall, "infelix." There is also a curious mixture of the sacred and the profane in the manure

and sacrificial blood in which Nisus lands. This perhaps indicates the noble intentions of aiding Euryalus to victory but the ignoble means of executing this in the tripping of Salius. Statius modeled his own Hopleus and Dymas on Virgil's Nisus and Euryalus. See Legras (1905) 115–17, Krumbholz (1955) 94–101, and Williams (1972) 76–86. The *Doloneia* of *Iliad* 10 is another important model. See Legras (1905) 115–17, Juhnke (1972) 144–7, and Ganiban (2007) 3. For Virgil the integration of prefiguring into the games is markedly less elaborate.

4 Legras (1905) 82–3. See also Vessey (1973) 210–11. To this order we might recall that in the prologue the deaths are presented slightly out of order.
5 Holland (1976) 86.
6 See Holland (1976) 215–16.
7 Cf. Snijder (1968) 226, who comments on the ability of Statius to depict the rousing of war in two different locations, Argos and Thebes.
8 Vessey (1973) 217.
9 For discussion of the "catera" and its description of Centaurs and Lapiths see Holland (1976) 87.
10 Smolenaars (1994) 331ff. reviews the division among scholars on how to take Amphiaraus in light of this turn and he notes that eagerness is consistent with the theme of *furor*.
11 Ahl (1986) 2859.
12 This is a notable shift in characterization from Aeschylus' *Septem*.
13 Cf. DeJong and Nünlist (2007) 515: "Actorial external prolepsis can be a powerful tool to extend the fabula beyond the limits of the story."
14 McNelis (2007) 130–4.
15 See Lovatt (2005) 202–19.
16 Vessey (1973) 225.
17 Rankin (1969) 384 suggests that "particularly persuasive to Romans as a justification for anthropophagy would be stress of siege." Nothing so desperate appears here.
18 See Lovatt (2005) 106–13.
19 Lovatt (2005) 104–5. Vessey (1973) 219 suggests that "the ease with which Hippomedon beats his opponent is an obvious foreshadowing of his *aristeia* in *Theb.* 9."
20 As Vessey (1973) 221 suggests, "there is something bestial, less than human about him; his strength is his *esse*, unredeemed by other or finer qualities: it is as if some extinct monster had strayed into the world." See also Klinnert (1970) 88–94.
21 The scene is based on Achilles confrontation with the Scamander. See Dewar (1991) 102ff. on the importance of Homer to the development of Hippomedon's death scene. See also ten Kate (1955) 95, Kytzler (1969) 228, and Klinnert (1970) 79–132.
22 Dewar (1991) 102.
23 See Vessey (1973) 295–6 and Dewar (1991) 126.

24 The idea of a valiant and brave hero being struck down by someone of lesser worth seems to be particularly abhorrent. As Tacitus remarks of Civilis' assault on a Roman camp: "nihil prodesse virtus, fors cuncta turbare et ignavorum saepe telis fortissimi cadere" (*Hist.* 4.29).
25 Vessey (1973) 297.
26 Vessey (1973) 298.
27 Cf. Schetter (1960) 44–8, for whom Parthenopaeus is "ein hilfloser Knabe" (45).
28 Cf. Jamset (2004) 95–104 who explores the erotic aspects of Parthenopaeus and his association with Camilla. Hardie (1989) suggests Camilla as the dominant Virgilian model.
29 Cf. Dewar (1991) 188–9.
30 See Vessey (1973) 218–19 and Lovatt (2005) 55.
31 Lovatt (2005) 58 reads this as an intertextual moment; Adrastus (and Statius) are attempting to decide which of the epic predecessors to follow.
32 Cf. *Theb.* 6.569–73 where he is more comfortable.
33 Dewar (1991) 214 observes that the enjambment "stresses the shock of realization." Cf. Parkes (2005) 361 who notes Parthenopaeus' youthful delicacy.
34 Capaneus is described as a giant and likened in size to a Cyclops and in anger to Centaurs. The description, as Snijder (1968) 238 notes, is consistent with the description at *Sept.* 424. Cf. Euripides' *Phoen.* 1171ff. See also ten Kate (1955) 73–4 and 105–8, Klinnert (1970) 11–21, Vessey (1973) 118–23, and Franchet d'Espèrey (1999) 197–203, 333–4.
35 This is the position held by Vessey (1973) 118 who claims: "The contrast between 'pietas' and madness (*furor*) is perhaps nowhere more forcibly expressed in the *Thebaid* than at this climax." Vessey reads Capaneus as a counter-balance to the piety of Menoeceus. Farron (1979) 35 argues that Capaneus' death is heroic. Similarly, Leigh (2006) 227 champions Capaneus, declaring that despite his excesses he still possesses a deeper nobility of spirit.
36 See Williams (1978) 125–35, Leigh (2006) 228, and McNelis (2007) 141. As Mastronarde (1994) 475 notes, however, "there are no certainly identifiable close imitations of [Euripides'] passage." Legras (1905) 215-17 suggests Mezentius as a model for Statius' Capaneus.
37 Cf. Dominik (1994) 32.
38 Vessey (1973) 221. See also Klinnert (1970) 32–8.
39 Legras (1905) 88.
40 Vessey (1973) 223 notes that the boxing match also foreshadows Alcidamas' death. While Capaneus does not kill him during the games, he is partly responsible for his end. At 10.498–507 Alcidamas is one among several others who die at the front line, urged on by Capaneus.
41 Cf. Olivi (1996) 135–6.

42 McNelis (2007) 144–5 connects Jupiter's amusement to *Theb.* 8.74 where Dis commands Tisiphone to provide deaths even the king of gods would enjoy.
43 Vessey (1973) 164.
44 Lovatt (2005) 278.
45 Legras (1905) 90.
46 Vessey (1973) 227.
47 Burgess (1971) 56.
48 On the necessity for effective communication within armies see Tacitus who discusses the disorder of the army at Cremona: "utque exercitu vario linguis moribus, cui cives socii externi interessent, diversae cupidines et aliud cuique fas nec quicquam inlicitum" (*Hist.* 3.33). Indeed, the instability of the army at Cremona are also seen in the attitude that the leaders must take to control it. As a massacre is getting underway, soldiers are entreated by their leaders: "nec procul caede aberant, cum precibus ducum mitigatus est miles" (*Hist.* 3.20). The use of entreaties to direct soldiers would be out of place in a more ordered force.
49 See in particular *Theb.* 2.145–8, 3.714–21, and 8.262–3.
50 See also *Theb.* 4.38–40.
51 A point of contact may be found in Euripides' *Hypsipyle* in which Amphiaraus, in his search for clear water in order to perform religious ritual, complains that the marching army has dirtied the waters at 752h 31–2.
52 A similar description of disorder comes in the first melee between Thebans and Argives. After Jocasta fails to mediate an initial peace and Bacchus' tigers maul Amphiaraus' charioteer, the council is broken up and Tydeus calls for war. Here again we find "duces" confused with common soldiers in a disordered fray (7.616–24).
53 For further instances of military disorder see *Theb.* 2.583–93, 7.616–24, and 8.350–3.
54 Notably, the Argives are not very far into their journey to Thebes. Such obstacles and setbacks seem somewhat premature to go astray. Cf. Parkes (2012) 284.
55 Parkes (2012) 282 suggests a key engagement with Lucan 4.292–336 in which Caesar relieves the Pompeians thirst.
56 Naturally, Polynices bears the most fault here: "formidine cauta, | sed iuuenem durae prohibebant discere Parcae" (6.324–5).
57 Since the games are a prelude to the war this particularly bodes ill since in battle there are seldom opportunities for a second effort.
58 This feature of Adrastus' rule is also in strong contrast to Tacitus' Antonius who is capable of restoring order with nothing more than a glance: "aspectu et auctoritate silentium fecerat" (*Hist.* 3.20).
59 McGuire (1997) 115.
60 See also Hill (1996) 37 who sees Tydeus's praise of Adrastus at 2.181ff. as evidence that "Jupiter is clearly revealed as a governor whose judgment on who is worthy to be granted authority is deeply flawed."

61 To be fair to Adrastus and the Argive forces, such scenes of disorder also extend to the Theban forces. The ambush against Tydeus demonstrates the hero's physical prowess, certainly, but part of his victory is attributable to the poor planning and incompetence of his enemies. Initially, Tydeus demands open ground when facing his attackers: "ferte gradum contra campoque erumpite aperto!" (2.547). When he realizes, however, the numbers against him he seeks a tactical advantage in higher ground (2.555ff.). He dislodges boulders from the mountain face that crush several and send them off in a disordered rout (4.576-7). Yet, the Thebans foolishly "iterum densi glomerantur in unum | Ogygidae firmantque gradum" (2.585-6). The leaders plan their attack poorly, and their increased numbers work against them (2.590-3). It is worth noting, however, that such incompetence is not limited to the ambush party. In another instance, during the war against Argive forces, Bellona rouses them and Thebes empties itself so fast that: "turbat eques pedites, currus properantibus obstant, | ceu Danai post terga premant: sic omnibus alae | artantur portis septemque excursibus haerent" (8.350-3).
62 Cf. Moore (1921) 168.
63 Vessey (1971a) 236-43 and Vessey (1973) 117-31.
64 Billerbeck (1986) 3143-5 maintains a Stoic interpretation of Menoeceus. Fantham (1997) 186 disputes Billerbeck's conclusion of Menoeceus, and a Stoic ethos in the *Thebaid* generally. See also Legras (1905) 117-21, Schetter (1960) 41-2, McGuire (1997) 198ff., Ripoll (1998) 219-20 and 292.
65 Vessey (1971a) 236. Ganiban (2007) 137-42 provides an exceptional reading of this scene which probes some of its ambiguities demonstrating that "pietas" is not as well-defined as Vessey suggests.
66 Vessey (1971a) 240.
67 Cf. Ganiban (2007) 139-40 who reads this falsehood in terms of fraternal rivalry.
68 The role of "pietas" in the *Thebaid* is conspicuously elusive. Kytzler (1996) examines "pietas" as it works against Oedipus' "confusa domus." Georgacopoulou (1996) 182 rightly identifies it as "un sujet par excellence tragique." See also her review of similar occurrences of the phrase in Greek tragedy (182 n.48). Burgess (1971) 48 defines the term: "'pietas' for a Roman consisted in the fulfillment of obligations to family, country, and gods, to one's leader or those who rely upon one as a leader and to those who had done a service." Burgess continues to say that "the basic dramatic tension of the *Thebaid* is to be found rather in the role played by 'pietas' in the epic." Ripoll (1998) 287 contends the question is not so clearly defined: "La problmatique de la 'pietas' dans la *Thebaid* passe donc par la redefinition du concept et la determination precise de son rôle dramatique."
69 So Vessey (1971a) 238 suggests: "Creon's doubts and fears, his 'pietas incerta,' are a sad contrast with the fixed and heroic 'pietas' of his son."
70 The brothers' rejection of Jocasta's advice and Polynices' choice to ignore the advice of Adrastus about Arion, for instance. Granted, it is fairly certain that Creon's counsel

is biased, he lights onto a fairly practical position—how can Menoeceus be certain that Tiresias' prophecy is legitimate and not part of a plan by Eteocles to eliminate a threat to his power (10.699 ff.)?

71 For discussion of Menoeceus' sacrifice in Euripides' *Phoenissae* see Foley (1985) 132-9. Foley further argues: "Menoeceus' death is presented as a cruel and ideally unnecessary one. Human sacrifice is clearly a legendary and literary cure for the evils of political life. Yet, when Euripides invents the human sacrifice of Menoeceus to redirect his sick plot to the outcome prescribed by tradition, he seems to make a marginal gesture of confidence in ritual and in the poetry that incorporates this sacrificial cure" (146). In Euripides' treatment of the story Menoeceus is entirely forgotten after his self-sacrifice and leaves us with the sense that the value of his act was meager. Cf. O'Connor-Visser (1987) 83 who suggests that, in characterizing Eteocles in such a negative light, the dramatist "had to give to someone else the heroic task of saving the city."

Chapter 7

1 Held (1984) 174.
2 Cf. Davis (1994) 483.
3 The pursuit of a personal happiness is also central to Aeschylus' *Septem*. Golden (1964) 87 concludes: "What has been portrayed in the *Septem* has been a contest for power that is fought out within the limited horizon of self-interest."
4 Legras (1905) 33, Juhnke (1972) 53-4, and Vessey (1973) 79-80 suggest that the critic approximates Thersites at *Iliad* 2. What the Thersites episode offers is the willingness of the principal chieftains and the army to follow Agamemnon and their willingness to quell dissent after order has been restored among the army. The criticisms of Statius' critic, however, are consistent throughout the *Thebaid*. I do not see a strong connection with Thersites, unless we reduce the Theban's criticisms to mere complaint. This, however, would not be an effective way of reading his vituperation.
5 Coffee (2006) 432 suggests that Eteocles lives up to the accusations of this figure. Gossage (1972) 195 suggests this is the voice of Statius. Ahl (1986) 2828, however, feels that "the critic's annoyance is obvious and reflects what probably passed through many an Italian mind during the year of the four emperors."
6 As O'Gorman (2005) 32-3 suggests: "Eteocles is represented as a tyrant, while Polynices differs from him not because he his Polynices but because he is not yet a tyrant." On differences between the two see also Helzle (1996) 180 and Coffee (2006) 415. See also Franchet d'Espèrey (1999) 30-31 who suggests: "Dans le conflit les deux sujets, Etéocle et Polynice, sont interchangeables dans leur relation à l'objet, c'est à

dire au pouvoir, au trône de Thèbes: quel que soit le premier qui le désire, le second le désirera aussi, devenant ainsi son rival et son double."

7 This unfortunate defect appears to run in the family (*Theb.* 1.227). Creon also shows diminished capacity: the persistent visions of Menoeceus' death (11.264–7), his antagonism toward Eteocles (11.269ff.), and his hallucinations (12.695–7).

8 Statius' own criticism of the critic (1.171–73) troubles Ahl (1986) 2829 since the poet and the anonymous Theban clearly hold the same views: "The snake-like poison Statius finds in his critic is hard to reconcile with the similarity between the critic's views and the poet's own pronouncements. Is Statius seriously questioning the right of the politically powerless to complain, since he certainly is not questioning the substance of the observations?"

9 Steiner (1996) 536.

10 Sophocles *OC* 1225–8.

11 Eteocles also notes this problem in changing rulers *Theb.* 2.448.

12 See Suet. *Dom.* 10.2–3 and 14.4, Dio 67.12.2–4 and 14.4, and Philostr. VA 7.8.

13 See discussion at pp. 32–4.

14 Lovatt (2005) 243.

15 See p. 112.

16 For discussion of the Phaethon simile see Vessey (1973) 215–16, Ahl (1986) 2869, and especially for the Ovidian intertext see Lovatt (2005) 32–9. See also Rebeggiani (2013) 190–93 who situates Polynices' contest within the context of succession.

17 Cf. Venini (1970) 106.

18 As Tacitus remarks: "et quia in metu consilia prudentium et vulgi rumor iuxta audiuntur" (*Hist.* 3.58). See also *Hist.* 3.67 where Tacitus comments: "Surdae ad fortia consilia Vitellio aures: obruebatur animus miseratione curaque."

19 There is a characteristic over optimism in Eteocles as well, as he supposes his brother dead during the duel and prematurely begins to despoil him. Tydeus, another exile, also has ambitious imaginings (3.418–9). As De Jong and Nünlist (2007) 7 note: "a narrator may sovereignly, perhaps even moralizingly, anticipate the outcome of events, while a character optimistically or anxiously looks ahead to the future."

20 Argia later recalls how he often looked back when he departed for Thebes, a "mitis coniunx" (12.191).

21 See Coffee (2006) 444–5, O'Gorman (2005) 35, and Bonds (1985) 234. Ahl (1986) 2885 suggests that he comes to the realization that his violent ambitions threaten to ruin his life.

22 Ahl (1986) 2883.

23 The notion parallels Thomas Middleton's pun that "banquets, ease, and laughter | Can make great men..." (*The Revenger's Tragedy* 1.1.47–8). Argia describes Eteocles, about whom she heard through Rumor, as "tumidum" (3.346).

24 See Coffee (2006) on similarities and differences between the two brothers.

25 Golden (1964) 81 maintains that Aeschylus' Eteocles operates within "a soldier's *Weltanschauung* in which all considerations are subordinated to the demands of the immediate tactical situation."
26 O'Connor-Visser (1987) 83 refers to Euripides' Eteocles in the *Phoenissae* as a "selfish creature" who is "not interested in the welfare of the city." In the *Thebaid* Eteocles' concern for Thebes beyond his own self-interest is doubtful.
27 Tarrant (1985) 106.
28 Cf. Vessey (1973) 79.
29 "utque rudis fandi pronusque calori | semper erat" (2.391-2). Cf. Dominik (1994b) 189-90.
30 Statius relates that Eteocles has governed cruelly and remained beyond the agreed year: "iura ferus populo trans legem ac tempora regni" (*Theb.* 2.386).
31 As Fantham (1997) 191 notes, "an Eteocles resolved to kill his own brother will go as far as…he can to render this (essentially self-destructive) enmity intelligible in terms of social rights and wrongs. But, ultimately, the division of the hater's own personality, and the externalization of his passion, become a necessary strategy for warranting the action that passion demands."
32 Mulder (1954) 251 reads Statius' development of this simile through *Aen.* 2.471-5; however, Vessey (1986) 2981 suggests *Geor.* 3.414-34 as the appropriate source.
33 See Seneca *de clem.* 1.20-1 on slowness of revenge, and condemnation of revenge by cruel rulers *de ira* 3.16.2-21.5. Compare also Juno's anger at *Aeneid* 1.36.
34 See McGuire (1997) 147-84.
35 Toolan (1988) 56. See also Rimmon-Kenan (1991) 53.
36 Cf. Quintilian (8.3.72) who notes the power of similes to make arguments vivid. For further discussion see Dominik (2015) 271 on "linking similes" which "strengthen the connection between individuals, images, scenes, and circumstances."
37 On stigmatism cf. Plautus *Persa* 298 and *Aen.*1.680-2. The tendency is well-known in Euripides. See Parker (2007) 65, Page (1938) 476, and Mommsen (1895) 668-76.
38 As Snijder (1968) 76 notes: "This phrase seems to imply that Eteocles commands his wrath in an unnatural way: he rouses it expressly in order to punish more cruelly."
39 On the happiness (*laetus*) that shades toward sadism for Eteocles as he stabs his brother see Franchet d'Espèrey (1999) 162-3.
40 To be sure, other images illustrate Eteocles, especially vis-à-vis Polynices: Statius compares the brothers to bulls unduly yokes (1.131-6) and adverse winds (1.193-4).

Chapter 8

1 As do, of course, the conventions of Homeric and Virgilian epic closure as discussed by McNelis (2007) 152-77.

2   Hough (1974) 8 finds Statius' description of the Idalian doves unpardonable because it demonstrates a lack of true understanding with regard to the aggressive and hostile actions of the pecking order. We cannot be certain if Statius' mishandling of ornithological behavior in his poetic integration of birds stems from ignorance or license, but in addition to being an aggressive and hostile action among birds, pecking order establishes hierarchy and dominance. Perhaps in an idealistic or utopian flash, Statius mislays the aggressive aspects of the birds to provide an anthropomorphic metaphor of welcome.

3   So Lucretius portrays her at *De rerum natura* 1.31–40, an image Statius reworks when we find her recumbent in Mars' lap during the Theban conflict at *Theb.* 9.821–4. The image likely derives from a Hellenistic norm, so Edmunds (2002) 346.

4   Statius may be playing off the patrilineal connection between the Furies and Aphrodite as Hesiod tells at *Theogony* 182–206. The blood from Uranus' castration falls to the ground and fertilizes Gaia with the Chthonic giants and Erinys, while the severed genitals that splashed into the ocean produce Cythera.

5   So Ovid relates in the *Fasti* "ergo saepe suo coniunx abducta marito | uritur Idaliis alba columba focis," "That is why the white dover is taken from her husband and burned in Idalian fires" (1.451–2). See Green (2004) 208 for discussion of Ovid's violation of this traditional aspect of Venus.

6   See Propertius 4.5.65 on sacrificing a dove at Venus' altar.

7   Cf. *Il.* 2.299–329 and Aeschylus *Ag.* 48–54.

8   *Theb.* 11.264–7, where Creon is filled with grief and tormented by the persistent vision of Menoeceus' death. At 11.297 Statius informs us he speaks to Eteocles: "infrendens, miseraque exaestuat ira." Cf. Pollmann (2004) 258.

9   Dominik (1994) 89 notes "monarchal power foredooms its possessor and disposes him to a lack of feeling and humanity." The power of rule consistently anticipates ruin for those holding the "sceptrum exitiale," but in as much as those ruling appear to be pitiless and without mercy, when Creon makes his edict its callousness stems from his own grief, occurring, as it does, at the pyre of his dead son. His desire for the corpses to be desecrated and unmourned is human, just not particularly humane.

10 McNelis (2007) 152–3 also sees in this narrative decision Iliadic reminiscences with Achilles' refusal to bury Hector. See also Shapiro (2006) 119–34 who finds similarities between Hector and Polynices, as well as between Achilles and Creon. The cruelty of Creon's decision is also indirectly anticipated by Eteocles' forbidding burial for Maeon.

11 Similarly, Apollo preserves the corpse of Hector while Achilles attempts to mutilate it in his anger (*Il.* 24.18–21). On Iris as "nuntia" to Juno see Ovid *Met.* 1.270.

12 Pollmann (2004) 124 takes the divine intervention here as an implicit suggestion that the widows' mission will be successful. No doubt Statius' audience likely felt the same way, a position shaped by encounters with previous story-versions.

13 For a summary of their unfriendly natures see Pollmann (2004) 127-8.
14 On Theseus' *humanitas* see Bessone (2011) 116-22.
15 Gervais (2017b) explores the quickening of narrative pace in the final book of the *Thebaid*, primarily with an eye toward the Aeneian allusions that parallel Aeneas-Turnus and Theseus-Creon in their duel.
16 See p. 130.
17 Thebes is, to her mind, not the *patria* of Polynices but, as she calls it in her prayer to him, "hostiles agros" (12.209).
18 For discussion of how Argia and Antigone relate to each other within Statius' epic program see Korneeva (2011) 184-91.
19 Pollmann (2004) 174. See also Bessone (2011) 210-12 and Manioti (2016).
20 See Lucan's *BC* 1.550-2. Cf. Pollmann (2004) 30.
21 See pp. 83-9.
22 See Davies (2014) 53. See also Propertius 4.39 and Tibullus 1.5.51-52.
23 Pollmann (2004) 189.
24 The only possible exception is the Bacchant's prophecy at 4.404.
25 The bibliography on Theseus is extensive and divided, but a few samples should suffice. Vessey (1973) 316 champions him as "a man of steel, an instrument of divine justice and human clemency through whom the world is purified and improved." Similarly, Braund (1996) 13 suggests that Theseus is the representative of civilization. Ahl (1986) 2890-8, however, finds him flawed. Dominik (1994) 157 points out that "there lurk beneath the surface some fairly disturbing implications concerning the extremely violent manner in which Theseus restores order to Thebes." Hershkowitz (1998) 301 also sees the ending afforded by Theseus as ambiguous, where "he has become the instrument of the Furies themselves, and the world, though better off for the moment, perhaps has not been forever cleared of the infernal taint of the Furies or the madness the bring." See also Ripoll (1998) 177 and Delarue (2000) 372-4.
26 In Sophocles' *OC* Theseus diplomatically intervenes on Oedipus' behalf and without bloodshed. Ahrensdorf (2009) 78 suggests that though Athens is the lesser military power to Thebes, Theseus' diplomatic intervention and the return of Antigone and Ismene to Thebes at the end of the play "sets the stage for the further, and foreseeable, struggle within Thebes that we witness in *Antigone*," which "serves Athens' interests by fomenting strife within Thebes and thereby weakening Athens' powerful neighbor."
27 See *Oly.* 6.15-16 and *Nem.* 9.22-4.
28 Plutarch *Theseus* 29. Storey (2013) speculates that the edict forbidding burial rites may have first been developed in Aeschylus' *Eleusis*.
29 Isocrates does not mention specific leaders by name.
30 Cf. Collard (1975) 320.
31 Cf. *Supp.* 223-5.

32 See discussion pp. 114–16.
33 Vessey (1973) 164.
34 For more discussion of the role of lament, particularly among women in the *Thebaid* see Markus (2004) 105–35 and Dietrich (1999) 40–50. See also Lovatt (1999) 136–40.
35 See Moreland (1975) 30: "The abuses of power evident in the rules of Eteocles and Creon must be dispelled, and Theseus takes on a godlike role, almost in a Christian sense, as he avenges not only Thebes but the Argives whom he has come to aid." Braund (1996) 15 argues that the absence of the gods "leaves the field free for Theseus to be the 'good king' or the 'good emperor,' virtually with the status of deity." Hardie (1993) 46–8 finds Theseus an epic "man;" Ripoll (1998) 178 suggests he "représente une *virtus* humaine active" and is the model of the Flavian emperor (495–502). Theseus has also been equivocated with gods. Braund (1996) 14–17 and Delarue (2000) 300 read the Athenian closely against Jupiter. Ripoll (1998) 178 suggests he is closer to Mars.
36 Braund (1996) 4.
37 Ahl (1986) 2896 suggests: "We distort the *Thebaid* if we exaggerate Theseus' heroism so as to mold him into a last-minute moral hero for the epic."
38 This recalls the dream sent to Agamemnon by Zeus to advance the narrative pace at the beginning of *Il.* 2.
39 See also *Theb.* 2.415–20. See Coffee (2006) 420 and Helzle (1996) 176–88. Ahl (1986) 2873 suggests Tydeus "attacks in a blunt but not altogether honest speech" and this "weakens his own case in our eyes by lying."
40 Cf. McGuire (1997) 177–78. Criado (2015) 296 n.25 finds him "a rather counterproductive ambassador."
41 On Phegeus see Ripoll (1998) 438. Pollmann (2004) 256 suggests "having in mind Theseus' intentions, Phegeus is acting in accordance with them,' but while he does exaggerate Theseus' bellicosity, there is no substantial evidence to suggest that Theseus has intentions beyond his ultimatum" (Cf. *Theb.* 12.590–598).
42 Collard (1975) 233.
43 The decisive moment of Creon's willingness to engage Theseus is *Theb.*12.686–92. Cf. Vessey (1973) 130.
44 Vessey (1973) 316.
45 This has significance for Theseus as a leader. As Pollmann (2004) 240 indicates: "Such a 'movement of the people' was thought to be the highest expression of common determination and united will of a nation. The battle thus fought represents not just the interests of a minority but the conviction of a whole community." See also Braund (1996) 3.
46 See *Thebaid* 12.699–708.
47 A scene patterned after Aeneas' slaying of Turnus. See McNelis (2007) 161–2.

48 See Bessone (2011) 128-99.
49 Pollmann (2004) 277.
50 "perdomita Britannia et statim omissa" (*Hist.* 1.2).
51 Cf. McGuire (1997) 125: "Thebes' 'sceptrum exitiale' awaits another claimant at the close of the epic." See also Dietrich (1997) 180-1.

Bibliography

Aélion, R. (1983), *Euripide héritier d'Eschyle*, Paris: Les Belles Lettres.
Ahl, F. (1986), "Statius' Thebaid: A Reconsideration," *ANRW II*, 32 (5): 2803-2912.
Ahrensdorf, P. (2009), *Greek Tragedy and Political Philosophy: Rationalism and Religion in Sophocles' Theban Plays*, Cambridge: Cambridge University Press.
Aricò, G. (2002), *Crudelis Vincit Pater*: Alcune note su Stazio e il mito tebano. *I Sette a Tebe. Dal mito alla letteratura*. Atti del Seminario Internazionale, Torino 21-2 Febbraio 2001. A. Aloni, E. Berardi, G. Besso and S. Cecchin. Bologna, Pàtron Editore.
Aricò, G. (1961), "Stazio e l'Ipsipile Euripedea: note sull'imitazione Staziana," *Dioniso* 35: 56-67.
Arthur, M. (1977), "The Curse of Civilization: The Choral Odes of the *Phoenissae*," *Harv. Stud.* 81: 163-85.
Augoustakis, A. (2016), *Statius, Thebaid 8*, Oxford: Oxford University Press.
Augoustakis, A. (2010), *Motherhood and the Other: Fashioning Female Power in Flavian Epic*, New York: Oxford University Press.
Bal, M. (1985), *Narratology: Introduction to the Theory of Narrative*, Toronto: University of Toronto Press.
Barchiesi, A. (2001), Genealogie letterarie nell'epica imperiale: Fondamentalismo e ironia, *L'histoire litteraire immanente dans la poesie latine*, Entretiens Fondation.
Beecher, D. (2007), "Suspense," *Philosophy and Literature*, 31: 255-79.
Bernstein, N. (2008), *In the Image of the Ancestors: Narratives of Kinship in Flavian Epic*, Toronto: University of Toronto Press.
Bernstein, N. W. (2003). "Ancestors, Status, and Self-Presentation in Statius' Thebaid," *TAPhA*, 133: 353-79.
Bessone, F. (2002), "Voce femminile e tradizione elegiaca nella 'Tebaide' di Stazio," in A. Aloni, E. Berardi, G. Besso and S. Cecchin (eds), *I Sette a Tebe. Dal mito alla letteratura*, 185-217, Bologna: Pàtron Editore.
Bessone, F. (2011), *La Tebaide di Stazio: epica e potere*, Pisa/Roma: Fabrizio Serra editore.
Billerbeck, M. (1986), "Aspects of Stoicism in Flavian Epic," *Papers of the Liverpool Latin Seminar*, 5: 341-56.
Bond, G. W. (1963), *Euripides, Hypsipyle*, Oxford: Oxford University Press.
Bonds, W. S. (1985), "Two Combats in the *Thebaid*," *TAPhA*, 115: 225-35.
Boyle, A. J. (1988), "Senecan Tragedy: Twelve Propositions," in A.J. Boyle (ed), *The Imperial Muse: Ramus Essays on Roman Literature of the Empire: To Juvenal through Ovid*, 78-101, Victoria, Australia: Aureal.

Bramble, J. C. (1974), *Persius and the Programmatic Satire: A Study in Form and Imagery*, Cambridge: Cambridge University Press.
Braswell, B. (1998), *A Commentary on Pindar Nemean Nine*, Berlin: Walter de Gruyter.
Braun, W. (1867), "Der Oedipus des Seneca in seinen Beziehungen zu den gleichnamigen Stücken des Sophokles und Euripides und Statius' *Thebais*," *Rh. Mus.*, 22: 245-75.
Braund, S. (2006), "A Tale of Two Cities: Statius, Thebes, and Rome," *Phoenix*, 60: 259-73.
Braund, S. (1996), "Ending Epic: Statius, Theseus and Merciful Release," *PCPhS*, 42: 1-23.
Bremer, J. M. (1985), "The Popularity of Euripides' Phoenissae in Late Antiquity," in *Actes du VIIe Congrès de la Fédération Internationale des Associations d'Études Classiques*, 281-88, Budapest.
Bremer, J. M. (1987), "Stesichorus: The Lille papyrus," in J. M. Bremer, S. R. Slings and A. Maria Erp van Taalman Kip (eds), *Some Recently Found Greek Poems: Text and Commentary*, 128-72, Leiden: Brill.
Bridgeman, T. (2005), "Thinking Ahead: A Cognitive Approach to Prolepsis," *Narrative*, 13: 125-59.
Brooks, P. (1992), *Reading for the Plot: Design and Intention in Narrative*, New York: Random House.
Brown, J. (1994), *Into the Woods: Narrative Studies in the Thebaid of Statius with Special Reference to Books IV-VI*, Ph.D., Cambridge University.
Bruner, J. (1991), "The Narrative Construction of Reality," *Critical Inquiry*, 18: 1-21.
Burgess, J. F. (1971), "Pietas in Virgil and Statius," *PVS*, 11: 48-61.
Burnett, A. P. (1988), "Jocasta in the West: The Lille Stesichorus," *ClAnt*, 7: 107-54.
Butler, H. E. (1909), *Post-Augustan Poetry from Seneca to Juvenal*, Oxford: Oxford University Press.
Calder, W. M. (1976), "Seneca: Tragedian of Imperial Rome," *CJ*, 72: 1-11.
Cantarella, E. (2003), "Fathers and Sons in Rome," *CW*, 96: 281-98.
Carrara, P. (1986), "Stazio e i primordia di Tebe: Poetica e polemica nel prologo della Tebaide," *Prometheus*, 12: 146-58.
Carroll, N. (2001), *Beyond Aesthetics*, Cambridge/New York: Cambridge University Press.
Casali, S. (2003), "Impius Aeneas, Impia Hypsipyle: Narrazioni Menzognere Dall'Eneide Alla Tebaide Di Stazio," *Scholia*, 12: 60-8.
Cave, T. (2009), "Towards a Pre-History of Suspense," in N. Kenney and W. Williams (eds), *Retrospectives: Essays in Literature, Poetics and Cultural History*, 158-67, London: MHRA.
Caviglia, F. (1973), *P. Papinio Stazio. La Tebaide: Libro I*, Rome: Edizione dell'Ateneo.
Chong-Gossard, J. (2013), "Mourning and Consolation in Greek Tragedy: The Rejection of Comfort," in H. Baltussen (ed), *Greek and Roman Consolations: Eight Studies of a Tradition and its Afterlife*, 37-66, Swansea: The Classical Press of Wales.

Chong-Gossard, J. (2009), "Consolation in Euripides' Hypsipyle," in J. Cousland and James Hume (eds), *The Play of Texts and Fragments: Essays in Honor of Martin Cropp*, 11–22, Leiden/Boston: Brill.

Coffee, N. (2009), *The Commerce of War: Exchange and Social Order in Latin Epic*, Chicago: University of Chicago Press.

Coffee, N. (2006), "Eteocles, Polynices, and the Economics of Violence in Statius' *Thebaid*," *AJPh*, 127: 415–52.

Coffey, M. and Mayer, R. (1990), *Seneca: Phaedra*, Cambridge: Cambridge University Press.

Collard, C. (1975), *Euripides, Supplices: Edited with an Introduction and Commentary*, Groningen: Bouma's Boekhuis.

Conacher, D. J. (1967), *Euripidean Drama: Myth, Theme, Structure*, Toronto: Toronto University Press.

Craik, E. (1988), *Euripides: Phoenician Women*, Warminster, UK: Aris & Phillips Ltd.

Criado, C. (2015), "The Constitutional Status of Euripidean and Statian Theseus: Some Aspects of the Criticism of Absolute Power in the *Thebaid*," in W.J. Dominik, C. Newlands, and K. Gervais (eds), *Brill's Companion to Statius*, 291–306, Leiden/Boston: Brill.

Criado, C. (1998), "El proemio de la Tebaida Estaciana. Una estructura no virgiliana," *FlorIlib*, 9: 111–40.

Criado, C. (1996), "Notas sobre la cronología de la Tebaida Estaciana," *FlorIlib*, 7: 53–76.

Cribiore, R. (2001), "The Grammarian's Choice: The Popularity of Euripides' *Phoenissae* in Hellenistic and Roman Education," in Y. L. Too (ed), *Education in Greek and Roman Antiquity*, 241–59, Leiden, Brill.

Davies, M. (1989), *The Epic Cycle*, Bristol: Bristol Classical Press.

Davis, P. (2003), *Seneca: Thyestes*, London: Duckworth.

Davis, P. (1994), "The Fabric of History in Statius' *Thebaid*," in C. Deroux (ed), *Studies in Latin Literature and Roman History* 7, 464–83, Bruxelles: Latomus.

Davis, P. (1993), Tyranny in Seneca's *Thyestes* and Statius. A paper presented at Cornell University (unpublished).

de Filippis, G. (1901), "La Tebaide di Stazio e la Tebaide di Antimacho," *Atene e Roma* 4: 125–28.

de Jong, I. (2004), *Narrators and Focalizers: The Presentation of the Story in the Iliad*, Bristol: Bristol Classical Press.

de Jong, I. and Nünlist, R. (eds), (2007), *Time in Ancient Greek Literature*, Leiden: Brill.

Dee, N. (2013), "Wasted Water: The Failure of Purification in the *Thebaid*," in A. Augoustakis (ed), *Ritual and Religion in Flavian Epic*, 181–98, Oxford/New York: Oxford University Press.

Delarue, F. (2000), *Stace, poète épique: originalité et cohérence*, Leuven: Editions Peeters.

Dewar, M. (1991), *Statius: Thebaid 9*, Oxford: Oxford University Press.

Dietrich, J. (1999), "The *Thebaid*'s Feminine Ending," *Ramus*, 28: 40–53.

Dietrich, J. (1997), *Thebais rescriptrix: Rewriting and Closure in Statius' Thebaid 12*, Ph.D. Dissertation, University of Southern California.
Dixon, S. (1988), *The Roman Mother*, Kent: Croom Helm.
Dominik, W. J. (2015), "Similes and their Programmatic Role in the *Thebaid*," in W.J. Dominik, C. Newlands, and K. Gervais (eds), *Brill's Companion to Statius*, 266-90, Leiden/Boston: Brill.
Dominik, W. J. (2005), "Statius," in J. Foley (ed), *A Companion to Ancient Epic*, 514-27, Malden, MA: Blackwell.
Dominik, W. J. (2003), "Following in whose Footsteps? The Epilogue to Statius' *Thebaid*," in A. F. Basson and W. J. Dominik (eds), *Literature, Art, History: Studies on Classical Antiquity and Tradition in Honour of W.J. Henderson*, 91-109, Frankfurt: Peter Lang.
Dominik, W. J. (1996), "A Short Narrative Reading of Statius' *Thebaid*," in F. Delarue, S. Georgacopoulou, P. Laurens and A.-M. Taisne (eds), *Epicedion: Hommage à P. Papinius Statius 96-1996*, 55-69, Poitiers.
Dominik, W. J. (1994a), *The Mythic Voice of Statius*, Leiden: Brill.
Dominik, W. J. (1994b), *Speech and Rhetoric in Statius'* Thebaid, Hildesheim: Olms-Weidemann.
Duchemin, J. (1968), *L'Agôn dans la tragédie grecque*, Paris: Les Belles Lettres.
Duckworth, G. (1931), "ΠΡΟΑΝΑΦΩΝΗΣΙΣ in the Scholia to Homer," *AJPh*, 52: 320-38.
Duckworth, G. (1933), *Foreshadowing and Suspense in the Epics of Homer, Apollonius, and Vergil*, Princeton: Princeton University Press.
Duff, J. W. (1960), *A Literary History of Latin in the Silver Age: From Tiberius to Hadrian*, London: Ernest Benn.
Dunn, F. (1996), *Tragedy's End: Closure and Innovation in Euripidean Drama*, New York/Oxford: Oxford University Press.
Edmunds, L. (2002), "Mars as Hellenistic Lover: Lucretius, *De Rerum Natura* 1.29-40 and its Subtexts," *IJCT*, 8: 343-58.
Else, G. (1986), *Plato and Aristotle on Poetry*, Chapel Hill: University of North Carolina Press.
Falkner, T. (1995), *The Poetics of Old Age*, Norman: University of Oklahoma Press.
Fantham, E. (2006), "The Perils of Prophecy: Statius' Amphiaraus and His Literary Antecedents," in R. Nauta, H.-J. VanDam and J. Smolenaars (eds), *Flavian Poetry*, 147-62, Leiden: Brill.
Fantham, E. (2004), *Ovid's Metamorphoses*, Oxford: Oxford University Press.
Fantham, E. (1999), "The Role of Lament in the Growth and Eclipse of Roman Epic," in M. Bessinger, J. Tylis and S. Wofford (eds), *Epic Traditions in the Contemporary World: The Poetics of Community*, 221-35, Berkeley: University of California Press.
Fantham, E. (1997), "Envy and Fear the Begetter of Hate: Statius' *Thebaid* and the Genesis of Hatred," in S. Braund and C. Gill (eds), *The Passions in Roman Thought and Literature*, 185-212, Cambridge: Cambridge University Press.

Fantham, E. (1983), "Nihil iam iura naturae ualent: Incest and Fratricide in Seneca's *Phoenissae*," in A. J. Boyle (ed), *Seneca Tragicus: Ramus Essays in Senecan Drama*, 61–76, Victoria, Australia: Aureal.

Farron, S. G. (1979), "The Roman Invention of Evil," *Studies in Antiquity*, 1: 12–46.

Feeney, D. (1991), *The Gods in Epic*, Oxford: Oxford University Press.

Fernandelli, M. (2000), "Statius' *Thebaid* 4.165–72 and Euripides' *Phoenissae* 1113–18," *Symb. Osl.*, 75: 89–98.

Fiehn, K. (1917), *Questiones Statianae*, Ph.D. diss. Berlin.

Flint, W. W. (1921), *The Use of Myth to Create Suspense in Extant Greek Tragedy*, Ph.D. diss. Princeton University.

Foley, H. (1985), *Ritual Irony: Poetry and Sacrifice in Euripides*, Ithaca: Cornell University Press.

Fortgens, H. (1934), *P. Papinii Statii de Opheltis funere carmen epicum, Thebaidos liber VI 1–295*, Zutphen: Nauta.

Franchet d'Espèrey, S. (2001), "La causalité dans le chant I de la Thebaide de Stace: Ou commence la Thebaide?" Revue des Etudes Latines 79: 188–200.

Franchet d'Espèrey, S. (1999), *Conflit, violence et non-violence dans la Thébaïde de Stace*, Paris: Belles Lettres.

Frank, E. (1965), "La Composizione della Tebaide di Stazio," *RIL*, 99: 309–18.

Frank, M. (1995), "The Rhetorical Use of Family Terms in Seneca's *Oedipus* and *Phoeinissae*," *Phoenix*, 49: 121–30.

Frings, I. (1992), *Odia fraterna als manieristiches Motiv—Betrachtungen zu Senecas "Thyest" und Statius' Thebais*, Stuttgart: F. Steiner.

Fuchs, A. (2000), *Dramatische Spannung: moderner Begriff—antikes Konzept*, Stuttgart: J. B. Metzler.

Ganiban, R. T. (2007), *Statius and Virgil: The Thebaid and the Reinterpretation of the Aeneid*, Cambridge/New York: Cambridge University Press.

Ganiban, R. (2013), "The Death and Funeral Rites of Opheltes in the *Thebaid*," in A. Augoustakis (ed), *Ritual and Religion in Flavian Epic*, 249–66, Oxford/New York: Oxford University Press.

Genette, G. (1980), *Narrative Discourse: An Essay in Method*, Ithaca: Cornell University Press.

Georgacopoulou, S. (1996), "Clio dans la Thébaïde de Stace: à la recherche du kléos perdu," *MD*, 37: 167–91.

Gerrig, R. (1989), "Reexperiencing Fiction and Non-Fiction," *The Journal of Aesthetics and Art Criticism*, 47: 277–80.

Gerrig, R. (1993), *Experiencing Narrative Worlds: On the Psychological Activities of Reading*, New Haven, Yale University Press.

Gervais, K. (2015), "Parent-Child Conflict in the *Thebaid*," in W.J. Dominik, C. Newlands, and K. Gervais (eds), *Brill's Companion to Statius*, 221–39, Leiden/Boston: Brill.

Gervais, K. (2017a), *Statius, Thebaid 2: Edited with an Introduction, Translation, and Commentary*, Oxford: Oxford University Press.

Gervais, K. (2017b), "Odi(tque moras): Abridging Allusions to Vergil, *Aeneid* 12 in Statius, *Thebaid* 12," 38: 305-29.

Gibson, B. (2004), "The Repetitions of Hypsipyle," in M. Gale (ed), *Latin Epic and Didactic Poetry: Genre, Tradition and Individuality*, 149-80, Swansea: The Classical Press of Wales.

Gibson, B. (2013), "Hymnic Features in Statian Epic and the Silvae," in A. Augoustakis (ed), *Ritual and Religion in Flavian Epic*, 127-44, Oxford/New York: Oxford University Press.

Golden, L. (1964), "The Character of Eteocles and the Meaning of the Septem," *CP*, 59: 79-89.

Görschen, F. C. (1966), "Der Hypsipyle-Prolog," *Hermes*, 94: 297-307.

Gossage, A. J. (1972), "Statius," in D.R. Dudley (ed), *Neronians and Flavians*, 184-235, London: Routledge.

Gostoli, A. (1978), "Some Aspects of the Theban Myth in the Lille Stesichorus," *GRBS*, 19: 23-7.

Götting, M. (1969), *Hypsipyle in der Thebais des Statius*, Wiesbaden.

Goward, B. (1999), *Telling Tragedy: Narrative Technique in Aeschylus, Sophocles, and Euripides*, London: Duckworth.

Green, S. (2004), *Ovid, Fasti 1. A Commentary*, Leiden: Brill.

Grenfell, B. and A. Hunt (1908), "Euripides, Hypsipyle," *POxy*, vi (852): 19-106.

Gruzelier, C. (1994), "The Influence of Virgil's Dido on Statius' Portrayal of Hypsipyle," *Prudentia* 26: 153-65.

Gunderson, E. (2003), *Declamation, Paternity, and Roman Identity: Authority and the Rhetorical Self*, Cambridge: Cambridge University Press.

Hall, E. (2010), *Greek Tragedy: Suffering under the Sun*, New York/Oxford: Oxford University Press.

Hall, J. B., Ritchie, A. L., and Edwards, M. J. (eds), (2008), *P. Papinius Statius: Thebaid and Achilleid*, Volume 3, Newcastle: Cambridge Scholars Press.

Hardie, A. (1983), *Statius and the Silvae: Poet, Patrons, and Epideixis in the Graeco-Roman World*, Liverpool: Francis Cairns.

Hardie, P. (1989), "Flavian Epicists on Vergil's Epic Technique," *Ramus*, 18: 3-20.

Hardie, P. (1990), "Ovid's Theban History: The First Anti-Aeneid?" *CQ*, 40: 224-35.

Hardie, P. (1993), *The Epic Successors of Virgil: A Study in the Dynamics of Tradition*, Cambridge: Cambridge University Press.

Hartung, I. A. (1843), *Euripides Restitutus*, Hamburg: F. Perthes.

Heath, M. (1989), *Unity in Greek Poetics*, Oxford/New York: Oxford University Press.

Held, G. (1984), "Spoudaios and Teleology in the Poetics," *TAPhA*, 114: 159-76.

Helzle, M. (1996), *Der Stil ist der Mensch: Redner und Reden im römischen Epos*, Stuttgart: De Gruyter.

Henderson, J. (1993), "Form Remade / Statius' *Thebaid*," in A. J. Boyle (ed), *Roman Epic*, 162-91, London/New York: Routledge.

Henry, D. and E. Henry (1985), *The Mask of Power: Seneca's Tragedies and Imperial Rome*, Chicago: Bolchazy-Carducci.

Herington, C. J. (1966), "Senecan Tragedy," *Arion*, 5: 422-71.

Herman, D. (1997), "Scripts, Sequences, and Stories: Elements of a Postclassical Narratology," *PMLA*, 112: 1046-59.

Herman, D. (2002), *Story Logic: Problems and Possibilities of Narrative*, Lincoln: University of Nebraska Press.

Hershkowitz, D. (1997), "Parce Metu, Cytherea: 'Failed' Intertext Repetition in Statius' *Thebaid*, or, Don't Stop Me If You've Heard This One Before," *Materiali e discussioni per l'analisi dei testi classici*, 39: 35-52.

Hershkowitz, D. (1998), *The Madness of Epic: Reading Insanity from Homer to Statius*, Oxford: Oxford University Press.

Heslin, P. J. (2008), "Statius and the Greek Tragedians on Athens, Thebes, and Rome," in J. J. L. Smolenaars, H.-J. v. Dam and R. Nauta (eds), *The Poetry of Statius*, 111-28, Leiden: Brill.

Heuvel, H. (1932), *Publii Papinii Statii Thebaidos liber primus. Versione Batava commentarioque exegetico instructus*, Zutphen: Nauta.

Hill, D. E. (1996), *Thebaid I Revisited*, in F. Delarue, S. Georgacopoulou, P. Laurens and A.-M. Taisne (eds), *Epicedion: Hommage à P. Papinius Statius 96-1996*, 35-53, Poitiers: La Licorne.

Hogan, J. C. (1973), "Aristotle's Criticism of Homer in the *Poetics*," *CP*, 68: 95-108.

Holford-Strevens, L. (2000), "Poplios Papinios Statios," Hermathena 168: 39-54.

Holland, J. E. (1976), *Studies on the Heroic Tradition in the Thebaid of Statius*. Ph.D. diss. Missouri.

Hough, J. (1974), "Bird Imagery in Roman Poetry," *CJ*, 70: 1-13.

Hubert, A. (2013), "*Malae preces* and Their Articulation in the *Thebaid*," in A. Augoustakis (ed), *Ritual and Religion in Flavian Epic*, 109-26, Oxford/New York: Oxford University Press.

Hulls, J. M. (2014), "Greek Author, Greek Past: Statius, Athens, and the Tragic Self," in A. Augoustakis (ed), *Flavian Poetry and its Greek Past*, 193-213, Leiden: Brill.

Hutchinson, G. O. (1993), *Latin Literature from Seneca to Juvenal: A Critical Study*, Oxford: Clarendon Press.

Jamset, C. (2004), "Death-loration: The Eroticization of Death in the *Thebaid*," *Greece and Rome*, 51: 95-104.

Juhnke, H. (1972), *Homerisches in römischer Epik flavischer Zeit*, Munich: Beck.

Keith, A. (2002), "Ovidian Personae in Statius' *Thebaid*," *Arethusa*, 35: 381-402.

Keith, A. M. (2000), *Engendering Rome: Women in Latin Epic*, Cambridge/New York: Cambridge University Press.

Kennedy, D. (2013), *Antiquity and the Meanings of Time: A Philosophy of Ancient and Modern Literature*, London/New York: I.B. Tauris.

Kitto (1939), *Greek Tragedy: A Literary Study*, London: Methuen.
Klinnert, T. (1970), *Capaneus-Hippomedon: Interpretation zur Heldendarstellung in der Thebais des P. Papinius Statius*, Ph.D. diss. Berlin.
Korneeva, T. (2011), *Alter et ipse: identità e duplicità nel sistema dei personaggi della Tebaide di Stazio*, Pisa: Edizioni ETS.
Krumbholz, G. (1955), "Der Erzählungsstil in der Thebais des Statius," *Glotta*, 34: 93–138; 231–60.
Kytzler, B. (1960), "Beobachtungen zum Prooemium der Thebais," *Hermes*, 88: 331–54.
Kytzler, B. (1969), "Imitatio und aemulatio in der Thebais des Statius," *Hermes*, 97: 209–32.
Kytzler, B. (1996). "Pandere Thebas: Welches Thema hat Die Thebais," in F. Delarue, S. Georgacopoulou, P. Laurens and A.-M. Taisne (eds), *Epicedion: Hommage à P. Papinius Statius 96-1996*, 25–34, Poitiers: La Licorne.
La Penna, A. (1994), "Me, me adsum qui feci, in me convertite ferrum …! Per la storia di una scena tipica dell'epos e della tragedia," *Maia*, 46: 123–34.
Lamari, A. (2010), *Narrative, Intertext, and Space in Euripides' Phoenissae*, Berlin: De Gruyter.
Legras, L. (1905), *Étude sur la Thébaïde de Stace*, Paris: G. Bellais.
Leigh, M. (2006), "Statius and the Sublimity of Capaneus," in M. J. Clarke, B. G. F. Currie and R. O. A. M. Lyne (eds), *Epic Interactions*, 217–42, Oxford: Oxford University Press.
Lesueur, R. (1992), "Les Femmes dans la Thébaïde de Stace," in M. Woronoff (ed), *L'univers épique: Rencontres avec l'antiquité classique II*, 229–42, Paris: Les Belles Lettres.
Lloyd, M. (2007), *Time in Euripides*, in I. de Jong and R. Nünlist (eds), *Time in Ancient Greek Literature*, 293–304, Leiden: Brill.
Lovatt, H. (1999), "Competing Endings: Re-Reading the End of the *Thebaid* through Lucan," *Ramus*, 28: 126–51.
Lovatt, H. (2005), *Statius and Epic Games: Sport, Politics, and Poetics in the Thebaid*, Cambridge: Cambridge University Press.
Lovatt, H. (2010), "Cannabalising History: Livian Moments in Statius' *Thebaid*," in J. F. Miller and A. J. Woodman (eds), *Latin Historiography and Poetry in the Early Empire: Generic Interactions*, 71–86, Leiden: Brill.
Lovatt, H. (2013), Competing Visions: Prophecy, Spectacle, and Theatricality in Flavian Epic, in A. Augoustakis (ed), *Ritual and Religion in Flavian Epic*, 53–70, Oxford/New York: Oxford University Press.
Lowe, N. J. (2004), *The Classical Plot and the Invention of Western Narrative*, Cambridge: Cambridge University Press.
Luschnig, C. A. E. (1995), *The Gorgon's Head: Studies in Alcestis, Electra, and Phoenissae*, Leiden: Brill.
Martin, R. (2007), "Stesichorus and the Voice of Jocasta" *Proceedings of the 11th International Meeting on Ancient Greek Drama, (2002: The Theban Cycle)*, Delphi: The European Cultural Center.

McGuire, D. (1997), *Acts of Silence: Civil War, Tyranny, and Suicide in the Flavian Epics*, Hildesheim: Olms-Weidemann.
McNelis, C. (2007), *Statius' Thebaid and the Poetics of Civil War*, Cambridge: Cambridge University Press.
Maignon, A. (1989), "Form and Content in the Lille Stesichorus," *Quaderni Urbinati di Cultura Classica*, 31: 31–56.
Mandler, J. M. and N. S. Johnson (1977), "Remembrance of Things Parsed: Story Structure and Recall," *Cognitive Psychology*, 9: 111–51.
Manioti, N. (2016), "Becoming Sisters: Antigone and Argia in Statius' Thebaid," in N. Manioti (ed), *Family in Flavian Epic*, 122–42, Leiden/Boston: Brill.
Marinis, A. (2015), "Statius' Thebaid and Greek Tragedy: The Legacy of Thebes," in W. J. Dominik, C. Newlands, and K. Gervais (eds), *Brill's Companion to Statius*, 343–61, Leiden/Boston: Brill.
Markantonatos, A. (2002), *Oedipus at Colonus. Sophocles, Athens, and the World*, Berlin/New York: de Gruyter.
Markus, D. (2004), "Grim Pleasures: Statius' Poetic Consolations," *Arethusa*, 37: 105–35.
Mastronarde, D. (1994), *Euripides: Phoenissae*, Cambridge: Cambridge University Press.
Matthews, V. J. (1996), *Antimachus of Colophon: Text and Commentary*, Leiden: Brill.
Mendell, C. (1967), *Latin Poetry: The Age of Rhetoric and Satire*, London: Archon Books.
Mikalson, J. D. (1989), "Unanswered Prayers in Greek Tragedy," *JHS*, 109: 81–98.
Moerner, F. (1890), *De P. Papinii Statii Thebaide Quaestiones criticae, grammaticae*, Ph.D. diss., Königsberg.
Mommsen, T. (1895), *Beiträge zu den Lehre von den griechischen Präpositionen*, Berlin: Weidmannsche Buchhandlung.
Moore, C. H. (1921), "Prophecy in Ancient Epic," *HSCP*, 32: 99–175.
Moreland, F. L. (1975), "The Role of Darkness in Statius: A Reading of Thebaid I," *CJ*, 70: 20–1.
Morson, G. P. (1994), *Narrative and Freedom: The Shadows of Time*, New Haven: Yale University Press.
Mozley, J. H. (ed and tr) (1928), *Statius* 1-2. Cambridge: Harvard University Press.
Mulder, H. M. (1954), *P. Papinii Statii Thebaidos Liber II commentario exegetico aestheticoque instructus*, Ph.D. diss. Groningen.
Myers, K. S., (2015), "Statius on Invocation and Inspiration" in W. J. Dominik, C. Newlands, and K. Gervais (eds), *Brill's Companion to Statius*, 31–53, Leiden/Boston: Brill.
Natanblut, E. (2005), *The Seven Against Thebes in Greek Tragedy*, Montreal: Laodamia Press.
Newlands, C. E. (2012), *Statius, Poet between Naples and Rome*, London: Bristol Classical Press.

Nugent, S.G. (1996), "Statius' Hypsipyle: Following in the Footsteps of the *Aeneid*," *Scholia*, 5: 46–71.

Nünlist, R. (2009), *The Ancient Critic at Work: Terms and Concepts of Literary Criticism in Greek Scholia*, Cambridge: Cambridge University Press.

O'Connor-Visser, E. A. M. E. (1987), *Aspects of Human Sacrifice in the Tragedies of Euripides*, Amsterdam: B. R. Grüner.

O'Gorman, E. (2005), "Beyond Recognition: Twin Narratives in Statius' *Thebaid*," in M. Paschalis (ed), *Roman and Greek Imperial Epic*, Herakleion: Crete University Press.

Ogilvie, R. M. (1980), *Roman Literature and Society*, London: The Harvester Press.

Olivi, M. -C. (1996) "Amphiaraos: un exemple de récriture d'un personnage mythique dans la Thébaïde," in F. Delarue, S. Georgacopoulou, P. Laurens and A. -M. Taisne (eds), *Epicedion: Hommage à P. Papinius Statius 96–1996*, 135–44, Poitiers: La Licorne.

O'Neill, P. (1996), *Fictions of Discourse: Reading Narrative Theory*, Toronto: Toronto University Press.

Ortony, A., Clore G., and Collins A. (1988), *The Cognitive Structure of Emotions*, Cambridge: Cambridge University Press.

Page, D. (1938), *Medea*, Oxford: Clarendon Press.

Papadopoulou, T. (2008), *Euripides: Phoenician Women*, London: Duckworth.

Parker, L. P. E. (2007), *Euripides Alcestis*, Oxford: Oxford University Press.

Parkes, R. (2005), "Men from Before the Moon: The Relevance of Statius *Thebaid* 4.275–84 to Parthenopaeus and His Arcadian Contingent," *CP*, 100: 358–65.

Parkes, R. (ed and tr) (2012), *Statius, Thebaid 4: Edited with an Introduction, Translation, and Commentary*, Oxford: Oxford University Press.

Podlecki, A. (1962), "Some Themes in Euripides' *Phoenissae*," *TAPhA*, 93: 355–73.

Poe, J. P. (1983), "The Sinful Nature of the Protagonist of Seneca's *Oedipus*," in A. J. Boyle (ed), *Seneca Tragicus: Ramus Essays on Seneca Drama*, 140–58, Victoria, Australia: Aureal.

Pollmann, K. (2004), *Statius, Thebaid 12: Introduction, Text, and Commentary*, Paderborn: Ferdinand Schöningh.

Pratt, N. T. (1939), *Dramatic Suspense in Seneca and in His Greek Precursors*, Princeton: Princeton University Press.

Prince, G. (1988), "The Disnarrated," *Style*, 22: 1–8.

Rankin, H. D. (1969), "Eating People Is Right: Petronius 141 and a Topos," *Hermes*, 97: 381–84.

Rawson, E. (1970), "Family and Fatherland in Euripides' *Phoenissae*," *GRBS*, 11: 109–27.

Rebeggiani, S. (2013), "The Chariot Race and the Destiny of the Empire in Statius' Thebaid," *IJCS*, 38: 187–206.

Reussner, A. (1921), *De Statio et Euripide*, Ph.D. diss., Halle.

Ricouer, P. (2002), "Narrative Time," in B. Richardson (ed), *Narrative Dynamics*, 35–46, Columbus: The Ohio State University Press.

Rimmon-Kenan, S. (1991), *Narrative Fiction: Contemporary Poetics*, London: Routledge.
Ripoll, F. (1998), *La morale héroïque dans les épopées latines d'époque flavienne: Tradition et innovation*, Louvain-Paris, Peeters.
Robert, C. (1915), *Oidipus: Geschichte eines poetischen Stoffes im griechischen Alterum*, Berlin: Weidmann.
Rosati, G. (2002), "Muse and Power in the Poetry of Statius," in E. Spentzou and D. Fowler (eds), *Cultivating the Muse: Struggles for Power and Inspiration in Classical Literature*, 229–51, Oxford: Oxford University Press.
Rutherford, R. B. (2012), *Greek Tragic Style: Form, Language and Interpretation*, Cambridge: Cambridge University Press.
Ryzman, M. (1989), "The Curse, the Oracle, and the Sisters in Aeschylus' *Septem*," *Revue Belge de philologie et d'histoire*, 67: 18–29.
Schachter, A. (1967), "The Theban Wars," *Phoenix*, 21: 1–10.
Schetter, W. (1960), *Untersuchungen zur epischen Kunst des Statius*, Wiesbaden: Harrassowitz.
Schetter, W. (1962), "Die Einheit des Prooemium zur *Thebais* des Statius," *Museum Helveticum*, 19 (4): 204–17.
Schiesaro, A. (1994), "Seneca's Thyestes and the Morality of Tragic Furor" in J. Elsner and J. Masters (eds), *Reflections of Nero: Culture, History, and Representation*, 196–210, Chapel Hill: The University of North Carolina Press.
Scodel, R. (1993), *Theater and Society in the Classical World*, Ann Arbor: University of Michigan Press.
Segal, C. (1983), "Greek Myth as a Semiotic and Structural System and the Problem of Tragedy," *Arethusa*, 16: 173–98.
Segal, C. (1992), "Tragic Beginnings: Narration, Voice, and Authority in the Prologues of Greek Drama," in F. Dunn and T. Cole (eds), *Yale Classical Studies XXIX, Beginnings in Classical Literature*, 85–112, Cambridge: Cambridge University Press.
Sewell-Rutter, N. J. (2007), *Guilt by Descent: Moral Inheritance and Decision Making in Greek Tragedy*, Oxford: Oxford University Press.
Shapiro, H. A. (2006), "The Wrath of Creon: Withholding Burial in Homer and Sophocles," *Helios*, 33: 119–34.
Sheppard, J. T. (1913), "The Plot of the Septem Contra Thebes," *CQ*, 7: 73–82.
Smolenaars, J. J. L. (1994), *Statius Thebaid VII: A Commentary*, Leiden: Brill.
Smolenaars, J. J. L. (2008), "Statius *Thebaid* 1.72: Is Jocasta Dead or Alive? The Tradition of Jocasta's Suicide in Greek and Roman Drama and in Statius' *Thebaid*," in J. J. L. Smolenaars, H. J. v. Dam and R. Nauta (eds), *The Poetry of Statius*, 215–37, Leiden, Brill.
Snijder, H. (1968), *P. Papinius Statius, Thebaid: A Commentary on Book III with Text and Introduction*, Amsterdam: Adolf Hakkert.
Soerink, J. (2014), "Tragic / Epic: Statius' *Thebaid* and Euripides' Hypsipyle," in A. Augoustakis (ed), *Flavian Poetry and its Greek Past*, 171–91, Leiden: Brill.

Soubiran, J. (1969), "De Coriolan à Polynice: Tite-Live modèle de Stace," in J. Bibauw (ed), *Hommages à Marcel Renard*, 689–99, Bruxelles: Latomus.

Steiner, G. (1996), "Tragedy, Pure and Simple," in M.S. Silk (ed), *Tragedy and the Tragic: Greek Theatre and Beyond*, 534–46, Oxford: Oxford University Press.

Sternberg, M. (1978), *Expositional Modes and Temporal Ordering in Fiction*, Bloomington: Indiana University Press.

Storey, I. (2013), *Euripides: Suppliant Women*, London: Duckworth.

Sussman, L. (1995), "Sons and Fathers in the Major Declamations Ascribed to Quintilian," *Rhetorica*, 13: 179–92.

Taisne, A. -M. (1994), *L'esthétique de Stace. La peinture des correspondances*, Paris: Belles Lettres.

Tan, E. (1996), *Emotion and the Structure of Narrative Film: Film as an Emotion Machine*, New York: Routledge.

Tarrant, R. J. (1995), "Greek and Roman in Seneca's Tragedies," *HSPh*, 97: 215–30.

Tarrant, R. J. (1985), "Seneca's Thyestes," Atlanta: Scholar's Press.

Tarrant, R. J. (1978), "Senecan Drama and its Antecedents," *HSCP*, 82: 214–64.

ten Kate, R. (1955), *Quomodo heroes in Statii Thebaide describantur quaeritur*, Groningen: J. B. Wolters.

Thalmann, W. (1982), "The Lille Stesichorus and the *Seven against Thebes*," *Hermes*, 110: 385–91.

Toolan, M. (1988), *Narrative: A Critical Linguistic Introduction*, London/New York: Routledge.

Tsitsibakou-Vasalos, E. (1989), "The Homeric ἄφαρ in the Oedipus Myth and the Identity of the Lille Mother," *Glotta* 67 (4): 60–88.

Tversky, A. and D. Kahneman (1974), "Judgement under Uncertainty: Heuristics and Biases," *Science* 185 (4157): 1124–31.

Venini, P. (1970), *P. Papini Stati Thebaidos Liber XI: Introduzione, Testo, Critico, Commento e Traduzione*, Florence.

Vessey, D. (1970a), "Statius and Antimachus: A Review of the Evidence," *Philologus*, 114: 118–43.

Vessey, D. (1970b), "The Games in *Thebaid VI*," *Latomus*, 29: 426–41.

Vessey, D. (1970c), "Notes on the Hypsipyle Episode in Statius: *Thebaid 4–6*," *BICS*, 17: 44–54.

Vessey, D. (1971a), "Menoeceus in the *Thebaid* of Statius," *CP*, 66: 236–43.

Vessey, D. (1971b), "Exitiale genus: Some Notes on Statius, *Thebaid 1*," *Latomus*, 30: 375–82.

Vessey, D. (1973), *Statius and the Thebaid*, Cambridge: Cambridge University Press.

Vessey, D. (1986), "Pierius menti calor incidit: Statius' Epic Style," *ANRW II*, 32.5: 2965–3019.

Veyne, P. (1987), *A History of Private Life*, Cambridge, MA: Harvard University Press.

Watson, L. and P. Watson (2003), *Martial: Select Epigrams*, Cambridge: Cambridge University Press.

Williams, G. (1978), *Change and Decline: Roman Literature in the Early Empire*, Berkeley: University of California Press.

Williams, G. (1986), "Statius and Vergil: Defensive Imitation," in J.D. Bernard (ed), *Vergil at 2000: Commemorative Essays on the Poet and His Influence*, 207–24, New York: AMS Press.

Williams, R. D. (1972), *P. Papini Stati Thebaidos liber decimus*, Leiden: Brill.

Winnington-Ingram, R. P. (1983), *Studies in Aeschylus*, Cambridge: Cambridge University Press.

Zeitlin, F. (1986), "Thebes: Theater of Self and Society in Athenian Drama," in J. P. Euben (ed), *Greek Tragedy and Political Theory*, 101–41, Berkeley: University of California Press

Index

Adrastus 4, 31–7, 39, 41, 41, 51, 61–2, 73, 100, 108, 112, 114–20, 130–1, 152–4, 158
Aeneas 33, 113, 138, 168 n.12, 169 n.17, 170 n.2, 171 n.12
Alcidamas 112
Aletes 127
Amphiaraus 32, 40, 42–5, 50, 60–6, 100–2, 105, 107, 113, 119, 129, 140, 153
Amphion 2, 27, 108
anachrony 15–16, 19, 23, 163 n.1–2, 165 n.42
analepsis 15, 19, 20, 23, 150, 165 n.27
Andromache 41–2, 106–7
anonymous critic 46, 126–8, 137
anticipation 8–12, 16, 20–2, 25–8, 31, 37, 40–2, 47, 53, 55, 67, 69, 74, 80, 89–93, 99–124, 141, 143
Antigone 5, 18–19, 24, 28, 68, 72–7, 81, 88, 95–6, 132, 146–52, 165, 175
Antimachus 3, 10
Antiphanes 16
Antonius 116
Aphesas (Mount) 43
Apollo 32, 33, 50, 85, 89, 100–2, 109, 171 n.5
Archemorus (*see* Opheltes)
Ares (*see* Mars)
Argia 28, 32, 36–7, 38–42, 130, 133–4, 137, 143, 148–52, 155, 169, 186
Argos 31–7, 41–5, 89, 101, 129, 168 n.8, 181 n.7
Arion 100, 114, 119, 131, 132, 184 n.70
Athena (*see* Minerva)
Atreus 135–6
Atys 104

Bacchant 45–6, 54, 189 n.24
Bacchus 51, 55, 62, 64, 69, 116
Bellona 184 n.61
Busiris 148

Cadmus 17–19, 27, 54, 87, 126
Calliope 58
Capaneus 29, 44–5, 61, 105–7, 110–14, 131
Cato 33, 43, 47, 118
Centauri 33
chronotope 25
cliffhanger 76
Clio 28–9, 167 n.75
Creon 28, 32, 46, 73, 75, 79, 83, 108–9, 121–4, 139–40, 143, 146–50, 152, 155–9
Cyclopi 33

Deipyle 32, 36–8
Diana 109
Dido 79, 171 n.12, 180 n.3
Dionysus (*see* Bacchus)
disnarration 69, 71, 134
Domitian 28, 130, 159, 178 n.15
Dorceus 109–10
Dryas 109–10

Erinys 40, 52, 56, 84, 87, 90, 94 96, 133, 144, 156, 188
Eriphyle 40, 42
Eteocles 1–2, 10, 15, 22, 24, 32–3, 35–7, 44–7, 68–80, 83–9, 92–6, 99–104, 125–30, 134–42, 151–5
Eurydice 50, 51, 58, 60, 63–5

fabula 29, 76, 80
foreshadowing 15, 31, 99
Furies (*see* Erinys)

Gorges 56

Haemon 103–4, 122
happiness 95, 125, 128, 185 n.3, 187 n.39
Harmonia (necklace of) 18, 37, 39–42
Hector 41–2, 71, 106, 147
Helen 101, 172 n.28
Hercules 50, 103
Hermes (*see* Mercury)

Hippolyta 134, 158
Hippomedon 28-9, 61, 105-7, 113
Hypsipyle 49-66, 108, 116-19, 171-4

Idalian Doves 53, 144-6
Idas 107-8, 119
Iris 147-9, 154-5

Jocasta 16-24, 67-81, 87-9, 94-5, 108-9, 114, 132
Jupiter 31-6, 40, 43, 55, 63, 83, 112, 147, 154

Laconians 113
Laius 16, 22, 24, 32, 35-7, 46, 49, 79, 86, 134, 154
Langia (river) 36, 51, 59, 61, 65, 116, 118-19
Lemnos 51, 52, 54, 56-9, 64, 144
Lycurgus (Lycus) 54, 57-9, 61-5, 119

Maeon 127, 139-40, 170 n.38, 188 n.10
Manto 46, 121-2, 151
Mars 36, 39, 49, 70, 106, 121, 154, 188 n.3
Megaera 68-9, 77, 83, 93
Menoceus 108, 143, 146-7, 156
Mercury 36, 154
Minerva 43, 103-5
mora (delay) 36, 49, 66, 68, 103, 170 n.1

Necromancy 45-7
nefas 72, 93, 97, 100, 125, 143
Nemea 49-50, 51, 58

Odysseus 105, 171 n.12
Oedipus 1-4, 16, 19-27, 31-6, 57, 67, 71, 75, 79, 83, 87-97, 102, 122, 135, 146, 151
Opheltes 49, 51, 52, 54, 57-65, 99, 100, 112, 114
Oryntus 147-8
Otho 106, 130, 170

Paphos 53, 144
Parthenopaeus 106, 107-10, 113, 119
Pentheus 54, 73
Phaethon 131-2, 186 n.16
Phegeus 154-7
Phlegyas 105

Pholcis 20
Polynices 22-8, 32-7, 41-2, 69-74, 76, 83-4, 86-7, 90, 93-6, 100-3, 107-8, 119-20, 127-42, 147-58
Polyxo 53-7
ponoi (motif) 18
Ponticus 3
portentousness 10-11, 29, 31, 47, 86, 99
portents 31-2, 37-41, 47, 100
prolepsis 15, 22, 31, 41, 52-5, 147, 163 n.5
Prospect emotions 8, 79

recusatio 28

Sirens 148
sleep 55, 56, 155
Sphinx 19, 21
spoudaios 125
surprise 8-9, 11, 13, 17, 20-2, 25, 28, 69, 80, 101, 107, 139, 150
suspense 7-13, 25, 47, 53-4, 65, 69, 74-81, 124-5, 162 n.30
suspense paradox 8-9

Talaus 52
talking cure 53
Tantalus 34, 89
teichoskopia 24
Thaos 56-7
Theseus 46, 79, 120, 127, 143-9, 152-9
Thyestes 61, 88-9, 135-6, 178 n.23
Tisiphone 1, 31, 33, 36, 40, 68-70, 72, 80, 83, 85, 86, 89, 90, 93-5, 102, 104-5, 132, 148
Trivia 108
Tydeus 24, 32-6, 37, 42, 44-5, 61, 70-2, 102-7, 113, 127, 129-34, 136-40, 146, 150, 153-5, 157, 167

Ulysses (*see* Odysseus)
uncertainty 8-10, 12, 26, 68-9, 76-7, 80, 137, 144

Venus 40, 53-4, 56, 144-5, 188 n.4
Virtus (personification) 122, 124
Vulcan 39

Zeus (*see* Jupiter)